Social Failures of EU Enlargement

Routledge Research in Employment Relations

SERIES EDITORS: RICK DELBRIDGE AND EDMUND HEERY,
Cardiff Business School, UK.

Aspects of the employment relationship are central to numerous courses at both undergraduate and postgraduate level.

Drawing from insights from industrial relations, human resource management and industrial sociology, this series provides an alternative source of research-based materials and texts, reviewing key developments in employment research.

Books published in this series are works of high academic merit, drawn from a wide range of academic studies in the social sciences.

Social Failures of EU Enlargement

A Case of Workers Voting with their Feet

Guglielmo Meardi

Routledge
Taylor & Francis Group

NEW YORK   LONDON

First published 2012
by Routledge
711 Third Avenue, New York, NY 10017

Simultaneously published in the UK
by Routledge
2 Park Square, Milton Park, Abingdon, Oxon OX14 4RN

Routledge is an imprint of the Taylor & Francis Group,
an informa business

Typeset in Sabon by IBT Global.
Printed and bound in the United States of America on acid-free paper by
IBT Global.

Library of Congress Cataloging-in-Publication Data
Meardi, Guglielmo.
  Social failures of EU enlargement : a case of workers voting with their
feet / Guglielmo Meardi.
    p. cm. — (Routledge research in employment relations ; 25)
  Includes bibliographical references and index.
    1. Europe—Economic integration.   2. European Union countries—
Economic conditions.   3. European Union countries—Social conditions.
4. Social rights—European Union countries.   I. Title.
  HC241.M42 2011
  337.1'42—dc23
  2011023098

ISBN: 978-0-415-80679-4 (hbk)
ISBN: 978-0-203-15370-3 (ebk)

For Helen

In memory of Maisa Milazzo

Contents

Figures and Tables

FIGURES

TABLES

Abbreviations

AWS	Akcja Wyborcza Solidarności (Solidarity's Electoral Action)
CISL	Confederatione Italiana Sindacati Lavoratori (Italian Confederation of Labor Unions)
CGIL	Confederazione Generale Italiana del Lavoro (Italian Genderal Labor Confederation)
CGT	Confédération Générale du Travail (General Labor Confederation)
DGB	Deutsche Gewerkschaftsbund (German Trade Union Confederation)
EC	European Commission
ECJ	European Court of Justice
EES	European Employment Strategy
EIRO	European Industrial Relations Observatory
EMU	Economic and Monetary Union
ETUC	European Trade Union Confederation
EU	European Union
EWC	European Works Council
FDI	Foreign Direct Investment
FZZ	Forum Związków Zawodowych (Trade Union Forum)
GDP	Gross Domestic Product
GDR	German Democratic Republic
GMB	General, Municipal, and Boilermakers' Union
HRM	Human Resource Management
IF	Investuotojų Forumas (Investors Forum)
IG-BAU	Industriegewerkschaft Bauen-Agrar-Umwelt (Construction, Agriculture, and Environment Trade Union)
IG-Metall	Industriegewerkschaft Metall (Metalworkers' Trade Union)
ILO	International Labor Organization
IMF	International Monetary Fund

KOZ	Konfederácia Odborových Zväzov Slovenskej Republiky (Confederation of Trade Unions of the Slovak Republic)
LFS	Labor Force Survey
LPR	Liga Polskich Rodzin (Polish Families' League)
MEP	Member of the European Parliament
MIÉP	Magyar Igazság és Élet Pártja (Hungarian Justice and Life Party)
MNC	Multinational Company
MP	Member of Parliament
MSzOSz	Magyar Szakszervezetek Országos Szövetsége (National Confederation of Hungarian Trade Unions)
NAFTA	North American Free Trade Agreement
NATO	North Atlantic Treaty Organization
NGO	Non-Governmental Organization
OECD	Organization for Economic Co-operation and Development
OPZZ	Ogólnopolskie Porozumienie Związków Zawodowych (All-Polish Trade Union Alliance)
PKPP	Polska Konfederacja Pracodawców Prywatnych (Polish Confederation of Private Employers)
PiS	Prawo i Sprawiedliwość (Law and Justice)
PO	Platforma Obywatelska (Civic Platform)
PSL	Polskie Stronnictwo Ludowe (Polish People's Party)
SLD	Sojusz Lewicy Demokratycznej (Alliance of the Democratic Left)
TUC	Trades Union Congress
UK	United Kingdom
UNCTAD	United Nations' Conference on Trade and Development
UP	Unia Pracy (Labor Union)
US	United States
USSR	Union of Socialist Soviet Republics
VAT	Value-Added Tax
WRS	Worker Registration Scheme
ZNP	Związek Nauczycielstwa Polskiego (Polish Teachers' Trade Union)
ZSSS	Zveze Svobodnih Sindikatov Slovenije (Association of Free Trade Unions of Slovenia)
ZZPR	Związek Zawodowy Pracowników Rolnictwa (Agriculture's Workers Trade Union)

Acknowledgments

This book has its roots in years of collaborative research across Europe, during which I had the luck and pleasure of working beside fantastic colleagues. I shared pains and joys of research, from fieldwork to ideas and impressions, with Michael Fichter, Marcin Frybes, Miroslav Stanojević, András Tóth, Manfred Krenn, Sonja Strohmer, and Juliusz Gardawski. Parts of this book are so rooted in collaboration with them that it has become impossible for me to precisely distinguish and acknowledge which ideas were originally mine, which theirs, and which just eclectic mixes: the whole book owes a lot to them, while remaining my responsibility for its limits and mistakes. I am confident that my fellow researchers will find limitations in this work so that I can continue to benefit from their honest, competent, and constructive criticism.

Sadly, one criticism will be missed: that of Franz Traxler, with whom I collaborated on an important project on employee participation rights in the Czech Republic. From his best Viennese observation point, Franz was an attentive observer of post-communist transformation since the beginning and had an important inspirational role in enlarging the European Sociological Association and its Research Network on industrial relations to colleagues from Central Eastern Europe. His sudden passing away while I was writing this book leaves a huge empty space in European debates about work.

Most of the work has been possible thanks to the generous and friendly support from the Industrial Relations Research Unit (IRRU) at the University of Warwick, especially its subsequent directors Paul Edwards and Paul Marginson: encouraging at stages that I thought nobody would ever be interested in, let alone sponsor, my exotic research in peripheral countries, generous dispensers of gentle advice and corrections whenever I indulged in disproportionate logical leaps in my ideas or simply in excessively bad English. If IRRU is a research center where the word collegiality becomes tangible, Warwick University has also offered wider opportunities for intellectual exchanges, especially with Colin Crouch, Simon Clarke, Claudio Morrison, and Teresa Staniewicz. Not to speak of the generous study leaves that allowed me the time to write up.

The writing up benefited from the superb hospitality from the Industrial Relations Department of Université Laval and the Centre de Recherche Interuniversitaire sur la Mondialisation et le Travail, Québec, and from the 'Institutions et Dynamiques Historiques de l'Economie' Unit at Ecole Normale Supérieure de Cachan. They provided tranquility, critical distance from the subject, and intellectual inspiration: Jacques Bélanger, Gregor Murray, Elodie Berthoux, Claude Didry, and Annette Jobert were magnificent. The Francophone world also confirmed to me that books—reduced to the status of unfashionable 'outputs' in Anglophone academia—still have an unsurpassed power for developing ideas and describing the world. I only hope this one will not ruin that reputation.

Many of the ideas in this book were developed through conferences and workshops across the world, where I benefited from important suggestions and feedback from colleagues. Again, some of the ideas in this book, maybe the most original ones, are actually the product of dialog with others. Magdalena Bernaciak, Dorotheee Bohle, Enrica Capussotti, Jon Erik Dølvik, Line Eldring, Roland Erne, Ian Fitzgerald, Steve French, Kasia Gajewska, Béla Greskovits, Jane Hardy, Richard Hyman, Steve Jefferys, Marta Kahancová, Ewa Kamińska, Maarten Keune, Martin Krzywdzinski, Adam Mielczarek, Adam Mrozowicki, Philippe Pochet, Magda Pustoła, David Ost, Alina Surubaru, Jochen Tholen, Vera Trappmann, Paulina Trevena, Aurora Trif, Jeremy Waddington, and Charles Woolfson have been particularly remarkable. In the Polish trade unions—those strange things I elected as my main research interest two decades ago—Andrzej Matla and Andrzej Adamski from Solidarność and Piotr Ostrowski from OPZZ were extremely helpful.

I am also grateful to the organizations that made the research possible: the British Academy, the Polish Academy of Sciences, the Hungarian Academy of Sciences, the Slovenian Academy of Sciences and Arts, the Economic and Social Research Council, and the Austrian Federal Ministry for Science and Research for their financial and organizational support; and a number of companies for the research access to their operations. I wish I could thank personally all managers, unionists, and workers I interviewed across so many countries, for sharing their precious time and unique knowledge.

Sections of this book appeared in previous versions in articles or book chapters. In particular, parts of Chapters 1, 2, 4, and 7 appeared in 'More Voice after More Exit?', *Industrial Relations Journal* (2007); part of chapter 2 in 'Keep Trying? Polish Failures and Half-Successes in Social Pacting' (with Juliusz Gardawski) in Philippe Pochet, Maarten Keune, and David Natali (eds) *After the Euro and the Enlargement: Social Pacts in Europe* (2010); part of Chapter 3 in 'Varieties of Multinationals' (with Paul Marginson, Michael Fichter, Marcin Frybes, András Tóth, and Miroslav Stanojević), *Industrial Relations* (2009); part of Chapter 6 in 'Multinationals' Heaven?', *International Journal of Human Resource Management* (2006); part of Chapter 7 in 'Multinationals in the New EU Member States and the Revitalisation of Trade Unions', *Debatte* (2007); parts of Chapter 8 in 'The Complexity of Relocation and the Diversity of Union Responses' (with Paul Marginson, Michael Fichter, Marcin Frybes, András Tóth, and Miroslav Stanojević), *European Journal of Industrial Relations* (2009) and in 'Union Immobility?', *British Journal of Industrial Relations* (2012). I am grateful for the permission to re-use these materials.

Last, but not least, my wife Helen is behind these pages through her contagious passion for books, her linguistic advice, and her emotional support.

Introduction

A LABOR QUESTION IN THE 'NEW EUROPE'?

Officially, the eastward expansion of the European Union (EU) in 2004–2007 was a success, only dented by the external shock of the later economic crisis. Whether it uses the term enlargement (from the point of view of the West), or the term accession (from the point of view of the East), the dominant narrative has been triumphant. In a frenzy of new zoological taxonomy, the new member states have been called economic big cats: the Slavic tiger (Poland), the Pannonian puma (Hungary), the Baltic tiger (Latvia). If the Pannonian puma and the Baltic tigers have been drastically tamed with the crisis, Poland may still be proud of being the only EU economy to have grown in the *annus horribilis* 2009.

The geopolitical and economic gains of the enlargement have been advertised by European institutions (e.g. European Commission [EC] 2006a), national governments, and most media and academics: increased investment, increased trade, increased labor mobility, and business opportunities (corresponding to the four 'freedoms of movement' the EU is based on, those of capital, goods, workers, and services). And as a result, falling unemployment, a reasonable pace of economic convergence, and a greater weight of the EU in international matters. The alternative and more pessimist popular narratives have been easily dismissed as uninformed, narrow minded, or even xenophobic. After all, none of the disasters Europhobes feared (a wave of barbarians invading the West or a wave of cosmopolites corrupting the East) materialized. But this book proposes, starting from the labor question (Kaufman 2007), a different perspective that provides a much more mixed assessment: if we consider social welfare, social order, and employee voice, the much proclaimed success of the enlargement looks very fragile and hardly sustainable—and the crumbling in 2009–2010 more understandable but also more worrying.

Employers, governments, and the EU neglect the labor question at their own peril. This book argues that labor relations are not just a private matter between two sides of a contractual relation. They also have an inherent, unavoidable political dimension; however they are regulated, they always affect public goods such as social cohesion, productivity, consent, social welfare. Broadly speaking, they affect citizenship, as work (or its denial in the form of unemployment) is too important a social situation for most citizens for it to be left entirely beyond the realm of democracy without undermining democracy altogether.

There are three problems with narratives that look only at GDP, volumes of trade and numerical employment indicators, and neglect labor relations as a citizenship issue. First, absolute figures are not always what matters to individuals, who think in relative terms. Economic growth does not necessarily make people happier if it is associated with growing inequality and increased contacts with much richer people—and may not help democratic and social cohesion. Ost (2005), looking at the Polish transition, detected a similarity with the social history of nineteenth-century Britain, where fast economic development did not preclude workers' anger, but the opposite, as, in Edward P. Thompson's (1963) words, 'most people were 'better off', but they had suffered and continued to suffer this slight improvement as a catastrophic experience' (12).

Second, even though workers' opinions do not need consideration from EU Commissioners, journalists or economists, still they matter in the national electoral processes. Repeated 'no' in referenda on EU Treaties have not impeded the ratification of the Lisbon Treaty, eventually. But the process has taken nine years and has drained the energies of Eurofederalists. Moreover, populist vote is strong in both Western and Eastern Europe, and electoral abstention is on the increase and has gone beyond 50% in some of the new member states. Populism and abstention are not always linked to the enlargement, but it has to be asked why the declared success of the enlargement has not translated into popular confidence in democratic processes. This is particularly important for social issues: having neglected the opinions of workers and their representatives during the process of EU integration, governments find that they have nobody to speak to once their consent is required for passing socio-economic reforms.

The third problem is specific to labor. The overwhelming focus on quantitative indicators of employment treats labor as a commodity that is easily priced and traded. Hence, the enthusiasm for labor and capital mobility, which facilitate the encounter of jobs and workers. But this is forgetting the insight by classic social scientists, such as Marx and Polanyi, that labor is a fictitious commodity. At the very least, it is also a resource with a variable value, but it also has an opinion of its own, unlike less problematic commodities such as potatoes and chairs. This means that making it continuously, inherently mobile, at least in potentiality, is not necessarily a good thing for it as a resource. It may be a good thing for some workers indeed: many do learn a lot from moving. Yet it should at least be asked whether the mobility of well-qualified people who move from the new to the old member states to work with limited rights in the food industry or in cleaning, learning little English, and leaving part of their families abroad, is actually a good thing for them, for their countries and for Europe. The fact that they earn more than they used to, and that they make unemployment rates decline, may be enough to satisfy economists—but not those concerned with issues of welfare, sustainability, and capacities.

Moreover, if labor has opinions, neglecting it is not just a potential problem for governments. It is a problem for organizations, too. Consent of labor to capitalist restructuring has been apparent for a while during post-communist restructuring, as I had tried to describe and explain in my 'Trade Union Activists, East and West' (2000). Workers were willingly submitting themselves to their own subordination. After all, as it is ironically said, the only thing that is worse than being exploited by capitalists, is *not* being exploited by capitalists, as it had happened to Eastern Europeans before 1989. Such willingness has come to be taken for granted in the process of EU integration. This has progressed in parallel to continuing undermining of employee representation, employee rights, and social consultation and negotiations—what the EU calls 'social dialog'. Yet if employers have been happy to marginalize worker opinions in terms of resistance, they still need worker opinions in terms of participation and commitment and active contribution during restructuring. But having fostered a system where the market only matters, they have been bitterly surprised by employees taking them at their word. Hence the increase in turnover and the lack of organizational commitment: if employment is just a 'contract' for meeting economic interests, it is then only natural for workers not to show any psychological commitment and to be ready to quit as soon as another employer offers a better contract. Or even to quit the country altogether.

MARKETIZING EMPLOYMENT RELATIONS

It did not have to be so. Historically, employee participation and institutional voice, through trade unions or works councils, have played a positive role in important cases of democratization, reform, and federalist integration. In their classic comparative analysis of works councils, Rogers and Streeck (1995) mentioned the case of negotiated reforms in post-Franco Spain, when the works councils played an important role. They added the then recent case of transition Poland, in which the works council was transformed from a state-union body into a platform for privatization and became an important vehicle for modernization processes (308). Yet, while Rogers and Streeck were writing those words, Polish works councils were being abolished. In another important work, Rueschemeyer *et al.* (1992) showed how labor (which in most cases means labor unions) has played a leading role in all waves of democratization of the twentieth century: in the 1920s, in the 1940s, and then in Latin America in the 1980s. But this role has been neglected and marginalized in the EU and especially in its new member states. As Erne (2008) has discussed, the EU preference for technocracy rather than democracy in employment issues remains a central cause for the democratic deficit of the EU itself.

What has emerged in Central Eastern Europe during the period of EU integration (before and after accession) is an employment regime that differs from the western one and continues to develop in a different direction. The core of it is the weakness of institutions for employee participation, and especially for employee representation. The crisis of trade unionism is not exclusive to the new member states, of course, but there it is much more pervasive, and it is not compensated by other institutions, be they works councils, state-supported collective bargaining or centralized social negotiations. Take Poland, the first mover in post-communist transformation and a frequently mentioned neo-liberal model. In 2000, when negotiations on EU accession were coming to a close, only 10% of owners and managers agreed that there should be union representation in private companies (Gardawski 2001). In other words, only 10% of them agreed with what in the same year was being ratified as a fundamental right of the European Union.

The outcome (Table I.1) is a clear gap between the new and old member states in terms of industrial relations, and most importantly, the gap is not narrowing with EU integration (whether measured from 1998, the start of the accession negotiation, or 2003, last year before accession). The European Commission's Industrial Relations in Europe Report of 2008 noted that in 2004–2006 in the new member states (weighted average according to country population) union density was only slightly below the old member states (22% against 25.8%), but collective bargaining coverage was much lower (42.5% against 68.8%), wage co-ordination was poorer, strikes were rarer and works councils had fewer right (EC 2008a). Experts had already described such labor weakness in the region extensively (e.g. Kohl and Platzer 2004). In summary, in the new member states, compared to Western Europe, unions are weaker, are more isolated in certain sectors, decline faster, affect working conditions through collective bargaining less, and have less capacity to challenge this situation through industrial action. And the trend is divergence, not convergence with the West.

The state does not compensate for the weakness of associational industrial relations, as Kohl and Platzer (2007) or Bluhm (2006) have hoped. The OECD Index of Employment protection legislation (Table I.1) shows that employment protection is generally poorer in the new member states than in the old ones—without even starting considering the greater problems of actual implementation (which I will discuss in Chapter 2). If on this dimension there is some convergence with the old member states, it is because some old member states (especially Italy, Germany, and Sweden) have recently moved decisively towards Eastern European standards, rather than the opposite. As a combined effect of industrial relations and state regulations, the last columns of Table I.1 report the enthusiastic assessment of the conservative Fraser Institute, which evaluates employers' 'freedom' worldwide. The Fraser index for labor market regulation is, like the OECD one, based on the legal rather than the actual situation on six dimensions

Table 1.1 Industrial Relations in New and (Selected) Old Member States

	Union density			Collective bargaining coverage			Employment protection legislation*			Labor market regulation freedom	
	2009	± from 2003	± from 1998	2009	= from 2003	± from 1998	2008	± from 2003	± from 1998	2008	± from 2000
Estonia	6.7	-3.9	-10.4	19.0	-9.0	-10.0	2.39			5.56	+0.82
Lithuania	9.5	-6.8	-17.5	15.0	+2.5	+7.5				5.59	+1.36
Poland	15.1	-8.6	-13.5	38.0	-2.0	-4.0	2.41	+0.25	+0.50	6.52	+2.32
Latvia	16.1	-1.8	-13.2	25.0	+7.0					7.13	+2.60
Hungary	16.8	-1.1	-10.8	33.5	-10.0	-18.5	2.11	+0.13	+0.38	7.08	+1.49
Slovakia	17.2	-8.9	-18.9	40.0	-5.0	-11.0	2.13	+0.10	-0.36	7.65	+3.11
Czech R.	17.3	-5.0	-14.8	42.5	-3.5	-4.5	2.32	+0.06	+0.06	7.67	+2.45
Slovenia	29.7	-8.9	-18.9	92.0	-8.0	-8.0	2.76			5.43	+1.83
Bulgaria	19.8	-8.3	-15.9	30.0	-10.0					7.75	+2.83
Romania	32.8	-5.5	-12.3	70.0						6.69	+0.41
France	7.6	-0.4	-0.6	90.0	=	=	3.05	=	+0.07	5.62	+0.64
Spain	15.9	+0.1	-0.4	84.5	-3.5	-7.5	3.11	=	+0.05	5.14	+1.22
Germany	18.8	-4.2	-7.1	62.0	-4.0	-8.0	2.63	=	-0.22	3.94	+1.09
UK	28.7	-1.0	-2.0	34.8	-1.1	+2.5	1.09	=	+0.15	7.98	+1.06
Italy	34.7	+1.0	-1.0	80.0	=	-1.0	2.58	+0.07	-0.81	6.30	+2.77
Sweden	68.4	-9.6	-12.7	91.0	-3.0	-3.0	2.06	-0.37	-0.37	5.13	+1.75

Data in italic are from the nearest available year.
Source: Union density and collective bargaining coverage: Institutional Characteristics of Trade Unions, Wage Setting, State Intervention and Social Pacts (ICTWSS) Database, Amsterdam Institute for Advanced Labour Studies (AIAS), Amsterdam, 2011 (Visser 2011); Employment protection legislation: OECD Database (OECD 2010a); Labor Market Freedom: Fraser Institute (Gwartney et al. 2010).
* Change from 2003 and 1998 refers exclusively to dismissal protection, due to data availability

(minimum wage, hiring and firing regulations, centralized collective bargaining, mandated cost of hiring, mandated cost of worker dismissal, and
conscription), and gives a maximum of 10 in the case of absolute employer
freedom. Not only do the new member states generally provide employers with more 'freedom' than the old ones (except the UK), but they have
increased this 'freedom' particularly generously between 2000 and 2007.
The EU accession has been a great present for employers—not necessarily
for employees.

There are differences among new member states, of course. The Baltic
states present the biggest challenges to those who hope for an assim-
ilation to Western European standards: Soviet Union legacies, ethnic
divides, and very dependent economies combine in creating much worse
employment regimes than in the so-called Visegrád group (Poland,
Czech Republic, Hungary, and Slovakia). There is then the exception of
Slovenia, which belongs to a different tradition, and I hope it will not
feel offended for having been included in this book and put alongside
the other, messier, new member states. In fact Yugoslavian and even
Austro-Hungarian institutional legacies, cohesive 'valley' communities,
national creation myths, and a strong export economy have combined
in making Slovenia one of the best, rather than worst, EU countries in
terms of social development. The reason for including the post-Yugoslavian state in this book is that the book is more about the direction
of change, than about the static situation. The problem discussed in my
argument is not that the new member states have poorer social standards than the old ones—this is self-evident, is not the fault of the EU,
and is not necessarily a political or theoretical problem. It is about the
fact the EU accession has failed in its implicit promise to upgrade those
social standards in order to fulfill expectations in the East and not to
disrupt the status quo in the West: it has not promoted social arrangements but rather disrupted the existing ones. Given this focus, Slovenia,
even in its uniqueness, is a telling confirmation of the general trend:
Europeanization has involved very serious strains on Ljubljana's welfare
state and the corporatist institutions.

A RESIDUAL WELFARE STATE

The weakness of employee representation is an aspect of a broader weakening of labor. The new employment regime implies not only poor representation rights but also poor social rights altogether. This is particularly
apparent in the welfare state. The welfare state in the new member states
may seem relatively generous, in relation to the level of economic development. After all, social expenditure is a 'luxury' item that is typically
higher, as a proportion of the GDP, in richer countries (except the US)
than in poorer ones, and in most new member states, it is higher than

in countries of comparable economic standing in Latin America, Middle East, or Asia, even if it is lower than in Western Europe. More concerning is the fact that while in the EU15, social expenditure has been constant since the 1990s, and in most new member states, it has been declining since accession into the EU, faster than it would have been justified by falls in unemployment (Table I.2). Again, as in industrial relations, the trend is divergent rather than convergent—and this would be even clearer if statistics also considered the dismissal of company-based welfare provisions inherited from communism.

Yet the most important distinctive feature of social protection in the new member states is its very heavy unbalanced structure as it focuses on the aged population, through old-age pensions, incapacity benefits, and healthcare, and neglects the new generations. Post-communist welfare states are largely 'residual welfare states' that combine legacies from the communist times with social programs that were introduced at the time of transition to limit mass unemployment and prevent protest from core workforces (Vanhuysse 2006). Countries differ: Slovenia, as mentioned, is an exception with a relatively strong 'continental-type' welfare state, and the three Baltic countries have an extremely minimalistic welfare state with massive poverty, while the other countries have some residual welfare state, the Hungarian one being the most generous (Klenner and Leiber 2009; Cerami 2009; Cerami and Vanhuysse 2009; Keune 2009; Bafoil 2009).

Table I.2 Social Expenditure in the New and Old Member States

	Social expenditure in % of GDP		
	1998	*2003*	*2008*
Latvia	14.7	13.1	10.7
Estonia		12.4	12.3
Lithuania	14.7	13.1	13.9
Slovakia	18.8	17.6	15.4
Poland		20.7	17.8
Czech Republic	17.9	19.5	18.0
Slovenia	23.6	23.2	20.8
Hungary		20.8	21.9
Bulgaria		15.5	14.6
Romania		12.7	12.6
EU15	26.0	26.6	25.9

Source: Social expenditure: Eurostat (2009a)

The protection afforded by this welfare state is of a very unbalanced kind. Beneficiaries from Central Eastern European welfare states are mostly the old generations. These are the people that inherited almost-free housing (however modest), had enjoyed employment security, and received relatively generous early retirement or incapacity benefits around 1990, so that they would not oppose their massive expulsion from the labor markets. But on the other side, those who are at work today in the new member states have no access to public housing—as it has been privatized and virtually nothing new has been built—have no employment security—due to the liberalization of labor law—are only offered expensive and unsecure contribution-based pensions and are faced with increasingly privatized health and education services (informal cash payments being often required for both) and worsening childcare for their children (except in Hungary). And if they are unemployed or poorly paid, they receive extremely poor benefits, generally below subsistence levels, and suffer from a regressive tax system that includes in many countries 'flat tax' on income, low corporate tax, high employee social contributions, and high indirect taxes.

The effect is clearly visible if one disaggregates the rates of poverty by age, as for instance Romano (2009) has discussed. In the aggregate, poverty risk (according to the Eurostat definition as disposable income below 60% of the national median) is similar in the East and the West of the EU, although absolute poverty is obviously much higher in the new member states: the risk of poverty, for decision of the European Council, is measured by Eurostat relative to the situation of each country. But while in Western Europe it is higher for those over 65 than for those under 18, the situation is different in the new member states (Table I.3). First we have the Baltic countries and the Eastern Balkan ones, where inequality and poverty risk are very high. In the most typical post-communist welfare states, the Hungarian and the Polish ones (and to a lesser extent the ex-Czechoslovakian ones), there is a distinctive inverse correlation between poverty risk and age. The poverty risk is relatively low, and much less than the EU average, for those aged more than 65. These are the people who have benefited from the 'residual welfare state'. Even if poorer than their western counterparts in absolute terms, they have a safety net under which they fall only vary rarely. But if one looks at youth, the risk of poverty is much higher: the younger the person, the higher the risk of poverty. Slovenia is, as usual, an outlier.

The implications of this social regime are serious. The residual welfare state has provided a near-decent safety net for a generation that was socially and politically crucial—the one with the highest participation in elections, and that was the core of trade unions and workforces at the end of socialism. This generation, which had the potential for political mobilization and was not so interested in emigration, has been gently invited to 'exit' the labor market without protesting and accommodated to benefits. By contrast, the younger generations, those who have entered the labor market

Table I.3 Poverty Risk by Age Group, 2008

	<18	18–24	25–49	60–64	>64
Bulgaria	26	21	6	17	34
Czech Republic	13	12	8	7	7
Estonia	17	15	13	20	39
Latvia	25	17	18	25	51
Lithuania	23	18	15	20	29
Hungary	20	18	12	9	4
Poland	22	20	16	15	12
Romania	33	23	21	17	26
Slovenia	12	10	10	12	21
Slovakia	17	12	10	8	10
EU15	19	20	14	14	20

Source: Eurostat (2009b).

since the 1990s, and even more those who are entering the labor market now, have been left in the most powerless position. To survive, they have to accept any job, at any pay rate. No benefits exist to provide a 'reserve wage', and trade unions are too weak to monitor and negotiate working conditions collectively, while minimum wages exist, but are low and grow slowly: in 2009 they range from 0.36% of average wages in the Czech Republic to 0.49% in Slovenia, as against an average of 0.50% in the old member states, and the trend since EU accession has been downwards in half of the new member states (OECD 2010a). To get housing, they have to take mortgages on conditions that are much worse than in the West, and often (especially in Hungary and the Baltic states) take on all of the exchange rate risk as credit is denominated in foreign currencies.

A EUROPEAN 'SOCIAL' MODEL

The social function of the welfare state and of the broader social system of industrial relations and political representation has been very different from the one we know from Western Europe. In Western Europe, specific European developments in the areas of management, employment, and welfare (Carpenter and Jefferys 2000) have acted as social compromises that have partially 'decommodified' labor (Esping-Andersen 1990), making capitalist social relations more socially bearable and providing some political and social gains for workers (Wright 2000). But in the new member states social and labor policies have fostered labor's maximal commodification. Social policies removed the resistance of older generations, while tripartite centralized social dialog in the 1990s co-opted trade unions, leaving privatization, extreme decentralization of wage setting, and minimalistic social security to consolidate the dominance of the market.

While there is no common social and employment regime to Western Europe (Crouch 1993, 1999), all of the continental Western European countries (and to some extent even the UK) share the presence of one or another 'functionally equivalent' institutions that moderate the impact of the market on the lives of workers. Whether these institutions are, country by country, a large welfare state, statutory regulations, strong associations, centralized collective bargaining, political concertation, local associational micro-corporatism, strong labor parties, or a mix of some of these devices, matters for the form of the resulting regulation but does not change their shared broad function: compensating the market with some social and political principles in the regulation of employment. This has been named 'mid-century social compromise' (Crouch 1999, 34), and it has undergone severe strains since the 1970s. It has entered competition with a different social compromise, adopted by countries such as US, UK, and Ireland, based on private consumer credit, which has been called 'privatized Keynesianism' and has shown its unsustainability with the 2008 crisis (Crouch 2008).

Despite these strains, the legacies of the western social compromise is still clearly visible in Western Europe, whether through the welfare state, associations, rights of employee information and consultation, and protective employment law. On all these dimensions, the 'old' EU (EU15) still looks clearly different from the US or Japan, so it is possible to speak, analytically, of a 'European Social Model' combining them (Ferrera *et al.* 2000). Interestingly, the more this model is being challenged, the more the EU feels the need to mention it and define it. The EU official declarative definition is as a model 'based on good economic performance, a high level of social protection and education and social dialog' (European Council 2002, §22).

One challenge to the pertinence of the 'European Social Model' concept comes from the new member states. These countries are distinctive in lacking not just some but all of these devices. Even if centralized collective bargaining exists in some countries, it has none of the incidence that is registered in the West; if the welfare state exists, it does not protect workers; labor law is important and some (e.g. Bluhm 2006) see it as reminiscent of a 'statist' system like the French one, but apart from the notorious implementation and enforcement weaknesses, it contains remarkably little on the crucial aspects of the employment relations, i.e. employment protection and pay. Workers are left in a situation of maximum vulnerability and lack of voice. Growing inequality and democratic deficit are the results, hitherto obscured by the apparent economic success.

The impact for workers' livelihoods is major. Working conditions are more onerous and hazardous (Burchell *et al.* 2009) and social inequality, despite the rather 'equal' starting points from communist times, is now much higher than in Western Europe, and it is rising faster (Table I.4). At the micro-level, the weakness of industrial relations, welfare state and statutory protections for employees have resulted in a recent 'explosion' of wage inequality, for instance in Poland (Newell and Socha 2007). Inequality, in turn, reduces social capital and support for the welfare state even further—so that a vicious cycle has been activated.

Of course, even the new member states are not realizations of the abstract (and impossible) ideal neoclassic model of unregulated markets, as some of their governments wish they were. There are some strong product market regulations, creating something that has been defined 'embedded capitalism' (Bohle and Greskovits 2007)—but these protect the elites much more than the workers. There are various social ties, especially at the very micro-level (family, local, and religious communities) that guarantee some solidarity and some social order—but none of these functions on the basis of democratic principles. The pervasive 'economic and industrial democracy' idea that has been present in Western Europe has been largely ignored.

We are therefore left not just with countries with weaker trade unions. We also have extensive use of atypical work, large informal economy sectors, extensive inequality—and popular anger and dissatisfaction with democratic institutions.

The most frequent explanation of labor weakness still blames the communist past (e.g. Crowley and Ost 2001). Over 20 years after the fall of Berlin Wall, this is less and less convincing. History does matter, of course. But first of all, it is imprecise to assume that workers under communism had no power or did not protest. Power and resistance did take place, mostly informally but, as only the opportunities arose, very explicitly too.

Table I.4 Social Inequality (Ratio of Gross Earnings between Decile 9 and Decile 1)

	2007	*Change from 2003*
Czech Republic	3.11	+0.11
Hungary	4.56	+0.18
Poland	4.21	+0.13
Germany	3.26	+0.09
France	2.91	−0.06
Sweden	2.31	+0.01
UK	3.59	+0.07

Data in italic are from the previous year.
Source: OECD.

See Poland, and not just the long list of its worker revolts: 1956, 1970, 1976, 1980–1981, and 1988. There is also much evidence of labor power in the 1980s in spite of martial law and political repression: real wages kept increasing, the underground union had a near veto power on directors' appointments in large companies, important reforms such as privatization and pension cuts were blocked.

Even if the communist past may be a part of the explanation for labor weakness, it is no explanation for the worsening trend. Historical legacies should count less and less over time. But the disorganization of society and of working lives in Central Europe has progressed and even, in many regards, accelerated. The accession to the European Union in 2004 and 2007 should have countered the trend. But as Tables I.1 and I.2 show, it clearly has not.

It is therefore more useful to turn our attention to what has happened to the new member states more recently. These countries are now strongly internationalized and integrated in the world economy—there is very little left from 'communism' economically. However, their position has been defined as 'dependent market economies' (Nölke and Vliegenthart 2009), and more specifically the Baltic states have been named 'peripheral economies' dependent on financialized growth (Myant and Drahokoupil 2010), while the Visegrád countries have deserved the better label of 'liberal dependent capitalism' (King 2007). In these definitions, dependence relates to the prominence of foreign ownership and limited sovereignty in economic and social policy. In these cases, capital has much less interest in compromises with labor, as production is largely for exports and local politics are nearly irrelevant (Bohle and Greskovits 2006). The main limit of such model, according to Myant and Drahokoupil (2010) is instability: extreme liberalization was accompanied by state break down and as a result no high-value activities—those that provide more sustainable and secure development—have been transferred by multinational companies (MNC) into Central Eastern Europe.[1]

THE TROJAN HORSE FOR THE
AMERICANIZATION OF EUROPE, REVISITED

During the long period of 'negotiations' of EU accession, European institutions often promised, to both Eastern and Western European citizens, social, and not merely economic convergence. For instance a European Commission report of 2002 stated that 'economic convergence in itself is not enough; it should be accompanied by progressive convergence in the social field' (EC 2002, 11). This was based on trust in a 'catching up' process and in the easy effectiveness of transferring a few formal institutions eastwards, while simultaneously avoiding open social debates. Yet this promise has been betrayed. It is not a matter of social standards remaining, in the new member states, below the western ones: none would expect miracles. It is much more about the direction and about the quality of change.

The EU enlargement, given the inherited gap in social and working conditions (Vaughan-Whitehead 2003) has provided a tough test of whether the so-called 'European Social Model' can be enlarged beyond the narrow boundaries of (most of) Western Europe. The marginalization of social issues during the accession process suggested the hypothesis that the enlargement could therefore threaten the 'European Social Model', or at least the aspiration to one. This is the reason why I dared ask the question, still during the negotiations, of whether the new member states could turn out to be a 'Trojan Horse for the Americanization of Europe' (Meardi 2002). This book tries to answer that question.

'Americanizing' European industrial relations refers to a growing diffusion of typical characteristics of the US: decentralization of wage bargaining, weak trade unions, high and growing inequality. The integration of the new member states into the EU included a number of specific risks for EU industrial relations and especially trade unions (Meardi 2002). First, the increased scope for 'coercive comparisons' of employment conditions by MNCs that may make workforces of different countries compete for investment and jobs by making concessions to the employer. Second, a power unbalance between labor and capital given mobility restrictions (so-called temporary arrangements) on the former, combined with increased space for xenophobia. Third, the increased scope for difficult-to-monitor movement of services and worker posting. In addition, the enlargement could diminish labor's institutional resources: it had the potential to hamper EU decision making on social matters and to shift the political equilibrium to the Right, especially on issues such as equal opportunities and economic liberalization. All this could lead, in the worst scenario, to the emergence of *liaisons dangereuses* between eastern trade unions and western employers on single market policies—which, in turn, would undermine cross-border trust and co-operation between trade unions of the two sides of the former iron curtain.

Nine years after my article of 2002, all those risks have materialized—but some have been counteracted by social and political forces. The EU institutions and policies have been mostly unable or unwilling to transfer the western social dimension to the East, and European social initiatives, after the very active late 1990s, came to nearly total standstill after 2004. The three risks linked to freedoms of movement materialized quickly. With regard to capital mobility, immediately after the enlargement, high-profile cases of coercive comparisons across East and West occurred in well-known companies such as General Motors, Bosch, and Siemens. The industrial relations implications have been particularly sharp for Germany (Fichter and Meardi 2008; Jürgens and Krzywdzinski 2010) but are best exemplified by the Fiat case in Italy in 2010–2011: to avoid relocation to Poland (and elsewhere), Italian workers had to accept not just work intensification:

this is no novelty in the internationalized economy. Most notably, they had to accept a reduction of collective bargaining and representation rights: a downturn for industrial democracy.

Freedom of movement of services and posting of workers have led to tensions in the transport and construction sectors (Cremers 2011). In this regard, the alarm bell for the until then rather aloof Western European labor organizations rang in 2007–2008 with the European Court of Justice's (ECJ) rulings on the Laval, Viking, Rüffert, and Luxembourg cases, which undermined western unions' efforts to protect, through collective bargaining and industrial action, established worker rights from undercutting by Central Eastern European providers (Dølvik and Visser 2009). Those rulings not only dealt with cases involving the new member states and issues that were not new as such but also had taken an unprecedented magnitude due to the social gap between eastern and western member states. They also revealed an East-West divide within the ECJ itself, and its transformation following the enlargement (Kilpatrick 2009) as well as among member states: of the governments that made submissions to the ECJ, those of Latvia, Czech Republic, Estonia, and Poland (plus UK and Finland) sided with employer's freedoms, while those of Italy, France, Austria, Ireland, Norway, and Sweden sided with union rights (Bercusson 2007).

But the freedom of movement of workers—which was by far the biggest social concern among populations and trade unions—failed to confirm the worst fears, at least until the economic downturn starting in 2008. Large migration did take place, but without causing social conflicts, and actually leading to some positive developments. Some common union reactions to further liberalization of economic freedoms took place, with at least partially successful union protests against the 'Bolkestein' Directive liberalizing cross-border service provision (Gajewska 2009). The social issues marginalized by the enlargement could re-emerge even more strongly because of it.

The situation on migration is made more complex because of the different regulations that the various old member states have introduced. Some countries (UK, Ireland, and Sweden) opened their borders to workers from the new member states immediately. Between 2006 and 2009, most other old member states followed this example, leaving only Austria and Germany to apply restrictions until the latest deadline of 2011. As an effect, there has been a movement of workers unprecedented (in absolute and relative terms) in the EU, and estimated around 1 million towards the UK, and 200,000 towards Ireland. For the first time in the EU, the assumption that mobility is a prerogative of capital but not labor has been proved wrong, and this has not failed to impact on power relations between capital and labor. Even if the 'voice' of employees in the new member states has remained feeble, their massive 'exit' has forced employers, and to a lesser extent governments, to important concessions, leading to higher than expected wage growth and even some improvements in employment conditions

This book, while focusing on the new member states, raises therefore broader questions for the EU as a whole. The social dimension of the EU and its, already weak, democratic credentials have been affected by the enlargement. Its ambition to foster 'upwards' harmonization working conditions, evident in the occupational health and safety programs since the 1980s and in the 'European social dialog' set up by Jacques Delors, has been seriously undermined. Rather than creating a 'bottom floor' for employee rights, the ECJ rulings on Laval, Rüffert, and Luxembourg suggest an opposite 'upper ceiling' beyond which worker rights should be capped so that they do not hamper the economic freedoms of employers. If the EU develops in this direction, it's often proclaimed social superiority in comparison to the North American Free Trade Agreement (NAFTA) becomes less credible. While NAFTA does not contain transnational minimum social rights, at least it does not impose maximum limits to those rights, in the way the ECJ has done. In fact, after the enlargement the EU looks more similar to NAFTA: the economic gap between Germany and Romania and the population ratio between old and new member states are comparable to those between US and Mexico. And the EU increasingly prioritizes economic freedoms over social rights in the way NAFTA does. In this way, the scenario for the new member states could be more and more similar to that of Mexico, where economic integration within NAFTA did produce economic benefits, but at huge social costs in terms of inequality and insecurity (Bayón 2009), and with a promotion of emigration as best option for Mexican workers.

The limits of so-called 'social Europe' have been known for long. Streeck (1998), in particular, pointed to the fact that in the multi-level institutional structure of integrated Europe, pressures for political defense of social cohesion tend to be deflected to national systems and are mostly compartmentalized in them, given that supranational institutions are far removed from and structurally de-sensitized to such pressures. The European Commission, on one side, engages in technocratic policy making with no social responsiveness, while national governments engage in ineffective populism or, in the best scenario, in 'competitive solidarity' strategies (Streeck 1999), which is in essence internalization of the constraints of international competition. This process is exacerbated by EU enlargement and brought to another level, where the EU liberal dimension increasingly undermines, rather than fosters, its democratic dimension, and thereby undermines its legitimacy (Scharpf 2009). Not only has the ECJ taken a more prominent role. The new European Commission chaired by Barroso, that took office in 2004 just after the enlargement, is more openly committed to the 'negative' market-making integration, as contrasted to positive market-correcting integration, than the previous ones. And the suddenly increased diversity among member states makes international competition more socially sensitive, as immediately evident in tax competition (Vliegenthart and Overbeek 2009) and in policies to attract foreign investors (Bohle 2009). The EU employment policies after the enlargement have been dominated by the idea of 'flexicurity', but if convergence has occurred, it has been more in the direction of eastern flexibility than in that of western security. Once welfare states and industrial relations have become competitiveness factors, it has not taken long before the Baltic nations, with their unilateral draconian wage and job cuts were presented as 'role models' for Western European countries in economic trouble: as Nobel Prize Krugman has noted, 'it says something about the current state of Europe that many officials regard the Baltics as a success story' (2011).

With the enlargement, the EU is becoming, for all its complex structure, a version of globalization, in the sense of placeless powers (EU institutions and MNCs) contrasted to powerless places (the member states; Castells and Henderson 1987, 10). The EU's motto *unitas in pluralitate* ('United in Diversity') sounds increasingly like meaning *unitas in inaequalitate* ('United in Inequality'): the diversity of social systems is removed by the overarching market rationality as 'only way' and replaced by stark and increasing inequalities as those between East and West.

The interrelations between EU, national, and local levels are stronger than assumed by Streeck, though. The story of the EU's new member states over the last 20 years is clearly that depoliticization has occurred at all levels, not only in the EU, but also at national and company levels. This has meant disaffection from both national politics (low turnout in elections) and the workplace (high turnover of employees). Eurobarometer surveys regularly show that the populations of the new member states are much less satisfied with their democracies—not just the EU's—than the European average. The fast-growing development of 'gated communities' in Central and Eastern Europe, so strikingly contrasting with Western European urban places and so closely reminiscent of the US and developing countries, is the special representation of a pervasive 'cancer' 'Americanizing' European democracy that acts not just in Brussels (Gądecki 2009). In the same way as the problem is at multiple levels, so can democratic responses occur at local and national levels, as well as transnationally. It is a multi-level approach that is needed for a robust critique of the EU, as it is for its understanding as an industrial relations system (Marginson and Sisson 2004).

This book, by presenting research from company and national levels, combined with analysis of EU policies and of transnational forces, attempts to contribute to such a multi-level approach, and thereby to a more comprehensive picture. It is based on different research projects I have been involved in the last 10 years, and by combining them into an integrated interpretation, including all main players (EU, MNCs, national politics, unions, workers, and other social movements), it aims to overcome limits of previous specific writings that, taken in isolation, could lead to partial interpretations. In particular, I hope it will become clear that this book is not against EU enlargement or the EU as a whole—as the question on the Trojan Horse had sometimes been seen. It is not just the case that at midnight of 1 May 2004, I was, in the company of 100,000 other people, on Budapest's Hősök tere, or Heroes Square, celebrating EU accession. It is, more importantly, the case that this book proposes an interpretation of EU enlargement as a contested terrain that should be re-politicized rather than rejected or idolized. It creates a space for social forces, from multinational companies to migrant workers, and it is on these social forces that the book focuses. Even more, I hope that it will become clear that this book is not against migration. Again, it is not just the case that I am myself a migrant, who has 'exited' not one but three countries. It is that the possibility of migration, while not an optimal solution given its individual, disorganized nature, and the social implications, first of all for the migrants themselves, is at least an option for workers trying to improve their conditions, when other options appear barred, and free movement of workers is the one important social advantage left of the EU compared to NAFTA. This book will not argue against workers' possibility of 'exit' through migration, but rather for creating the institutional and political conditions for migration to become 'vocal exit', whereby migrants can have a say in their situation (whether in the host country, the home country or at transnational level).

A BOTTOM-UP CASE STUDY RESEARCH PERSPECTIVE

Critiques of the new member states as 'dependent economies' are useful but, in their structuralism, are prone to the risks of economic determinism and stop short of understanding what actually happens to workers and how they might react: why, for instance, don't workers protest? And are we sure that they don't protest? Or that employers' and EU strategies are coherent and even 'hegemonic'? Workplace studies have the capacity to raise and answer these question marks and to root macro-level trends in actual social processes. While contextualization of the political economy of EU enlargement is important, more is needed to bring social forces into the picture, combining the analysis of actors with that of structures in a constructivist, rather than deterministic or merely interpretative, approach (Berger and Luckmann 1967).

This book includes social actors through materials accumulated during case study research: a total of 32 company case studies in the new member states, plus one case study of national-level social dialog (Poland) and one case study of Polish migrants in the UK (see Annex for details). Twenty-four company case studies, as well as the national-level and the migrants' one have been conducted after EU enlargement in Poland, Hungary, Slovenia, and Czech Republic, and these will constitute the core of the book's empirical material. Yet on some issues my interpretation also benefits from earlier case studies, in particular two in-depth ones in Poland in the second half of the 1990s (Meardi 2000) and six others conducted in Poland in 2001 (Meardi 2004).

Case studies' utility for understanding societal issue has strong traditions. In particular, Burawoy (2009a) developed across three decades and three continents the 'extended case study' method, linking the understanding of factory regimes to the understanding of social structures. An essential requirement for such use of case studies is careful contextualization and theoretical selection. If the relations between the case and the context are clearly investigated and understood, through background and insiders' information as well as through triangulation of methods involving actors outside the cases, the commonly asked skeptical question ('how do we know if the case is representative?') can be by-passed. Because the case is significant, not on the grounds of its statistical representativeness, but because of the investigated links with the context and the specific questions that it allows to answer about that context. In my specific case, the case studies would not have been that useful had I not spent the best part of the 1990s (and of my 20s) in Poland and then extended periods in Hungary, Slovenia, and Czech Republic, and had I not benefited from the collaboration of excellent local experts, as well as, in the case of studies of Austrian and German companies, of Austrian and German colleagues.

Through careful contextualization and theoretical framing, workplace case studies can be effective to address issues as broad as globalization (Bélanger *et al.* 1994). Case studies allow, in particular, to discover hidden, hitherto unknown forms of behavior and to identify and explore critical cases (*ibidem*). Company case studies, and more specifically case studies of multinational companies, have also proved their usefulness for the understanding of the link between European integration and industrial relations (Marginson and Sisson 2004). In this book, the selection of critical cases follows two rules, depending on the research questions: when testing the limits of social transfers by MNCs, the focus is on companies that are known for their 'best practices' (Chapter 3); and when testing the limits of transnational union action, the focus is on companies that are particularly internationalized, in the geographically and economically closest country to Western Europe, the Czech Republic (Chapter 8). These are the critical cases that shed light on broader issues: if transfers do not occur in successful, 'benchmark' companies, they are unlikely to occur elsewhere; and if transnational union action is fragile in integrated companies in the Czech Republic, its prospects must be grim in other situation too.

Of course, case studies also have limitations. They do not discover everything and the ideal methodological criterion of 'saturation' (implying the research is complete when new data do not change the overall picture any more) is hard to meet in practice. In this specific case, the focus is mostly on the automotive and banking sectors, which are rather overstudied in industrial relations, while it would be interesting to know more about other sectors such as retail, construction, and the food industry, on which the book has to rely on fragmentary sources. And it is mostly on the four mentioned central European countries. The other new member states (Slovakia, the Baltics, and especially Romania and Bulgaria) receive here a more superficial treatment, based when possible on secondary literature and similar studies carried out by other researchers. Another limit is that while my case studies from the 1990s involved dozens of in-depth interviews each, and those of 2004–2005 were still about 10 interviews each, the last ones (in 2007–2008) were limited to four or five. This is partially justified by increasing familiarity with the terrain but unavoidably limits the depth of the findings. The book also draws extensively on document analysis for the discussion of EU and national policies, and on 'participant' observation in expert debates and meetings during the last decade.

BETRAYAL, EXIT, AND VOICE: A BOOK IN THREE PARTS AND A QUESTION MARK

Conceptually, the book in inspired by Hirschman's (1970) concepts of 'voice', 'exit', and 'loyalty', which come from behavioral economics and marketing but have been used extensively in industrial relations and human resource management studies (Freeman and Medoff 1984; Bennett and Kaufman 2007; Allen and Tüselmann 2009), as well as in the study of the Europeanization of welfare states (Ferrera 2005) and of European labor law (Maduro 1999). In industrial relations, in particular, 'voice' refers to 'collective voice/institutional response' (Freeman and Medoff 1984) through independent representation (unions or works councils), given that individual and direct 'voice' tends to be ineffective in such an uneven power relation as between employer and employee (the limits of individual, direct participation mechanisms are apparent in the new member states too, as will be shown in Chapter 3).

The book is organized around three concepts and divided in three parts, each comprising three chapters. While Hirschman started from the issue of loyalty and of its production and maintenance, I will start from the symmetric but equivalent issue: betrayal or absence of loyalty. The first part of the book ('Betrayal') will present the unfulfilled expectations of 'transfer' of the so-called 'European Social Model' to the new member states through regulations (Chapter 1), co-ordination (or 'soft regulations'), social dialog (Chapter 2), and foreign direct investment (Chapter 3). It is this betrayal of the proclaimed 'European Social Model' that lies at the roots of a lack of loyalty towards the emerging structures (EU, national politics ,and companies) in the new member states.

One might assume that people do not mind about this betrayal and that they have remained loyal and therefore that it does not constitute a problem. The problem with this statement is that it cannot be substantiated so long as people are not asked and have little way to make themselves heard. It is actually evident that in the few cases when people are asked, they do mind, but with no chance of expressing their dissatisfaction in alternative proposals. In Western Europe, repeated 'no' votes in EU referenda express dissatisfaction but contain no positive alternative proposal (so that those 'noes' combine opposite standpoints, from the extreme Right to the extreme Left). In the East, when workers are asked in surveys, they do express their dissatisfaction with working conditions: in the European Working Conditions Survey of 2005, in all new member states satisfaction with working condition was below EU average (Parent-Thirion *et al.* 2007, 78). But surveys do not contain any 'option for change' box to tick. What happens, in Hirschman's words, is that workers 'suffer in silence, confident that things will soon get better' (Hirschman 1970, 38). In the same way as within organizations, management can structure 'silence' (Donaghey *et al.* 2011); at the macro-level EU and national policies have powerfully limited the opportunities for employee 'voice'.

Workers' discontent with their conditions in the new member states has become apparent not in their opinions, therefore, but in their massive 'exit'. 'Exit' (title of the second part of the book) was defined by Hirschman as an economic, market-based response to dissatisfaction: to quit and go elsewhere. This was contrasted with 'Voice', a political response: expressing discontent and engaging with those in power in order to change things locally. Suggestively, Hirschman also defined 'exit' as typical of the US, a country having been founded on it (Hirschman 1970). In this sense, the prevalence of exit in the post-communist countries may be seen as an aspect of their 'Americanization'.

Such 'exit' is most visible in the massive migration eastwards: 10% of the workforces of several new member states within a short period. The UK received an inflow of workers that was about 10 times higher than its government expected, and the overall movement from the old to the new member states was at least twice that forecast by the European Commission. In Chapter 4, I discuss why migration can be theorized as 'exit' and with what social implications for our understanding of the labor markets in the EU. I will show the association of migration from the new member states with dissatisfaction with democracy, both at the national level (in terms in particular of minority rights) and in the workplace (in terms of industrial relations). As Piore (1979) had argued, migration acts as a 'safety valve' for political tensions. Broader implications derive from the fact that intra-EU migration is more 'transnational' than most previous migration waves, with specific consequences for the polity. As Standing (2009) put it:

> Migration in the Great Transformation is more migratory in the old sense of the term, being almost nomadic and "homeless", rather than about reconstructing home (. . .). Migrants who do not expect to stay where they are labouring, whose goal is to send money "home", or

who do not have a legal right to stay, cannot easily enter an indigenous community. Nor, unless it is internationalized, can they easily join an occupational community. (69)

Migration is not, however, the only form of 'exit' for employees. Chapter 5 will discuss political exit through the analysis of electoral abstention, which is rife in the new member states, and populism as a reaction that, while formally political, denies the democratic political process. Yet the form of exit that has received most attention in industrial relations is turnover and lack of organizational commitment, which, Freeman and Medoff (1984) argued, increase when employees have no right of 'voice'. These are dimensions that are difficult to detect and analyze, but Chapter 6 will present the existing evidence, both from fragmentary secondary sources and data and from workplace case studies.

The third and final part of the book is devoted to 'Voice' and to the possibility that it might emerge following the manifestation of massive 'Exit', as it has already happened in history. In particular, the labor market shortages and retention problems that have been caused by migration and turnover may create opportunities for labor assertiveness, and political crisis may pave the road to political and social movements. Chapter 7 will look at the possibilities of trade union revitalization suitable to democratize the workplace, Chapter 8 at transnational responses suitable to democratize the EU, and Chapter 9 at other social movements suitable to democratize the new member states. This third part is, unavoidably, more tentative and speculative than the previous two: this is why its title has a question mark: 'Voice?'

The conclusion will deal with this question mark more directly, reassessing the available evidence in a historical perspective, and linking the shift from exit to voice to Polanyi's idea of countermovement: a conceptually useful tool, although one that does not allow any precise forecasts on when a countermovement may start. But then, forecasts are not really the business of critical social sciences. More modestly, this book, as a critical social science-inspired analysis of current development, aims at fulfilling more realistic functions: demystifying myths, detecting hidden and emerging trends, interpreting them, and reporting voices that are rarely heard.

It is not clear where the saying 'voting with one's feet' originated—it is probably as old as the idea of voting. But one of the earliest recorded uses is by Lenin, in early 1918, commenting on Russian troops not waiting for elections to decide on continuing World War I but simply defecting and going home. Once again in the eastern part of Europe, major political change of a revolutionary nature with empowering potential has been turned into a situation in which the best option for people is defecting, and opportunities for democracy are limited. But unlike what the most absurd Euroskeptic conservatives argue, the EU is no Soviet Union and thanks to this the third part of this book can be sufficiently substantial.

Part I
Betrayal

1 The 'Hard *Acquis*' and Its Avoidance

At the time of the enlargement, many looked at the EU for hope with regard to social progress. Mailand and Due (2004) noted that the state of industrial relations in the new member states was so dismal that it could only be improved through a massive effort from the EU side. A similar argument, but in a more pessimistic tone, was made by Vaughan-Whitehead (2003). A top-down approach was invoked, sometimes even with educating, neo-colonial tones. It is now time for an evaluation, starting from the effects of the transposition of EU social regulations, technically called the social *acquis communautaire*, and sometimes qualified as 'hard' law to distinguish it from the 'soft', non-binding regulations that I will discuss in the next chapter.

Countries applying to access the EU must transpose all existing EU regulations into their legislations. This is the meaning of *acquis communautaire*: something established, which newcomers have to comply with and not change it. The EU social regulations are impressive, actually unique for an international organization, and not only on paper. They include dozens of directive and regulations on health and safety at work (including, crucially, working time), working conditions, non-discrimination (initially between men and women, now also on the ground of race, disability, age, and sexual orientation), information and consultation of employees, and integration of disadvantaged groups such as disables and freedom of movement of workers. Even if many of these regulations are often criticized for their ineffectiveness, there is a broad consensus that at least those on health and safety and those on equal opportunities have effectively avoided a 'race to the bottom' in social standards and even contributed to a degree of convergence towards the best practices.

It can be argued, reasonably, that EU 'hard' regulations are less and less important. Since the 1990s, EU social policy, and with it the 'European Social Model', is increasingly 'soft': a matter of co-ordination—whether positive or negative, whether direct or indirect—and of general principles or values. But this is not the view of policy makers in the new member states: on their part, they generally consider the 'European Social Model' as nothing more than a series of EU directives (Neumann 2007). This may be criticized as a narrow, legalistic approach (Keune 2009), but it is a fact. Therefore it makes sense for this book to start the assessment of the 'hard' *acquis communautaire*, consistently with local perspectives. Moreover, there is a logical reason: it is generally assumed, with few dissident voices (Heidenreich and Zeitlin 2009), that EU 'soft' regulations are implemented more slowly and less incisively than the 'hard' ones. When looking for EU social effects on the new member states, it is therefore correct to start from the 'hard' *acquis*. Even more so that the post-communist new member states have been often described as having a 'legalistic' system (e.g. Bluhm 2006), more conducive to hard regulations than soft ones.

So, how, and with what effects, were EU social regulations transferred to the new member states?

Before evaluating the experience of the new member states, we have to avoid the mistake of comparing them with an abstract ideal of implementation. The experience of the old member states, in fact, is already one of varied degrees of implementation, monitoring and sanctioning (Falkner *et al.* 2005). Still, the overall western EU experience is one of positive, if not full, effects of implementation. Accordingly, the new member states cannot be expected to perfectly fulfill all requirements and miraculously attain all social targets by simply passing new regulations. But it is legitimate to check whether the process of implementation is moving at all, and if so, in what direction: improvement or worsening of the hitherto existing social standards.

The 'hard' social *acquis communautaire* was imposed rather smoothly and quickly on the candidate countries during the pre-accession negotiations, in spite of some resistance from local employers, who requested some 'transitional periods' before being forced to adapt to EU standards (Meardi 2002). Overall, social regulations and issues played a marginal role in the whole enlargement process, in comparison to the political and especially economic ones. Gerda Falkner, expert of the Europeanization of social policy, warned of the negative side of such smooth, literal, and technical transposition process: it lacked debates, involvement of civil society, and consideration of how best to adapt the new regulations to the specific local circumstances (Falkner and Nentwich 2000; Falkner and Treib 2008). Also compared with the extended negotiations and the very long transition periods on environmental regulations, EU social regulations appeared much less problematic for the new member states. Maybe they were perceived as either not too costly, or not too binding, and therefore transposed as a matter of course. The result is that in terms of formal transposition, all new member states actually performed better than many old ones (Falkner and Treib 2008). As in a school, the new arrivals in the class feel a stronger pressure to conform than the already cynical old pupils; even more so, if the new arrivals' access is conditional: exactly the situation of the accession countries, whose accession to the EU was conditional on the closely monitored process of adopting the *acquis*. The problem is not the transposition but its form and the actual compliance with it: the experience of the first years after accession is that if the new member states are blameless in terms of literal transposition, theirs is just a 'compliance of dead letters' (Falkner and Treib 2008, 293), where transposition occurs in a minimalist way or is not followed by effective monitoring and sanctioning. This is worth investigating: is the social harmonization potential of EU law exhausted, exactly when it is most needed?

OCCUPATIONAL HEALTH AND SAFETY AND WORKING CONDITIONS

There is still a shortage of information on the effects of the EU *acquis* on occupational health and safety in the new member states, effects which are anyway likely to occur only in the medium to long term and to be affected by problems of figure reliability and under-reporting. What is available, however, is the widespread skepticism of social actors in the new member states, used as they are to more legalistic (precise professional standards rather than broader preventive principles) regulations in the field. In particular, in Poland there are fears that EU rules, rather than improving standards, could jeopardize the established role of the Polish Labor Inspectorate, which is still perceived as the main pillar of monitoring on health and safety. The Polish Labor Inspectorate is far from perfect, surely: it is largely insufficient and it is reported that inspectors often deliberately 'spare' companies in economic difficulties. However, before reducing its role, the new rules should be tested with more caution.[1] Even less promising has been EU accession for Slovakia, where the Dzurinda center-right government (2002–2006), in the name of free market and Economic and Monetary Union (EMU) convergence, reduced the number of labor inspectors (Falkner and Treib 2008).

It is difficult to evaluate whether the effects of EU regulations have improved workplace safety in the new member states, as statistics in this field are notoriously unreliable, distorted by under-reporting, and incomparable due to different collection methods. As acknowledged by the European Foundation for the Improvement of Living and Working Conditions, 'gentlemen agreements' among member states open the way to cosmetic improvements of official data (European Working Conditins Observatory [EWCO] 2008). Therefore, the same institution's evaluation that the gap in working conditions between East and West may be narrowing (Peña-Casas and Pochet 2009) can only be provisional and conditional. A proposed EU Regulation on statistics on health and safety, which might have paved the way to better data, has been proposed but not agreed upon: while the EU is keen on comparing and monitoring macro-economic indicators and public budgets, it considers fatalities and accidents at work not important enough to deserve attention and statistical rigor.

In 2005, figures on death fatalities per 100,000 workers across Europe reveal that an enduring 'iron curtain' between East and West in this regard: with the only exception of the Czech Republic, on one side, and of Ireland, Spain, and Portugal, on the other, occupational hazard is clearly worse in the new than in the old member states. Let us be clear: this is not the fault of the EU but is a result of a longer history. But is the EU contributing to narrow this gap?

It certainly isn't in the 'worst-case' Baltic states, where the European health and safety regulations' inadequacy has been well-documented by a number of studies, and notably the Baltic Working Environment and Labor survey (Woolfson and Calite 2008; Woolfson *et al.* 2008). Such inadequacy has been blamed on the actual 'softness' of these allegedly 'hard' regulations, that is the lack of credible enforcement and sanctioning mechanisms, and the large discretion margins for differing local interpretations (Woolfson 2006). In the years around EU accession (before the collapse of 2008), the Baltic states experienced very high, mostly double-digit economic growth but at the cost of unchecked work intensification with damaging health and safety outcomes. Survey data indicate that work intensification has slowed down after 2004 in comparison to the late 1990s to 2002, but this might be because an 'effort ceiling' is being reached (Woolfson *et al.* 2008, 319). The EU integration has not managed to improve working conditions or to correct a form of socially unregulated, and eventually unsustainable, economic development that contrasts with the 'European Social Model'. Data on mortality have remained nearly the same as in 1990. In Lithuania, between 2004 and 2006, the number of Labor Inspectorate inspections fell by 1.5 times, and no reported case of health and safety violations led to criminal proceedings, something that raised the concern of the International Labor Organization (ILO; Woolfson and Calite 2008).

The most important point made by Woolfson (2006, 199) with regard to the gap between eastern and western members of the EU is that, according to Eurostat data on fatal accidents at work, while the *acquis communautaire* was being introduced (1998–2002) occupational safety was improving more slowly in the new (–5%) than in the old member states (–25%), and in some countries (Hungary, Lithuania, and Latvia), it was even worsening in real terms.[2] The gap between East and West, instead of narrowing, was widening. After 2004, the overall situation has improved, and this divergent trend appears to have stopped but neither has it inverted into any sign of convergence (Figure 1.1.). Even the overall improvement is not specifically due to the EU: according to the ILO (2010) in the neighboring non-EU post-communist countries Russia, Ukraine, and Belarus improvements were similar, and even slightly better, than in the new EU member states. Among the new member states, in 2004–2006 improvements were registered in Hungary, Czech Republic, Slovakia, and Estonia but deteriorations in (still-to-join) Romania and Bulgaria, as well as in Slovenia. The EU effect, if it exists, is then a negative one in the stressful pre-accession period, and a neutral one after accession.

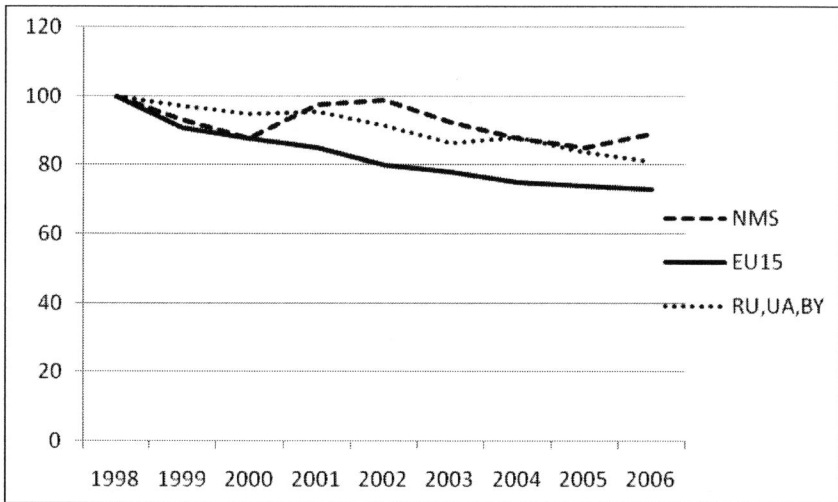

Figure 1.1   Fatal accidents at work (1998 = 100).
Data: Eurostat, ILO.

It is worth noticing a point I will get back to in Chapter 4: in 2004–2006 the worst increases in fatalities were in Sweden (+29% between 2006 and 2003) and UK (+16%), countries with high numbers of new migrants or contract workers from the new member states, especially in construction (Ireland, in a similar situation, shows highly volatile figures between 2003 and 2006, which do not allow to detect a clear trend). It may then be that the safety problem has been 'exported' rather than solved: accidents have travelled with the workers.

The impact of the Working Time Directive—legally part of the Health and Safety *acquis*—on local debates and regulations is more visible than that of the health and safety directives, and it is puzzling. The Hungarian case is particularly telling. The Working Time Directive was implemented in 2001, but Hungarian trade unions, rather than welcoming it as an example of 'Social Europe', opposed it and defined it as a unilateral governmental concession to the demands of employers, and especially multinational companies (Neumann 2007). The main measure introduced was the extension of the reference period for working time measurement, which translates into more working time flexibility under unilateral management control, associated with easy collective and individual opt-outs. In countries such as Germany, annualized working hours contribute to co-determination in the workplace. This is unlikely to happen in countries in which employee representation is much weaker.

The Hungarian case is not isolated in this regard. Similar transpositions, worsening rather than improving employees' prerogatives, took place in most of the new member states, meeting particular trade union opposition and employer enthusiasm in Estonia (Eamets and Philips 2004), Lithuania (Blažiene 2007), and Poland. In Poland, the Working Time Directive implementation was the opportunity, in 2002, for reducing minimum overtime payments from 100% to 50%, as well as extending the reference period for working time calculation, which was then further extended in 2009. It is true that, as highlighted by Leiber (2007), employers too complained about the Directive, because of the new rules on daily rests. But there is no evidence that those regulations actually made working time any less flexible. In Slovakia, the transposition included 'opening clauses' allowing employers to negotiate flexible working time with their employees without union involvement (Falkner and Treib 2008). The non-regression clauses of European health and safety regulations therefore proved unfit for the purpose of preventing national arrangements that autonomously worsen pre-existing provisions. Employee-friendly implementations occurred only in the Czech Republic and Slovenia (Falkner and Treib 2008), two countries that at the time of the enlargement were ruled by genuine center-left governments (the Czech social-democrats and Slovenian center-left coalition were not renamed former Soviet-bloc parties, such as those that had ruled on occasion Poland, Hungary, Bulgaria, and Romania, quickly moving from the old Eastern Orthodoxy to the new Western one).

Working time therefore remains a problematic feature in the region: in 2005, according to the European Working Condition Survey, in the A8, in comparison to the EU15, working hours were longer, shift work was more frequent, employees had less autonomy over working time and their health was more affected by it (Parent-Thirion *et al.* 2007; Morley and Sanoussi 2009). Moreover, there was no evidence of convergence between western and eastern member states since 2000 (Morley and Sanoussi 2009). Neither there has been convergence afterwards: the gap has remained virtually unaltered, on all these dimensions, in the 2010 European Working Conditions Survey (Eurofound 2011).

In terms of regulations, not only have nearly all new member states taken advantage of the opt-out from the 48-hour week. Six of them (Czech Republic, Hungary, Latvia, Poland, Romania, and Slovakia) count the limit by contract, not by worker. This allows workers to combine more employment contracts and thereby work over the limits: a legalized form of 'moonlighting'. Estonia, Hungary, Latvia, and Romania also have insufficiently transposed the night time work regulations, according to the European Commission's evaluation of December 2010.

Even the regulations that have been passed are met with huge problems of application and enforcement—something inherited from the previous situation, but which the EU failed to address. Often employees work longer hours than allowed by the law voluntarily, because they need the extra pay (Falkner and Treib (2008). In addition, the litigation system is very slow, with labor law courts being very slow: 14 months in Slovakia, one to two years in Hungary, up to three years in the Czech Republic, against the one-year average in Western Europe. No effective information campaigns were conducted, and the Labor Inspectorate are not only under-resourced, but specialized in technical health and safety issues only and they therefore neglect working time issues (*ibidem*). In the worst case of Lithuania, where 53% of employees declare working overtime, 42% of them add that overtime hours are unpaid (Woolfson and Calite 2008).

The detrimental effects go beyond the new member states' borders. There are also domino effects on Western Europe, due to the competitive pressure: concession bargaining on working time in companies threatening relocation, reforms of the 35-hour week in France and, above all, the shelving of the planned revision of the Working Time Directive.

Initially, the Directive was meant to be revised 10 years after its approval in 1993, with regard to the controversial possibility for member states to 'opt-out' from the 48-hour limit to weekly working time. In 2000, the UK was the only member state to make use of this 'opt-out', and it seemed to be alone in opposing the removal of this possibility, which could therefore be agreed by a qualified majority of the 15 member states in the European Council (the inter-governmental body with EU legislative powers). But the revision that started in 2003 slipped into the following year, and by then, with the enlargement, the UK gained several new allies. Bulgaria, Estonia, Cyprus, and Malta opted out from the 48-hour limit in all sectors, like the UK, while other six new member states (all except Romania and Lithuania) opted out in some sectors only, in the meanwhile also five old member states have done. These countries are enough to reach a blocking minority in the European Council. As a result, after five years of attempts by European Commission and European Parliament, the revision of the Directive ended in a total deadlock (the Commission's proposal even worsened the 1993 Directive, an unprecedented regressive attempt).

It is true that the conflict on the Working Time Directive cannot be entirely reduced to an East-West divide and the enlargement. By 2008, most western member states, and notably Germany, had also sided with the UK in defense of the opt-out. On the other side, the Hungarian socialist government has joined the small front, including Spain, Greece, Belgium ,and Cyprus, opposing the opt-out maintenance. But the enlargement precipitated a turning point on working time in Europe: after reduction until the late 1990s, in the 2000s, it started to be extended and made more flexible. The failure of the Directive revision is symbolic of how difficult any EU 'hard law' in social affairs has become after the enlargement, involving increased economic competition without social safeguards and as a shift in power in the European Council.

If EU regulations do not seem to have positively affected statutory substantive conditions, they might at least have fostered procedural changes, in the direction of stronger involvement of social dialog: a process that arguably could provide positive results in the medium-long term. A defining feature of the EU Occupational Health and Safety strategy is that in its aim of creating a

high level of 'risk awareness', it foresees a crucial role for employee representatives and thereby employee 'voice'. But this is a dimension that has not been
pushed through the local barriers that obstruct it. Procedures for involving
trade unions and civic society in monitoring and judicial proceedings have
remained minimalist in most new member states (Falkner and Treib 2008).
In the Czech Republic, the Chamber of Commerce filed a complaint with
the Constitutional Court claiming that the Czech transposition law of the
Working Time Directive is unconstitutional for giving trade unions rights
over health and safety matters (Hala 2007). In the Baltic States, the ineffectiveness of the foreseen participation and voice mechanisms on health and
safety has been documented most vividly: even if formal compliance with the
regulations seems good, in Lithuania 78% of employees do not know of any
Health and Safety reps in their workplace (Woolfson *et al.* 2008). Moreover,
a large majority of employers (91% in Estonia, 71% in Latvia, 60% in Lithuania) is opposed to the creation of such reps (*ibidem*). The weakness of trade
unions and employee workplace representation is reproduced, perpetuating
unhealthy and unsafe working conditions.

INFORMATION AND CONSULTATION OF EMPLOYEES

The most important directive in this field, in theory, should have been the
one on Information and Consultation of Employees (2002/14/EC), officially
meant to set a minimum floor of rights for employees in the EU. The Directive was expected to affect the new post-communist member states more
than the old ones, as in the majority of them (the exceptions being Hungary
and Slovenia), trade unions were the only channel of employee representation, which might now be replaced by a dual channel. However, such
transfer has not occurred, at least not in a way that makes the new member
states more similar to the German model (Rogers and Streeck 1995).

Some western observers have seen the transfer of the dual channel into
the new member states as a potential improvement for employees (e.g.
Tholen 2007). Such a view neglects that works councils have historically
been an effective channel for employee voice only in countries where they
have been preceded and supported by a strong labor movement as in Germany. In countries where union penetration is low, works councils have
mostly been manipulative tools in employers' hands (Freeman and Medoff
1984). The relationship between works councils and trade unions is problematic, and while being generally one of complementarity (Brewster *et al.*
2007), the actual dynamics depend on the specific and changing contexts
and legislations. Even in Germany, strains on the relation between works
councils and trade unions have recently appeared: it has been proposed
to give works councils a collective bargaining role, and there have been
instances of 'yellow' trade unions (that is, unions manipulated, controlled,
or funded by the employers) infiltrating works councils of companies such

as Siemens and Lidl. In post-communist countries (including in East Germany, where works councils depart from trade union positions more often than in West Germany), the context is unfavorable, as private employers are already reluctant to negotiate with trade unions. Given the weakness or inexistence of multi-employer collective bargaining, trade unions need workplace presence. Even in the 'best case' Hungary, where the dual system had been introduced 'endogenously' in the 1990s, works councils failed to play the expected role wherever unions were absent (Tóth and Neumann 2004a). In Estonia, research has found that non-union works councils were initiated, if at all, by the employers, and were dominated by middle managers (Kallaste et al. 2008). In Poland, interestingly, the pre-existing works councils, which in the 1980s had often played important functions against 'nomenklatura' management, had been abandoned soon after 1989 at the initiative of Solidarity (Weinstein 2000) and without any particular resistance: given this history of dismissal, it is naïve to expect positive developments from the Information and Consultation Directive.

While the Directive was officially meant to set a minimum floor of rights for employees in the EU, as happened with the Working Time Directive, several new member states' governments have been quick at exploiting the opportunity to undermine, rather than reinforce, employee prerogatives. Governments' initial proposals tried to replace the single channel with a dual-channel system in which the establishment of a works council could have easily made the unions disposable. The proposed laws allowing works councils to replace the prerogatives of existing unions were particularly dangerous, as they would have opened an avenue for union-avoidance techniques and management-controlled works councils. Although other possible transpositions introducing works councils *while* strengthening unions were available, for instance hybrid institutions along the Italian *Rappresentanze Sindacali Unitarie* or the South African Workplace Forums examples, both guaranteeing union presence in the works councils, this option was not considered. Union-threatening legislative proposals were pushed by governments in Poland, Slovakia, and Estonia. Only after strong union opposition (which in the case of Estonia, where the proposed law restricted the prerogatives of trade unions, also required the solidarity intervention of international unions) were such proposals amended and replaced by 'residual' works councils systems, which give priority to unions as employee representatives in workplaces (Carley and Hall 2008). Only Bulgaria and Estonia introduced a dual channel that guarantees union presence alongside employee trustees but still raises some union concerns. The Czech Republic is exceptional for two reasons. First, an early agreement between social-democratic government and trade unions led to a system foreseeing works councils only where there are no trade unions. Such mechanism involved minimal change to the pre-existing system, and it was eventually adopted by Estonia, Poland, and Slovakia, too, after more anti-union plans were defeated. Second, the

Czech Republic is unique in the EU for defining 'consultation' as 'negotiation': however, there is very little sign of any practical change.

The legal framework has since been changed in some countries by interventions from the Constitutional Courts, reintroducing threats for trade unions. In both the Czech Republic and Poland, in 2008 the Constitutional Court decided that a works council can be established at an employer's business and can also operate alongside a trade union. Thereby, a dual channel has been introduced by the back door, and over time the option for non-union representation may undermine independent employee organization: if even German trade unions struggle to fend off 'yellow' rivals and conservative reforms, the task will be even more difficult for their weaker counterparts in the new member states.

The implementation of the new information and consultation bodies has proceeded slowly. In the Baltic states, it is reported that employees lack the assertiveness and information to take action demanding information and consultation rights (Woolfson *et al.* 2008). In Bulgaria, Czech Republic, Romania, and Slovakia very few companies have introduced innovations, and Slovak trade unions believe that some employers are encouraging the establishment of works councils in preference to trade unions (Gładoch 2008; Hall and Purcell 2011). In Poland, according to data from the Ministry of Labor, about 3,000 Information and Consultation (I&C) bodies (out of 34,000 companies covered by the legislation, i.e. with over 50 employees) had been established by 2010. Until 2008, 90% of them were mere ratifications of previously existing union bodies, and the remaining 10% appeared to be weaker and less active than union bodies (Surdykowska 2008). After the law was changed due to the Constitutional Court intervention in 2008, the number of non-union works councils increased to about 30% in 2010. Gardawski (2009a) reports some gradual positive developments in the I&C bodies, but again, mainly when they are dominated by one strong pre-existing trade union. My research on employee participation rights in multinational companies in the Czech Republic, carried out in 2007–2008, found no effect of the Directive at all, as I will describe in Chapter 3. In February 2008, a review of the Directive's implementation by the European Commission (EC 2008c) reported no, or problematic, impact in Bulgaria, Czech Republic, Estonia, Lithuania, Poland, and Romania—and the positive impact reported in Latvia, Hungary and Slovakia was so generic to be possibly due only to national rose-tinted glasses. The Directive's failure to produce any tangible improvement in workplace employee participation rights is therefore plain.

Analogous problems are encountered by other, more specific pieces of EU regulations involving employment relations: in Hungary, for instance, the transposition of the Transfer of Undertaking Directive contains no clear definition of information of employees, making the norms rather hollow (Neumann 2007). By contrast, EU deregulation policies appear more incisive and disruptive of employee rights: in Hungary, a new Company Act was passed in 2006 reducing the role of board-level employee representatives, in the name of the freedom of investment.

In a similarly distorted way, the Charter of Fundamental Rights of the EU, which in the West is often portrayed as strengthening social rights including the right to strike, in the new member states is mentioned to limit it (e.g. the proposed restriction of the right to secondary action in Estonia) and to support the introduction of a different right to industrial action—that of lockout (in Poland and Lithuania). The feebleness of EU social rights protection is confirmed by the fact that in 2007 the populist government of Poland joined the UK in refusing (with a protocol) the Charter altogether, although for reasons of disagreement on civil rather than social rights (a decision confirmed by the following liberal government).

A more promising field for advances in employee consultations and information exists for that small minority of workforce who are employed by large multinational companies covered by the European Works Council Directive. In Chapters 3 and 8, however, we will review research in the field showing that the effects are strong only where employee initiatives manage to go beyond the narrow field of the Directive, and that there are no spill-over effects to the broader systems of industrial relations.

In the meanwhile, not only union membership, but also the perception of union rights keeps falling. In 2007, the Polish survey 'Working Poles' found that only 41.4% of employees believed that the right of unionizing is respected—a fall of 18.3 points in comparison to the same survey two years earlier (Męcina 2009a, 280).

EQUAL OPPORTUNITIES

European directives, community policies, and European Court of Justice's rulings on equal opportunities between men and women had a major impact in Western Europe in the late 1970s and early 1980s, notably introducing the principle of indirect discrimination. Undoubtedly, they are also contributing to shaping debates on equal opportunities and raising awareness about them in the new member states, especially with regard to sexual harassment and indirect discrimination and so are the more recent EU regulations on other forms of discrimination, especially on sexual orientations. Equal opportunities may remain exceptional as a 'success story' of EU social policy only because of its nature as '"cheap", relatively innocuous, even high-sounding platform for demonstrating the EC's commitment to social progress' (Ellis 1998, 22).

It has to be reminded that Central Eastern Europe has a different history on gender. During communism, formal equality and full (but not necessarily voluntary) female employment had been effectively achieved, despite a degree of enduring segregation and discrimination. Later, capitalist restructuring hit women employment and living conditions disproportionately, with the closure of entire female-dominated industries and services, serious cuts to childcare, and the individualization of employment relations (Pollert 2003; Hardy 2009). Such a history has resulted in some barriers to equal opportunities policies. On one side, their resemblance to communist-time policies and slogans allow opponents to discredit them, as with anything else related to the old system. On the other side, in some countries such as Poland and Slovakia, Romania Catholic and Orthodox churches have gained a strong position in the public sphere, which they use to defend traditional family values.

If the EU effect on this pre-existing situation appears to be positive, it still is below reasonable expectations of compliance. In the case of the Employment Framework Directive (2000/78/EC), introducing non-discrimination principles on age, religion, sexual orientation, and disability, only Hungary and Slovenia extended its scope beyond the required minimum, the area of employment. In the Baltic States, Czech Republic, Slovakia, and Poland, there was strong resistance from the Christian Democrats and the Christian Right, especially on sexual orientations (Falkner and Treib 2008). In the Czech Republic, the opposition from the Senate and from the President Vaclav Klaus impeded the adoption of a new bill, and transposition only occurred though a complex arrangement of individual provisions, that, according to Falkner and Treib (2008), 'are marked by several shortcomings if compared to the European standards', given that the country 'failed to create a proper Equal Treatment Body, which is meant to provide assistance to victims, conduct its own surveys and publish independent reports about equality issues'. Klaus' opposition to the Directive is resolute: in May 2008, he vetoed the new bill required by the EU as 'poor, counter-productive and unnecessary', and as a product of the Soviet mentality forcing equality of outcomes and social engineering (302). In the Czech Republic, but also in Romania, particular opposition is met by the idea of non-discrimination of the Roma minority.

In the other member states the situation is not necessarily better. Opposition to ethnic minorities or homosexuals affects large parts of local societies, and the Equal Treatment Bodies, even where introduced, lack visibility (Falkner and Treib 2008). Latvia in 2006 omitted sexual orientations from its implementation of the Framework Anti-Discrimination Directive. In Poland, the new rules' ineffectiveness is proved by the fact that senior Polish ministers can repeatedly call for a ban on homosexuals in occupations such as teaching, and that the country altogether 'opted out' (through a protocol limiting its scope) from the Charter of Fundamental Rights of the EU, seeing it as excessively protective towards homosexuals. In Lithuania, the parliament went even further by approving a 'censorship' law (so far vetoed by the president) forbidding any public demonstrations and any reference to homosexuality on TV before night time. Overall, a realistic assessment is that EU influence on gender equality is conditional: local compliance depends less on EU commitment (or rather, lack thereof), and more on mobilization of women's movements and reactionary forces within each member state (Avdeyeva 2009).

It is, as on health and safety, the application and enforcement that are particularly lacking: according to Falkner and Treib's account, enforcement bodies' resources and actual performance have lagged behind their formal competences (Falkner and Treib 2008). Sissenich confirms the same on Hungary and Poland (although Hungary has done a little more than Poland): on equal opportunities like on labor law, the 'adoption of the *social acquis* has focused on approximating secondary legislation, with behavioral adoption lagging far behind' (Sissenich 2005, 157). According to Sissenich (2007), the main reason relies in the weakness of labor and of non-state actors, resulting in a democratic deficit in the process of EU social policy transposition.

Besides the non-discrimination regulations, EU rules on sex equality include the Directive on pregnant workers, which provides for a minimum of 14 weeks maternity leave. In Poland, the transposition of the Directive in 2002 involved the *reduction* of maternity leave from 24 to 16 weeks (Leiber 2007). Again, like with the Working Time Directive, the non-regression principle of EU labor law was ineffective. Moreover, the Directive did not manage to affect the Polish system's 'protectionist', rather than equality-oriented, approach: Poland maintained its list of work prohibitions (e.g. night work) for pregnant workers, which is potentially discriminatory for the EC, rather than adopting the EU principle of individual risk assessments. The regulation of pregnancy is, by nature, complex and potentially a double-edged sword, in terms of sex equality, because of the competing aims of protection and non-discrimination. But Poland managed not to improve women treatments on either of these two sides: protection was reduced in terms of maternity leave, and discrimination risks were maintained in terms of work prohibitions.

As with health and safety and working time, there are knock-on effects on the EU as a whole, with a slowing down of initiatives in this field and even risks of political shifts towards more conservative approaches, as evident in the lack of progress on paid paternal leave proposals. A telling sign was the election, in 2004, to chair of the European Parliament's Committee on Women's Rights and Gender Equality, a hitherto instrumental body for promoting gender equality in the EU, of Slovak Christian democrat Anna Záborská, a traditionalist personality in striking contrast to her feminist predecessors. In 2009, however, the post went back to a left-wing member of the European Parliament (MEP).

CONCLUSION

The EU law has not had visible effects on the new member states with regard to employment conditions. In none of its main fields—health and safety, working conditions, information and consultation, and equal opportunities—it produced the qualitative changes that some had hoped. In some cases, as with the Working Time Directive, increased competition has led to more work intensification regardless of the new regulations, and in extreme cases, the new regulations have been used against their aims, with no concern with the non-retrogression clause. Overall, the disappointing effects of the 'hard' social *acquis* reveal that the problem is not simply one of 'compliance' by the new member states but involves the easily distortable nature of the regulations itself. The enlargement test has revealed that EU regulations on working conditions are so 'soft' that they can be bent into the opposite direction. As Bafoil (2009) has commented, with regard to social and employment issues 'the European project was barely distinct from the project of globalized liberalism' (163). According to an East-West comparison by Wallace and Pichler (2008), the resulting situation in the new member states is a combination of path-dependent poor nature of work, and new, imported insecurity. The only positive change EU regulations have provided to employees in the new member states is the one I will discuss in Chapter 4: the right to leave and work freely in Western Europe.

So, the race has not been towards the top, as the official story of the European common market tells. To the contrary, the enlargement has stopped social initiatives at community levels. In his excellent account of the 'long march' of social Europe, Barbier (2008) defines the period starting in 2004 as 'quasi-collapse' of social Europe. The enlargement coincided with the beginning of the new, neo-liberal-oriented, Barroso Commission. The two facts have been so simultaneous to be analytically inseparable: there would have been no Barroso without the enlargement, and the new member states would have experienced different EU policies without Barroso.

The 'quasi-collapse' of social Europe is evident in the lack of new meaningful EU social legislation since 2004, after the 12 years of legislative activism that followed the social protocol of Maastricht of 1991 (European Works Councils [EWC], non-discrimination, part-time, temporary work, information and consultation). No new social directives have been ratified between 2004 and 2008—with the exception of the directives on seafarers and on workers in cross-border railways of 2005. Some long-awaited acts, such as a directive on work-related musculoskeletal disorders, were stalled.

The trend may have changed in 2008, when the Temporary Agency Work Directive was passed, followed by more, if timid, acts in 2009 (EWC, parental leave) and with the more socially worded 'Europe 2020' Agenda. But to have Europe 2020 the shock of a major financial crisis had been needed. And the Temporary Work Directive, besides having its limitations (Countouris and Horton 2009), has a different story and is not the product of top-down EU policy but rather a first sign of the different, transnational bottom-up counter-processes—something we will see in Chapter 8.

2 The 'Soft *Acquis*' and Social Dialog As Talk Show

The results of the 'soft' social *acquis* appear as disappointing as those of the 'hard' *acquis* discussed in the previous chapter. The EU has promoted social dialog in the new member states in different 'soft' ways, formally: through their involvement in inter-sector and sectoral European social dialog, the European Employment Strategy (EES) and the promotion of social pacts in the process of convergence into the European Monetary Union (EMU).

Only the former of these means may have had substantial effects in promoting social partners' capacities, especially at the sector level (Kusznir and Pleines 2008). The EES has had a negligible impact and has been watered down and distorted concomitantly with, and in connection to, the enlargement. Social pacts have been bypassed or used very selectively.

Of course, the state of social dialog in the region cannot be blamed on the EU: there are deeper historical reasons, which can be traced back to the communist period, when there were no autonomous actors, and the transition phase, in which the idea of market transformation accepted little or no dialog with different perspectives or interests. But it can be asked whether the EU has had an overall positive effect at all. Results in terms of negotiations and agreements between employers and trade unions have been meager, in spite of the agenda being potentially very pressing: labor market reforms, welfare state reforms, income policies, and 'Lisbon Agenda' on competitiveness. Central and Eastern European governments, overall, have preferred to continue on their path of unilateral, top-down reforms, without recognition of 'voice' mechanisms for civil society and notably workers. If anything, reforms have been de-politicized even further, in the name of EU technocracy. The most visible aspect of this approach that distinguishes the new member states from many old ones is the repeated failure of comprehensive, tripartite social pacts. But first we'll turn the attention to the impact of EU employment policies.

EUROPEAN EMPLOYMENT STRATEGY

When the European Employment Strategy was launched in 1997, it included the formal promotion of social dialog. In the new member states, however, it has not favored social negotiations and regulation of the labor market. Even worse, since its redefinition in 2000 under the 'Lisbon Agenda' umbrella and the stress on 'competitiveness', it has had a deregulatory function, rather than a social one. Such a role is particularly visible in the new member states. The Polish Forum of the Lisbon Strategy, created in 2003 and promoted by the Ministry of the Economy, has as its core the neo-liberal Market Economy Research Institute, whose Director, Jan Szomburg, openly advocates an 'Americanization' role for Poland in the EU (Kowalik 2009). At its Conference on employment policy of 2005, the Forum recommended limiting trade union influence on the labor market and reducing the already very narrow scope for sector collective agreements (Sztanderska 2005).

The role of the EES has been increasingly marked by its focus on the Danish-inspired 'flexicurity', seen as a relevant solution for the weak labor markets of the new member states (Cazes and Nesperova 2007). The European Commission, in its 2006 'Employment in Europe Report' devoted to flexicurity, argued that 'progress on flexibility and security, together with the resources needed to implement comprehensive activation and lifelong learning policies, requires a well-developed tripartite social dialog' (EC 2006b, 110). The argument was based on the need of avoiding 'political difficulties' and 'social turmoil' and drew on the examples of Denmark and the Netherlands. While recognizing that corporatist structures are not present in all countries, the EC argued in that report that the crucial point is broadening the bargaining agenda to include employment, seen as a positive-sum game. The new member states entered the EU with weaker labor markets and, in particular, low employment rates: Hungary and Poland, together with Malta, took over from Italy the title of worst performers. So, in the new member states, there should be a particularly wide scope for change promoted by the EES.

Yet flexicurity leaves little space for union interest: the stress in the new member states is on the 'flexibility' side, while the 'security' one is hampered by structural long-term unemployment and budget constraints. The general doubts on flexicurity that have been expressed in the West (e.g. Funk 2008) acquire a more dramatic dimension in those Central Eastern European countries (Poland, Slovakia, Hungary) where unemployment is higher and the public budget smaller. In such situations, the Danish model of high unemployment benefits—developed in a country with high public expenditure and, even at its peak, low unemployment—is simply unrealistic, and as a matter of fact, it has not been taken seriously. In Poland, for instance, unemployment benefits' replacement and coverage rates have kept falling since their introduction by Labor Minister Jacek Kuroń in 1990: by 2007, only 14% of Polish job seekers received benefits, and these amounted to a meager 20% of the average wage (Spieser 2009). With EU accession, things have kept going in the wrong direction: unemployment benefits, now labeled as 'passive' policies, lost legitimacy, and the same happened to other benefits, which have often played a substitutive role to unemployment insurance: incapacity benefits were cut in Slovakia in 2004 (causing street protests in the east of the country), and early retirement was strictly limited in Poland in 2008 (despite large union protests). On the flexibility side of flexicurity, the new member states, even if employment protection law remains apparently strict, suffer from excessive, rather than insufficient, flexibility (Cazes and Nesperova 2007). If the flexicurity recipe could be judged as 'not balanced' in the West (Keune and Jespen 2007), the unbalance is even more striking in the East. In the extreme case of the hyper-liberal Baltic states, there is an entrenched insecurity system, as indicated by the very few ILO conventions that have been ratified, and both numerical flexibility and pay flexibility meet little institutional constraints (Eamets 2009).

As a 'soft policy', the EES affects member states through peer pressure and through resources—rather than financial, it is the case of 'symbolic' resources, which can be used strategically by national players. Mailand (2008) has detected that the EES has had more effect on Poland (and Spain) than the UK and Denmark. This would suggest that, somehow, the EES is succeeding in narrowing the gap between old and new members. But his analysis needs more careful investigation. The main reason of the bigger impact in Poland is simply the worse starting point in terms of compliance and performance: changes are more visible. But are these changes really significant, and are they likely to continue in the direction of convergence? Mailand reports positive effects on public employment services but fails to give any real example. His analysis is just a secondary report of other observers' opinions: it is more a rumor than an empirical test.

It is true that after 2004 TV troupes have rushed into filming new EU-funded services for the unemployed in Eastern Europe, especially if IT supported, as if this were a civilization shift. But my interviews in Warsaw's Job Centre in the summer 2009 downplay Mailand's positive evaluation of Polish advances through the EES massively. There are new resources thanks to the European Social Fund and new computers thanks to technological developments, but the activity in the cramped 1970s concrete building of the capital's Wola working class district has not changed qualitatively: officers are positive in saying that all of their current activities already existed before 2004. The only important change is international co-operation on migration, but this has nothing to do with the EES but much more with the 'exit' response, which will be analyzed in Chapter 4. In general, the EES in the new member states takes the form of old wine in new bottles.

Thanks to the EES and funding through the European Social Fund, funding for active labor market policies increased in comparison to that for 'passive' policies. In Poland, for instance, expenditure for active labor market policies jumped from 20% to 50% of total Labor Fund expenditures between 2003 and 2006—however, much of these policies are ways to artificially, and temporarily, 'delete' jobless people from unemployment statistics, and the impact of such policies for recipients' employability has remained 'very limited' (Portet and Sztandar-Sztanderska 2008, 156). Even in the 'best scenario' of the Czech Republic (low unemployment, relatively strong welfare state, and little competition from undeclared work) the results of 'flexicurity' are dubious: the number of people benefiting from Active Labor Market programs has nearly doubled between 2002 and 2007, but the total expenditure has hardly increased and the outcomes are indistinct, inducing strong union criticism (Janicko and Sirucek 2009). The new member states figure particularly badly on a core measure of the EES and the Lisbon Strategy, i.e. lifelong learning: they are not only the countries with the smallest share of adult workers in training (4.4% in 2006, against the EU average close to 10%), but they are also those with the slowest progress (a mere 0.1% in four years, against a two percentage point increase in the EU; EC 2008b). In part, this may be due to the emigration of those workers who might have been interested in lifelong learning: an issue that we will look at in Chapter 4.

With regard to peer pressure, the EES is a prominent example of the Open Method of Co-ordination as a new form of 'soft' governance in the EU. While the Open Method of Co-ordination may have its distinctive potential on issues in which transnational 'hard' regulation is not viable (Heidenreich and Zeitlin 2009), there are limits to how much countries can learn from each other through such mechanism (Casey and Gold 2005). These limits are selective: learning about the unavoidably complex social dimension of markets is more difficult, if just for linguistic reasons, than about quantitative targets and benchmarks—preferred by politicians and European officers alike.

If we analyze the new member states' National Reform Programmes (the documents member states have to elaborate every three years to comply with the Commission's 'Integrated Guidelines for Growth and Jobs'), we find regular ritual mentions to social dialog (a requirement), but we struggle to detect any meaningful outcome from it. In 2005 Poland failed to even mention any consultation in its National Reform Plan.

In 2005, The Commission's guideline 22 explicitly recommended collective bargaining as a tool for employment-friendly wage policy. Despite it, the Czech Republic and Poland failed to address the issue at all, not mentioning trade unions or collective bargaining in their National Reform Programmes. In the other countries, plans remained extremely vague (administrative support, information, promotion through small European Social Fund projects). The only exception in 2005 was the elaborated Hungarian program, which had some effects in creating sector social dialog committees and leading to the first private-sector collective agreement in construction; Romania and Bulgaria, that joined the process in 2007, also presented more specific programs. Moreover, where they mention collective bargaining, governments betray that they are concerned, rather than with its promotion as an autonomous process, with its control from a monetaristic perspective. This is most clear in the Estonian case, which introduced a limit to minimum wage increases (contrary to the social inclusion aim claimed by the EES), which is hardly surprising given the overall Commission's and European Central Bank's predicament.

At the following round of National Reform Plans in 2008, social dialog was further diluted into more generic consultations that neglected the centrality of negotiations with employer associations and trade unions, as representatives of the core productive forces in a capitalist economy. Despite two Commission guidelines (nr 21 and 22) calling, if vaguely, for social dialog, the Estonian and Polish programs do not mention either of the social partners, nor any social dialog initiative besides a generic broad consultation. Slovenia, Hungary, Bulgaria, and Romania remained the only country to include meaningful social dialog negotiations. In the extreme case of the Czech Republic, the unions had to express and register their formal disagreement on the 2008 National Reform Programme. It is worth citing the Czech National Reform Programme for its typical top-down, monetarist-biased interpretation of social dialog: 'the Czech Republic intends to provide quality information and analysis, which will allow for the social partners to become convinced of the need for moderate growth of salaries' (Czech Republic 2008: 23).

SOCIAL PACTS: A WESTERN RECIPE

National-level social dialog was not a distinctive feature of Central Eastern Europe before EU accession: tripartite institutions had been established everywhere in the early 1990s, but their actual functioning attracted dismissive definitions such as 'illusory corporatism' (Ost 2000), aimed at preempting possible union opposition. However, EU accession had been seen as an opportunity to strengthen social dialog (Mailand and Due 2004), part of the 'soft' *acquis communautaire*, and more specifically to promote the practice of 'social pacts'.

Social pacts are tripartite (state—unions—employer associations) agreements on income policies and the welfare state. They have been popular in Western Europe in the 1990s, especially in relation to the introduction of the EMU, although they have been used also later on, for instance in Ireland, in Italy in 2007 and in Spain, to face the economic crisis, in 2011. They are not part of the *acquis* and are not formally required by the EU: many old Member States have done without them. Yet, they appear to have been frequently recommended during 'peer reviews' at multiple levels, mostly by the ILO (e.g. Ghellab and Vaughan-Whitehead 2003, 28) but also by the EU. My interviews with social partner representatives in Hungary, Poland, and Slovenia reveal the suggestions come mostly from Irish and Italian counterparts. I witnessed such explicit recommendation, especially from representatives of the Italian tripartite body CNEL (Consiglio Nazionale dell'Economia e del Lavoro), at a European conference at the Ministry of Labor in Warsaw in March 2004, attended by officers of tripartite institutions from most of the EU. A comparative study by the European Foundation for the Improvement of Working and Living Conditions in 2004 promoted the idea that social pacts would be the most socially acceptable way to meet the Maastricht criteria (Tóth and Neumann 2004b), an opinion that is also expressed by academic observers (Donaghey and Teague 2005).

The argument in such promotion was that EMU reforms (notably, meeting the 'Maastricht criteria' on inflation and public deficit) are socially costly and require some co-ordination and restraint on wages: in order to avoid social protest or uncontrolled wage demands by groups of workers (so-called 'leapfrogging', continuous wage increases prompted by workers' fears, in each company, to receive lower wage increases than their neighbors), it is best to involve the social partners in centralized, national level negotiations in the name of national competitiveness. In Western Europe, social pacts have been popular in the 'periphery': Ireland, Finland, Portugal, Spain, and Italy. These countries were not already in the core of the 'D-Mark zone', used to discipline monetary policies, nor had the 'classic' features of corporatist governance, such as strong unitary trade unions and employee associations. In addition, in those countries trade unions were dominated by the protected public sector, rather than the exposed manufacturing and export one: therefore, they were not 'disciplined' by the market and needed some form of centralized involvement and control to behave responsibly. All these features correspond to the case of the new member states as 'new periphery', which could therefore imitate the path of the 'old' one. The best advertisement for social pacts were Ireland and Italy. Both 'sick' and ungovernable economies until the end of the 1980s, they eventually managed, thanks to centralized social dialog over wages and reforms, to enter the Euro: Ireland, as best performer, and Italy, as miraculously if suspiciously cured at the last minute. The limits of western social pacts, and the dubious advantages for labor (Meardi 2006a; Erne 2008), at the time, were not publicized.

Did those arguments convince local policy makers? The Polish case, where some political leaders did try to implement social pacts, is telling and deserves to be told in detail, before moving to a broader picture throughout the region.

THE POLISH EXAMPLE[1]

Poland has been considered as the worst performer in terms of social pacts among the Visegrád countries (Avdagic 2006). What is interesting, however, is that in Poland there had been some genuine political initiatives in terms of social pacts, by two eminent labor ministers who were keen supporters of corporatism. The first was Jacek Kuroń, legendary dissident, main figure in the 'Left' of Solidarity, and later of the Democratic Union/ Freedom Union part and Minister of Labor and Social Policy in 1989–1990 and 1992–1993. Kuroń wrote about corporatism in his books and was an important mediator in social conflicts at the beginning of the transition. After a wave of strikes in 1992, he prepared the 'Pact on the Transformation of State Enterprise' of 1993, which would remain the only important social pact in post-communist Poland and paved the road to the creation of the Tripartite Commission in 1994—which however would achieve very meager results (Gardawski and Meardi 2010). The second was Jerzy Hausner, a former communist but also an academic and economist linked with western international corporatist networks and author of publications on interest politics, who became Labor Minister and then Minister of Economics and Deputy Prime Minister in 2001–2005. So Polish failures cannot be blamed on ignorance or backwardness: the ideas were there but were not well received. Hausner's attempts at social pacts are particularly relevant here because they coincided with EU accession.

Hausner came to power in a new political, international, and economic situation. Politically, a new social democratic government was elected in the autumn of 2001, following the defeat of the previous Solidarity-led right-wing government. The political scene was redrawn with a drastic reduction in the direct trade-union influence that had characterized the Polish parliament throughout the 1990s, when large numbers of MPs were from the two largest and competing unions Solidarity and (post-communist) OPZZ (All-Polish Trade Union Alliance). This political change paved the way for the depoliticization of the same unions. The OPZZ was no longer an integral component of the post-communist party SLD (Democratic Left Alliance), and Solidarity, after failing to reach the 5% threshold, remained outside parliament and decided to withdraw from direct politics. A new, more pragmatic general secretary, Janusz Śniadek, replaced the strongly political Marian Krzaklewski at the head of Solidarity. The change at the top reflected deep changes at the grassroots: for the first time, opinion polls showed that a majority of Solidarity members had voted for the post-communists in the elections: for the first time, it seemed that the political divide inherited from the 1980s could be overcome.

Internationally, EU negotiations were coming to an end and the Copenhagen summit of December 2002 would decide on the accession of Poland from 2004. But rather than the end of the EU road, this meant Poland moving to the next step: monetary convergence in order to subsequently join EMU. The new member states, unlike old ones such as the UK, Sweden, and Denmark, are not allowed to opt out from the common currency, which is itself a constraint on their options and democratic self-determination. The Maastricht criteria were demanding. Inflation, at around 4%, was slightly higher than the Maastricht requirement and was driven by wage inflation, as wages, having been severely depressed in the 1990s, were now growing faster than prices (although slower than productivity). Public deficit was even more of a concern, at over 4%, with a large share of social transfers accounting for this, and it would become the main economic concern of the SLD-led government, causing much unpopularity.

Economically, after years of fast growth, Poland was facing a downturn, and unemployment, approaching 20%, had become a major problem. In Western Europe, especially since the launch of the European Employment Strategy in 1997, employment had been seen as an area in which social dialog would be particularly promising (Léonard 2005).

Soon, another important factor would have suggested the suitability of social pacts. After a landslide election victory in 2001, in 2002 the SLD-led government was shaken by a series of alleged corruption scandals and a dramatic fall in public confidence, from which it never recovered. In 2004, Prime Minister Leszek Miller had to resign and was replaced by the technocrat economist Marek Belka, the SLD had a crushing defeat in the European elections, and the government lost the support of the junior coalition party, the Peasant Party PSL (Polish People's Party) and thereby its majority in parliament: until the next elections in 2005, it had to rely on ad hoc agreements with the opposition parties. In the West, it has already been observed how government's political weakness increases the attractiveness of social pacts as 'a coalition of the weak' (Baccaro and Lim 2007), an argument also proposed on Central Eastern Europe (Avdagic 2006). The combination of corruption scandals, political fragmentation, and technocratic government resembled in particular the Italian government led by Azeglio Ciampi in 1993—the protagonist of the frequently acclaimed *concertazione* (Meardi 2006a).

Altogether, it seemed that Poland had a 'window of opportunity' for social pacts and that Hausner could have been the Polish Ciampi. Most institutional and political obstacles had been overcome, and the agenda, in terms of shared objectives (EMU convergence, employment), was most promising. Hausner, who soon became Minister of the Economy as well as Minister of Labor, invested much of his authority in achieving social pacts (Hausner 2007), seeing social dialog as a policy alternative to those of previous governments, but especially of the die-hard monetarist Polish National Bank, chaired by the author of the shock therapy, Leszek Balcerowicz. But the results were mostly disappointing. Hausner also identified in social dialog the potential for bypassing even more difficult negotiations within the ruling coalition, between the SLD and PSL. In such a situation, it was hoped that the Tripartite Commission could assume the role of a 'quasi-government'.

Hausner's first initiative involved strengthening multi-sector social dialog, bringing the sectoral committees under control. These had acquired increasing autonomy but, according to traditional corporatist policy and to the views of Vice-Minister Długosz (2005), such meso-corporatism was a threat to macroeconomic governance because of the high risk of externalities (see for instance Calmfors and Driffill 1988.) However, this initiative

already encountered resistance from organized interests and state administration bodies, and the only objective that was met was the harmonization
of sectoral social dialog committee regulations, not their co-ordination.

Hausner's quest for a social pact started in October 2002, when he prepared a document on the principles of social dialog, directly inspired by
Western European experiences of the 1990s, which was approved by the
cabinet. The document hoped to give social dialog a systematic role.

The next and most important initiative was the proposal, at the beginning of 2003, of a social pact known as the 'Pact for Work and Development'. The pact had to be regulatory and not distributive. A distributive
social pact on wages was seen by Hausner as barely achievable because of
the enduring disequilibrium among economic sectors in terms of the organization of interests: the interests of the organized sectors would always
prevail over macroeconomic interests.

The proposed social pact covered a number of issues and especially
reform of the public finances, employment, healthcare reform, and labor
law. The attractiveness for employers had to be the increase in flexibility
and control over the public deficit, while the trade unions were offered a
less clear procedural influence over the shape of reforms, which would have
replaced their diminished political-parliamentary power. At a special meeting in Sobieszów in May, the Tripartite Commission unilaterally signed
an agreement on the beginning of negotiations over the social pact. However, the very next day, the National Commission of Solidarity voted by a
majority to oust its president who had signed the agreement and decided to
withdraw from the negotiations. The decision was taken on two grounds.
First, in line with their traditional political standpoint, part of Solidarity
feared legitimizing and even strengthening a post-communist government,
which it opposed as a matter of principle. But also, the more unionist wing
of the union did not see what material benefits a social pact would entail
for employees. Solidarity would later return to the table to discuss what
was downgraded from a 'social pact' to a 'social agreement', but after eight
months of intensive negotiations, Hausner had to throw in the towel and
abandon his proposal. The employers' confederation PKPP (Polish Confederation of Private Employers) proposed to sign the pact even without
Solidarity's signature, but this was eventually deemed pointless by the government: a pact without the signature of the most active trade union would
not have protected the new policies from social resistance.

Among the causes of Hausner's failure, the enduring lack of trust between
Solidarity and the post-communist party is the most visible. Despite formal
political change—Solidarity having withdrawn from direct political participation in 2001, and the SLD having enthusiastically embraced NATO and
the EU and co-opted several former key Solidarity figures—such mistrust
seems to have a deeper cultural element, which is unlikely to change until
the generations who fought each other in the 1980s have left the scene. But
one can also see Solidarity's opposition in a different light: not simply as a

perpetuation of its ideological positions but as a learning process in terms of its union-political role. The new Solidarity leaders were all too aware of the heavy costs they paid, in terms of social support, for their support for the market reforms of 1997–2001 under the Solidarity-led government. Social acceptance for such concessions having been exhausted, Solidarity had to turn to a more intransigent role in the defense of workers' interests.

An additional explanation lies in the nature of the Pact for Work and Development itself, which would mostly have penalized the most organized sectors—heavy industry and state sector. Given the low level of the encompassing nature of Polish trade unions, in which the new private sector is almost nonexistent, such proposals were bound to run into resistance. Even the OPZZ eventually refused to subscribe to most of the government's labor law proposals, which were then implemented by the government with the support of the employers but against the opposition of all trade unions. The same occurred regarding the controversial issue of collective bargaining, with the introduction of 'hardship clauses' for the suspension of collective agreements.

Social dialog under Hausner was not entirely fruitless. More specific agreements were signed on a number of issues, from pay raise indicators (non-binding), to social security, entrepreneurship, and pensions. All of these agreements, despite being more numerous than at any time since 1989, fell well short of a comprehensive social pact, both in terms of scope and stability. The poor institutionalization of such deals could be seen in the agreement reached in 2002—after five years of failed negotiations—on the criteria for determining the minimum wage. Even before the agreement passed into law, the OPZZ protested against it (bringing some SLD MPs across to its positions) and embarked on new bilateral negotiations with the government, which were concluded by a new protocol and concessions to the unions, guaranteeing that the minimum wage would not decline in relation to the average salary. On many issues, it proved impossible to reach an agreement: proposals on tax credits for low-wage employees and on the reform of the national Social Fund for Guaranteed Benefits (which had been created by the social pact of 1993) were rejected by the trade unions, while those on social security contributions for the self-employed were blocked by the employers. On labor law, Solidarity even refused to negotiate.

The intensive contacts under Hausner did open the way to the development of some bilateral social dialog between employers and the trade unions, and especially between PKPP and OPZZ, which in December 2003—with strong public opposition from Solidarity—signed a bilateral understanding on a number of issues, such as temporary employment and conflict resolution. There was also a bilateral dialog in autumn 2004, when the social partners reacted to Hausner's proposal on the implementation of the Information and Consultation Directive, which would have introduced works councils (see Chapter 1). Both employers and trade unions felt threatened, whether by a loophole for employee co-determination or by competition from new institutions, and therefore agreed an alternative proposal, which minimized the role of works councils (the implementation law would not be passed until 2006, by the next right-wing government, without tripartite agreement, though in line with Solidarity's proposals.) Paradoxically, the main social dialog success of Hausner had been achieved *against* him rather than by him.

Hausner reacted to the frustration of the failed social pact by shifting the debate to a different area. Having established the impracticability of social dialog (Hausner 2007), he promoted a more generic 'civic dialog' involving a number of non-governmental organizations, as well as the traditional corporatist ones. Such a choice, as with the enlargement of concertation to civic society in Italy in 1998, watered down the social dialog and made it less relevant, rather than relaunching it in different ways. Hausner also promoted regional social dialog, seeing the local level as less ideological than the national one. Even at this level, however, the results were fairly limited.

Accession to the EU failed to introduce social dialog as a process for social and labor policies. The EU agenda has however at least promoted the institutional capacities of social partners through their inclusion in EU corporatist policies and institutions. The relevance of the agendas coming from the EU is clearly discernible within the Tripartite Commission, which from 2004 onwards, started debating all EU social policy initiatives—even if mostly still in a 'talk show', rather than policy-making manner.

Joining the EU was accompanied by an economic boom but also by a political counter-reaction. The presidential and parliamentary elections of 2005 were won by a traditionalist party, Law and Justice (PiS), led by the twin brothers Kaczyński (Lech, elected president and Jarosław, party leader and then prime minister), which formed a coalition with the extreme right League of Polish Families (LPR) and the anti-EU Peasant Party Self-Defense. This explicitly euroskeptic government had the external support of Solidarity and fulfilled some of the unions' demands through its program of a 'solidarity-based Poland', particularly as regards working hours and the minimum wage. However, the Kaczyńskis' conception of social dialog prioritized Solidarity over the OPZZ. The new government's anticommunism included a program of 'cleansing' the state administration and Polish society, which expanded to encompass post-communist trade unions. The teachers' trade union ZNP (the largest among OPZZ federations, and the most representative union in the education sector) in particular was the victim of ostracism by the new Minister of Education—and leader of the LPR—Roman Giertych. The unions' political divide was therefore reinstated and the OPZZ once again turned to principled opposition, despite agreeing to some of the new government's most pro-labor initiatives. The Tripartite Commission was sidelined, as the government preferred direct autonomous negotiations with Solidarity only. The government proposed a social pact under the title 'Economy—Work—Family—Dialog', once again inspired by Western European solutions (the government even created a website on social pacts, www.umowaspoleczna.gov.pl, devoting a great deal of space to stories from Western Europe). Solidarity itself, however, realized the risk of such close negotiations with the government and refused to sign the pact outside the Tripartite Commission and therefore without the OPZZ, showing that its trade union identity prevailed over the political one. This also proved that social dialog within the Tripartite Commission had reached a sufficient level of institutionalization to ensure that it could not be easily sidelined. The negotiations within the Tripartite Commission lasted, without making any real progress, from March 2006 until the summer of 2007 when the OPZZ and the employers withdrew because of the political crisis overtaking the PiS-LPR-Self-Defense coalition.

Early parliamentary elections were held in autumn 2007 and resulted in a landslide victory for the liberal opposition Civic Platform (PO), which formed a coalition government with the PSL. Although PO had had an extreme neo-liberal program on socio-economic issues, it moderated this in the electoral campaign, and rediscovered its roots in the Solidarity movement. Subsequently, PO watered the neo-liberal program down in order to obtain the support of the more socially oriented PSL. Most visibly, the initial flagship proposal of a flat-rate income tax was abandoned, as well as an early proposed law on industrial relations that would have allowed derecognition of trade unions in the workplace. The new government, led by Donald Tusk, proposed a new 'social agreement', authored by the Deputy Prime Minister and PSL leader Waldemar Pawlak. The project covered a number of core issues: wage policy, pensions, trade unions law, and employment. Negotiations started within the Tripartite Commission in April 2008.

For the first time since 1989, the government was not directly backed by any trade union and is not clearly positioned along the communist-anticommunist divide (the PSL is a former satellite of the communist party). Therefore, the OPZZ and Solidarity no longer occupied opposite positions with regard to it. Nonetheless, the negotiations on the new social pact soon came to a halt in the autumn, due to union opposition to one of its core elements: the reform of early retirement schemes. Here, the blame clearly cannot be placed on union political partisanships: Solidarity and the OPZZ acted together and co-operated in collecting 70,000 signatures against the government proposal, and they managed to obtain some government concessions over the initial plans. Union opposition was purely union-based: against unilateral concessions in a pact without any clear trade-offs. The failure of the pact lay in the government feeling stronger than its predecessors and therefore not needing to make any major concessions.

At the same time, a major contextual change occurred in the labor market and in the economic outlook. Following EU accession, economic growth and mass emigration caused unemployment to fall from 20 to 9.5% in five years. As a consequence, labor shortages became apparent and wages, previously depressed by unemployment, started growing in an uncoordinated way, creating a direct threat to employers' planning and competitiveness. Moreover, the re-appreciation of the Polish zloty started to harm Poland's foreign competitiveness. While the OPZZ launched a new campaign for increased wages, demanding compensation for the large productivity increases in the last few years (43% in 2000–2005, compared to 7% for real wages), the employers, for the first time, are now considering the usefulness of some form of co-ordinated income policy.

Economically, although Poland was hit less hard than the rest of the EU by the global financial crisis, growth prospects were suddenly downgraded at the end of 2008, from around 6% to 2–3%, the Polish zloty lost some of its value, and unemployment started increasing again. Government austerity plans to deal with lower tax revenues and currency devaluation faced immediate union protests. While making the social climate tense, the feeling of crisis has led to a widespread consensus on the emergency and the need for concerted action, as it had happened in Italy or the Netherlands in the past. Such a converging trend was visible first in the broadening support for adopting the euro and at sector level. The same export sectors that had benefited from EU accession were hit, leading to the novelty of the automotive-sector Solidarność and the OPZZ coming together with the employers' Automotive Industry Association (the same employers' association that until recently would not co-ordinate any relations with the trade unions) to seek a government rescue plan in December 2008.

In 2009, this new wave of social dialog fostered by the crisis and by the depoliticization of the unions reached the Tripartite Commission. Bilateral negotiations between trade unions and employers started in February within the Tripartite Commission on the crisis as well as on the issue of EU subsidies (on which the two sides agreed—an apparent similarity with past experiences in Ireland and Southern Europe) and led, this time, to the signing of an 'anti-crisis package' proposal of 13 points on 13 March, the most important being working time flexibility. However, the government was not a part of the agreement and, while initially expressing approval, eventually in June implemented the anti-crisis package by removing trade unions' requested points (guarantees on working time, temporary contracts, and minimum wage). This, unsurprisingly, led to an anger reaction by the trade unions and especially Solidarity. Even in this case, in a situation of shared economic concern, social dialog's limits in scope (the most controversial issue, such as the minimum wage, was removed from the negotiations) and capacity (encompassingness of the social partners, reliability of the government) have not been overcome. Within a few months, centralized social dialog all but stopped, because of the lack of interest by the liberal government, even though, by now, OPZZ and Solidarity had put their historical disagreements aside and had a common standpoint in the Tripartite Commission.

Social organizations still have too little power to force the government to negotiate when it does not want to. Poland, even if it had developed a unique 'underground' society in the 1980s, is characterized by the very low level of social association that is met in all post-Soviet bloc countries. On one side, even though trade unions remain the largest associations in Poland, most of their members come from just a few sectors, which are either state owned or recently privatized. On the other side, employers have been slow at organizing, and their associations have very little power over their members.

It is therefore no surprise that the Polish story is mostly a story of failures. The EU support of social dialog, by remaining limited to technical programs and committees in Brussels, has by-passed this crucial point: incentives to actors' organization and co-ordination. The specific obstacles to the conclusion of social pacts relate to all three actors involved.

The most visible obstacle, trade union politicization has kept weakening since 2001 and is no longer a crucial factor. It is no longer an automatic step for trade unions to oppose hostile governments' proposals and support friendly ones: Solidarity signed some agreements with the left-wing government of 2001–2005, and opposed some of the right-wing government's proposals in 2005–2007, while the OPZZ opposed some government proposals in 2001–2005; the two unions acted together after the 2007 elections. As Italy shows (Meardi 2006a), union political divides are no insurmountable obstacles for concertation; and as Spain shows, nor is it the abandonment of authoritarianism.

The government side, which had shown only occasional interest in social dialog in the 1990s, committed itself to social pacts with Jerzy Hausner in the social democratic period of 2002–2004, and the liberal government elected in 2007 showed interest in negotiations. However, in both cases the democratically elected governments were not ready to contradict the economic orthodoxy of the unelected Polish National bank—and indirectly, of the European Central Bank. The Polish National Bank also, especially while chaired by Leszek Balcerowicz in 2000–2007, adopted an inflexibly restrictive monetarist line, contributing to very high unemployment: in this way, trade union power was controlled, and there was no need to negotiate a transition from an accommodating to a restrictive monetarist monetary policy which, according to Hassel (2006), is one of the main reasons for the emergence of social pacts. When it came to taking decisions, the 'talk show' of tripartite negotiations was interrupted and unilateral decisions took place.

The employers' disorganization, which was understandable in the 1990s, when private capital was still emerging as a social force, can no longer be taken for granted. The PKPP, which was admitted into the Tripartite Commission in 2001, plays the role of a modern employers' confederation. Yet Polish business still prefers informal ways of interest representation, through lobbying and networks, than centralized dialog (McMenamin 2002). The lack of structures for multi-employer collective bargaining in the private sector is no longer a legacy of the past, as there have been nearly two decades in which to build them, and the reform of the Tripartite Commission in 2001 has been an important opportunity, with the effect of turning employers' associations into effective lobbying groups.

It seems therefore that an explanation of the Polish failures cannot be traced to single factors concerning one actor only but require a more thorough understanding of the *relationships* between the actors involved. As Bohle and Greskovits (2006) have argued, there is a new form of capitalism emerging in Central Europe, which has its own dynamics and power relations, distinct from the previous system. This form of capitalism is characterized by, among other things, an unequal balance of power between capital (and the shortage thereof) and labor (and the oversupply thereof): the resulting power relations bring Poland closer to a US-style deregulation than to a Swedish-style social compromise (Wright 2000).

The influence of foreign capital—dominant in the PKPP—in particular is a new factor. It then appears that the lack of co-ordinated bargaining structures is now to a large extent the outcome of specific strategies pursued by the employers, characterized by labor market power and by heterogeneity. In one of the most influential sectors, metalworking, the employers had actually created a federation in the late 1990s. They took the decision to dismantle it when faced with a request for a sector-level agreement from the trade unions: so it is not that they *could not* negotiate but that they *did not want* to. In a situation of very high unemployment and patchy unionization, single-employer negotiations were the best strategy for exerting employer power. Bohle and Greskovits (2010) report the same process in Slovakia and Hungary: the prominence of MNCs in the exposed sector of the economy means that other, company-specific forms of wage control, rather than co-ordinated social dialog, are preferred by the employers. These alternative instruments may be fast productivity increases or international coercive comparisons and will be discussed in Chapter 3.

To some extent, government policies have also strengthened this active refusal to engage in co-ordinated pay setting. Despite his intentions of favoring social dialog, Hausner did not introduce wages as an important topic for negotiations in 2001–2005. Moreover, his proposed weakening of sector-level committees within the Tripartite Commission, which were defended by the trade unions, although justifiable through the aim of avoiding meso-corporatism at sector level, was an additional action against the development of multi-employer bargaining. As a result, the step of combining the issues of incomes and social security, which was the characteristic of social pacts in Western Europe, was prevented in Poland. Once the social dialog was narrowed down to 'regulatory' issues only, and the distributional issues removed, the possibility of benefits for the trade unions was also narrowed down. Their opposition is therefore largely natural, and not only due to ideological positions. It would be ill-advised to keep blaming Polish labor.

THE MEAGER REALITY OF SOCIAL DIALOG
THROUGHOUT THE REGION

The relevance of EMU accession for social dialog varies country by country. In the Baltic states, macroeconomic convergence was not as compelling an issue because these young nations have not inherited high debt. In those countries, the Maastricht criteria were practically already met (Lithuania had expected to enter the EMU in 2007), apart from inflation which, in pre-credit crunch times, was not perceived as a warning sign of the underlying economic unsustainability. At the time, there was no social pact because, they said, there was no social problem, as an Estonian officer explained to me at a conference in 2007. When the Baltic bubble (caused by low-interest credit in foreign currency, dumped on the countries by foreign-owned banks thanks to the freedom of movement of capitals) eventually burst in 2008, governments started to need social pacts very much, just like Ireland and Spain in the West, to face protest and unpopularity, and negotiate the drastic reforms requested by the International Monetary Fund and the EU—Latvia, in the summer of 2009, cut state-sector wages by 15–27% and shut down 10% of state schools (Rekacewicz and Rucevska 2009). Social pacts were signed in the three Baltic states in 2009, in a situation of emergency and despite protests, when even the IMF asked for co-ordinated wage development negotiations (Gonser 2010). But, not having made any effort to build the necessary organizational capacities and dialog culture before, these social pacts were characterized by very poor governability capacity: cross-sector agreements that were not respected by sector-level employers and trade unions; therefore, in the public sectors hit by cuts protests and strikes went on, while in the private sector wages were not controlled. Nor were they respected by the governments, which in all three countries broke their commitments within months (Gonser 2010; Woolfson *et al.* 2011). The 2009 social pacts were no more than concession bargaining but in an ineffective way: they did not provide unions with any guarantees that concessions would be sufficient, and governments soon started planning even harsher reforms and cuts. Given such poor governability, a political crisis accompanied the economic one. Riots occurred in Riga and Vilnius, the Lithuanian government lost the elections in October 2008 (although, paradoxically, to a more pro-EU and neo-liberal coalition), the Latvian one fell in February 2009 and again in 2010. The Baltic states, as Bohle (2010) has argued, have found in identity politics useful substitutes for social dialog and social policy: social consensus and cohesion is obtained *against* others, that is through the exclusion of minorities, such as the Roma in Slovakia or the Russian speakers in the Baltic states. This feature of the Baltic political systems exacerbates illiberal risks (Ost 2005) and populism as an 'exit' strategy, which will be discussed in Chapter 5. It also explains why, in spite of the economic crisis and political failure, no social alternative has emerged in either the Lithuanian elections of 2008 or the Latvian ones of 2010: in both cases, the opposition is perceived as defending ethnic minorities (the Russians in Latvia, the Russians and the Poles in Lithuania).

In the Visegrád countries (Poland, Czech and Slovak Republics, and Hungary), by contrast, public debt (and to a lesser extent inflation) is an open problem, but governments have opted, rather than for social pacts, for two opposite strategies: unilateral enforcement of macroeconomic convergence, at the cost of electoral defeat (Slovakia, Poland, and Czech Republic) or a Maastricht-ignoring Euro deferral in order to ensure political survival (Hungary). Even more than in the West, then, EMU entry and socio-political stability are mutually irreconcilable: you cannot satisfy at the same time the electorate on one side and international financial institutions on the other—unless you have an instrument to involve society in the reforms and make the latter acceptable. This is what social pacts were meant to offer, and why governments should have looked for support from the social partners. However, this has not happened. Social pacts did not occur, or they occurred in one-sided, ineffective ways.

Among the Visegrád countries, at the EU accession, only in Hungary did the government prioritize social consent to Maastricht. The socialist-liberal coalition that narrowly won the 2002 elections engaged in populist concessions and especially wage increases in the public sector, disregarding the financial implication: unilateral concessions were the main strategy for political support (the same used to happen under the previous, right-wing, government). It also experimented, in November 2005, with a sort of tripartite social pact, including a three-year minimum wage agreement and pay policy guidelines (Tóth and Neumann 2006a). However, this pact responded to internal political considerations only (the imminent elections and the agreement between the MSzOSz union and the ruling Socialist Party) rather than EMU constraints. As a result, the government did, with an exceptional recovery of popularity, manage to win the elections of April 2006, but immediately after, it was punished by the international markets for the excessive budget deficit (7%), and a financial crisis followed, with the forint's value falling. A few months later, when, under direct international and EU financial pressure, the same government had to introduce a real economic program of monetary convergence, social dialog was promptly abandoned. The unions were left to protest against the government's unilateral and hard proposals, the employers considered terminating the 2005 agreement, and the president referred the draft laws on social dialog to the Constitutional Court with the aim of setting policy free from corporatist constraints. Violent riots accompanied the 2006–2007 period. A new national wage agreement was concluded in January 2007 only with much difficulty after the trade unions were threatened with the end of national negotiations. In 2008, public sector strikes hit the country, and the opposition called and won a 'social referendum' against some of the reforms. Hungary's curve in the EU was symptomatic of the instability that bypassing social dialog involves from populism, to futile electoral success, to financial crisis, and to social anger.

Slovakia's path was the opposite of the Hungarian and shows symmetric consequences of the lack of social dialog. The EU accession was immediately followed by the deterioration of social dialog: the conservative Dzurinda government in November 2004 repealed the Act on tripartism and replaced the Council for Economic and Social Concertation with a watered-down, consultation-only Economic and Social Partnership Council (Mansfeldová 2007). Socio-economic reforms pleased Brussels and foreign investors, the Slovak 'flat tax' of 19% for value-added tax (VAT), income tax, and capital tax became the flagship of liberal reformers across the whole region, and the country met the Maastricht criteria allowing it to enter the EMU in 2009. However, those reforms, involving drastic cuts to social expenditure, caused social discontent, from riots in 2004 to healthcare strikes in 2006 that led to Dzurinda's defeat in the 2006 elections (Bohle and Greskovits 2010), when a coalition of populist parties from the Right and the Left came to power. The path was, then, from financial orthodoxy, to EMU success, to social discontent, to populism, and to financial orthodoxy again after the 2010 elections.

The Czech Republic followed a more moderate path than Slovakia, Poland, and Hungary, given the weakness of its government coalitions. Negotiations with the trade unions took place and minor agreements were reached in 2006 and in 2010 (before the elections) but not on public expenditure cuts, which were implemented unilaterally (Myant 2010).

The fact that in the EMU macroeconomic social dialog (in spite of having been mentioned in the so-called 'Cologne Process' in 1999) remains no more than a disposable, optional extra is confirmed by the fact that in the only new member state where social dialog flourished in the 1990s and continued until 2004, it has been subsequently weakened. In Slovenia, a social pact on the EMU had been signed already in 2003, but the new right-wing government elected in 2004, while making EMU accession an urgent priority (the country became the 13th EMU member in 2007), disposed of social dialog in favor of unilateral neo-liberal and monetarist proposals. The EU had a direct impact on the deregulation of the previously corporatist Slovenia by requiring the separation of the Employer Confederation from the all-encompassing Chambers of Commerce and challenging state control on large firms, undermining in this way two important pillars of the Slovenian social model. Increased competition for foreign investment in the single market achieved the rest. The Slovenian unions were left with no other option than protesting, organizing the largest demonstration since independence in December 2005, and successfully opposing the introduction of a 'flat tax' in 2006. A new social pact was signed after EMU accession, in 2007 but under a strict subordination of social aims to the Maastricht criteria and international competitiveness considerations (especially inflation), unlike the pre-2004 social pacts that contained pay-off for labor as well (notably, generous pension reforms; Stanojević 2010). Interestingly, the one-sided pact of 2007 (unlike those of the 1990s) was not enough for the government to avoid electoral defeat the year after. With the arrival of the crisis, and a new center-left government, Slovenian social partners reached an agreement on austerity measures in February 2009, but subsequent negotiations over a new social pact broke down, and the employers left in protest the Economic and Social Council. Europeanization may have meant the end of the Slovenian brand of corporatism.

The real EMU effects are on wage growth and public expenditure controls. Their implementation through social dialog may have been a reasonable strategy for western unions with large loyalty reserves, but it is dangerous for unions in new member states, which would risk losing the little popularity they have—also because the euro has lost much of its attractiveness in the meanwhile.

The point of a negative EU effect can be proven even more strongly through an *a contrario* argument. If EU regulations and policies had a positive effect, these effects should be most visible where governments are EU-committed and compliant and least visible under EU-skeptic governments. However, the opposite is clearly the case. In Poland and Slovakia, the EU- and EMU-devoted governments were replaced, after the accession, by Euro-skeptic parties. In Poland, a coalition between the chauvinistic conservatives of Law and Justice, the anti-EU agrarian populists of Samoobrona, and the fundamentalist extreme right (publicly naming the EU as an organization led by sodomites and pedophiles) rules between 2005 and 2007. In Slovakia, a coalition of New Left, extreme right and nationalists (who when in power until 1998 had kept the country at the fringes of the EU integration process) was in office between 2006 and 2010. The revulsion these governments provoked abroad has overshadowed their labor policies. The winners in the elections were supported by the largest trade unions (Solidarity and KOZ, respectively) thanks to their pro-labor manifestos: the 2005 elections in Poland were portrayed as a 'solidaristic Poland versus liberal Poland' contest. While being explicitly Euro-skeptic and even refusing to subscribe to the Charter of Fundamental Rights of the EU, the Kaczyński twins showed an unusual consideration for labor rights. Even the post-communist trade union OPZZ (author's interview, 2009), which cannot be suspected of any sympathy for Law and Justice, appreciated the Jarosław Kaczyński's electoral commitment never to liberalize the Labor Code, a commitment he kept and that distinguishes his governments from all previous and later ones. After coming into power, while cold footed on EU policies, Law and Justice stopped some anti-labor proposals from the previous governments (e.g. the flat tax) and introduced more progressive measures in spite of business opposition. In Poland, these include a new Labor Code with more protection for atypical workers, more restrictive working time regulations (increased overtime bonus, limits to Sunday working), a union-friendly Information and Consultation Directive implementation, and the abandonment of the previous (EU-friendly and social democratic) government's proposal to introduce a right to lockouts. In Slovakia, they included a steep minimum wage increase, employee-friendly working time and health and safety regulations, a reformed Labor Inspectorate, and a new bill on tripartism to advance social dialog; moreover, a social pact on income policies and public expenditure was signed in February 2008 (Bohle and Greskovits 2010). In both countries, measures deemed unattainable when proposed by the EU were now easily implemented by local governments responding to internal social demands.

As Hassel (2009) has argued, when comparing social pacts in Central Eastern and in Western Europe, governments and trade unions had an interest in tripartism only in the initial phase of post-communist transformation, when they both needed legitimacy. Soon after, the strengthening of governments (allied with powerful international institutions such as EU and IMF), and the emergence of employers as a new assertive actor, have quickly marginalized social dialog. Symbolic tripartism has allowed unions to survive as organizations but nothing more. The EU accession—and Europeanization in general in the whole of the EU—may have fostered the 'expressive' functions of concertation and thereby guaranteed the survival of tripartism despite its apparent lack of results (Traxler 2010). But this has happened at the cost of concertation's instrumental functions in the actual regulation of labor, and therefore the content is increasingly nebulous. In this way, while tripartite social dialog may have contributed to limit the 'legitimation crisis' (Habermas 1973; Traxler 2010) of the state in the region, this has happened at the cost of deepening the 'legitimation crisis' of trade unions: increasingly associated to obscure central negotiation with the elites and thereby perceived as far away from the workplaces. Social dialog after EU accession, in this way, has reinforced the power unbalance as a structural problem to institutional employee voice.

THE WEAKEST LINK: MULTI-EMPLOYER BARGAINING

At least as far as wages are concerned, a precondition of co-ordinated social dialog is the existence of multi-employer collective bargaining, which in Western Europe tends to occur at the sector level. In the new member states it has been long noticed that this important prerequisite is nonexistent, with the exception of Slovenia, where, however as already mentioned, EU competition law jeopardized it by undermining employer organizations. Slovakia is sometimes mentioned as an additional example, but its numerous sector agreements have very little incidence. On the eve of EU enlargement, ILO experts had labeled sectoral social dialog in the region as the 'weakest link' and pointed at the meager content, low coverage, and poor enforcement of collective agreement (Ghellab and Vaughan-Whitehead 2003). As explanations for this dire situation, the weakness of the social partners, the ambiguous role of the state (at the same time too interventionist and too little facilitating) and the economic environment were mentioned (*ibidem*, 15–18).

As far as the social partners are concerned, it is employer organizations that constitute the crucial pillar of multi-employer bargaining: in some western countries such as Germany, it is the strength of employer organizations that allows sectoral level collective bargaining to survive in spite of rapid weakening of trade unions. In the new member states, until recently the weakness of employer organizations was blamed on, more generically, employers' organizational weakness due to their recent (post-1989) emergence as autonomous economic actors. For instance, in her study of Polish employer organization, Kozek argues that Polish business was not strongly organized because it was still 'in a developmental state', 'fighting for survival', faced with 'the challenges of the European market and globalization', still in search of its 'ethos', and 'social identity' (Kozek 1999, 102). Such an interpretation requires a fundamental revision: business in the new member states is not weak at all, and its disorganization is not a fate but a choice.

As Offe and Wiesenthal (1985) have argued, collective organization is actually simpler for employers than for employees. And in the new member states, it is not the weakest employers, such as small and medium enterprises, who hold back organization: it is, from the beginning, the multinational companies, who are neither weak nor unused to employer organizations. Moreover, employer organizations actually exist, and are highly efficient in other activities than social dialog, and especially in political lobbying—as in the case of the Polish Private Employers' Confederation (Behrens 2004).

The point is therefore not the capacity of employers to organize, but their choice of not doing it—and the failure of the EU to set up any incentive in the opposite direction. Collective bargaining in the new member states has actually declined with EU accession, at company as well as at sector level. In Poland, for instance, the decline in registered company-level agreements has been constant: from 1,389 in 1996, to 405 in 2004, and to 159 in 2009 (PIP 2009). Moreover, according to the State Labor Inspectorate, there is a tendency towards the reduction of provisions that are advantageous to employees and an increase in detrimental provisions, which have been allowed by the liberalization of the Labor Code (PIP 2008). The decline is associated with the privatization of the economy, something the EU has encouraged without setting any safeguard for employee rights. In the same way, sector-level bargaining has declined with the retrenchment of state-controlled sectors: in 2000, in Poland there still were six significant (i.e. not on small sub-sectors) sector-level agreements in the private sector. By 2008, half of them had disappeared due to employer withdrawal: road transport, cereal processing, and steel—all sectors in which major privatization took place. Only one case followed the opposite trend: previously state-owned railway workers managed to keep a sector-level agreement despite privatization. As a result all four surviving private sector agreements have their roots in the public one: railways, energy, mining, and military industry.

Private employers' active disinterest in co-ordinated bargaining is clear. In Poland, employer organization representatives from the private sector explicitly exclude relations with the trade unions from their functions, and some business organizations have gone as far as to forbid agreements with trade unions (Anacik *et al.* 2009). Gardawski (2009a, 487–488) reports the telling cases of Polish foundry, automotive, and retail sector. Despite union pressure and advanced negotiations, employers decided to withdraw or even, to avoid any risk of having to sign anything, to dissolve the employer associations themselves. It was not the lack of organization but the explicit choice to disorganize that prevented collective agreements.

Why, in spite of some institutional pre-condition through the discussion of minimum wages in tripartite institutions (Hassel 2009), is collective bargaining rejected by employer organizations, and industry-wide wage negotiations are seen as an infringement on entrepreneurial freedom, as for example by the Klaus government in the Czech Republic from 1992 to 1997 (Bluhm 2006; Stark and Bruszt 1998)?

Multinational companies, thanks to their 'systemic power' (Bohle and Greskovits 2007), have been the main actors behind this decision to avoid sector-level collective bargaining. Those operating in the export sectors, in particular, set their wage references cross-nationally, and they are largely uninterested in national developments. But even in the sheltered sectors, such as services, competition on wages is, rather than avoided, actively promoted by private companies—which betrays a focus on short-term predatory profit opportunities, rather than on long-term sustainable investment and competition on the basis of quality and efficiency.

If we look inside the companies, the rejection of co-ordinated social relations and social dialog actually goes even further and has even deeper roots. For not only is wage setting decentralized towards the enterprise but also very often towards the individual, especially in the extreme case of the Baltic states. Woolfson *et al.* (2008, 328) describe the informal individualistic approach to salary issues in Estonia, Latvia, and Lithuania, which leads to a drastic re-appraisal of the real impact of collective bargaining even in those companies where it occurs. The widespread practice of 'envelop wages', constitutes a barrier against formal negotiations of wages (Woolfson 2007a; Williams 2009). Wage secrecy is a very common company policy, even if it meets resistance on the employee side (see Chapter 6). The competition from the large informal sector is a major obstacle to effective formal collective bargaining. According to the most trustworthy estimates, in 2004, the informal sector accounted for between 17% (Slovakia) and 39% (Latvia) of the economy, all above the OECD High Income average of 15% (Schneider and Buehn 2007). There is little evidence that this has declined: actually, according to Schneider and Buehn, if there is a trend at all, it is towards increasing informality. In Poland, the Central

Statistical Office estimates that the number of workers in the informal sector has increased from 900,000 to 1.2 million between 2002 and 2008, with a further increase expected for 2009 due to the economic slowdown in the formal economy (GUS 2009). In Romania, a link has also been noted between emigration and informality, as circular migrants have a strengthened preference for short, informal jobs and tend to develop a 'culture of evasion' (Parlevliet and Xenogiani 2008). This hints to a link between Exit and lack of Voice that will be the topic of Chapter 4.

CONCLUSION

As Traxler (2010) has argued, European social dialog performs an 'expressive' function meant to compensate for the democratic deficit and the legitimation weakness of the EU. Nowhere is this more visible than in the new member states. Tripartism as a device has fulfilled this function to some extent but at the cost of depleting trade unions of their own, fragile, legitimation. The frequently heard criticism of trade unions in the region as excessively political is therefore misplaced: the problem is not that trade unions use politics (if anything, they should have used it more, given the magnitude of the political decisions that have been made) but that politics has used trade unions—to then dispose of them. The clearest contrast is between tripartism and social pacts—that have been formally sponsored by the EU, but with little content—and organized collective bargaining—that would have a major regulatory and civilizing role but has been further undermined.

If in the previous chapter we have seen that EU 'hard' policies are actually very 'soft', the paradox of the 'soft' policies seen in this chapter is that they have accompanied very 'hard' decisions: the single market and liberalization, the road to the EMU and the Maastricht criteria, and the competition for Foreign Direct Investment. As a result, another major actor has emerged in European integration: multinational companies.

3 The Hoped Transfer through Foreign Investment

There is a more indirect, or bottom-up, way in which EU integration might have led to employment relations in the new member states to converge towards Western European standards. The EU integration, by removing barriers to the mobility of goods and capitals, promotes foreign direct investment (FDI). It could therefore be hoped that those western companies with a tradition of social dialog and employee participation, could transfer those practices to the countries they would invest in, and even set a positive example for local employers. In particular, this should have happened in the case of companies from those countries where employee participation rights are most entrenched, such as Germany and Austria, which also happen to account, together with other so-called 'co-ordinated market economies' (Hall and Soskice 2001), for the largest share of FDI in the region (Rugraff 2006). In those countries it is often argued that 'codetermination' is good for companies' effectiveness and economic success. Peter Hartz, former personnel director of Volkswagen (but then advisor to Chancellor Schröder and eventually hit by corruption scandals), offers a particularly authoritative example when arguing that for German employers, 'if codetermination didn't exist, it should be invented' (Hartz 2007, 103). Why, then, not to reinvent it in the new company sites abroad?

Before the enlargement, an expert of the European Trade Union Institute speculated that:

> The activities of EU companies with their overwhelming share of FDI in each of the accession countries, have been assigned a key role in closing the various gaps between Central Eastern Europe and EU by the architects of transition; in other words, in improving company performance within an emerging culture of business ethics, corporate social responsibility and European labor standards (...) The overwhelming presence of EU companies has raised expectations that the European social model will have a strong impact on emerging structures and processes of social dialog. (Gradev 2001, 9,16)

Such expectations may seem naïve today (and in fact Gradev himself qualified them carefully), but they were not isolated, and actually inspired academic, public, and European debates of the last decade. They were particularly widespread, as I could notice directly, among Austrian and German experts and practitioners. Similar hopes of foreign companies introducing good practice had been raised in the broader area of corporate social responsibility (e.g. Koleva 2009). This chapter will discuss—through a review of data and literature and through case studies carried out between 2004 and 2008—how far FDI into Central Eastern Europe has actually been a potential 'bearer' of standards and practices associated with the 'European Social Model'.

THE COMPLEXITY OF FOREIGN DIRECT INVESTMENT

Even if the new member states, given the small size of their economies, are rather small players in global FDI flows, inward investment has been the dominant force of investment for them, accounting for around half of investment in manufacturing in Hungary, Czech Republic, and Estonia, and about a third in the other new member states (OECD 2010b). Growth of FDI inflows has been fast and is now well above world's average. The ratio of FDI stocks to the GDP in 1989 was less than 1% in Central Eastern Europe, and 8% in the world; by 2003, on the eve of EU accession, it was 39% in Central Eastern Europe and 22% in the world; by 2008, in all new member states except the Baltic states, it was well above the 'old' EU average of 35% (UNCTAD 2010). In spite of their later entry, the new member states have much higher penetration of FDI than the old member states. In terms of employment, OECD and UNCTAD data indicate that four new member states (Estonia, Latvia, Hungary, and the Czech Republic) are particularly permeated by FDI (mostly in the export sector): in these countries, MNCs employ over 40% of the manufacturing workforce and over 20% of the total. In the other new member states, figures are around the EU average, at 20–30% in manufacturing and 10–20% of total employment. The FDI is therefore an important factor in the labor market: being organization bound, it has more direct and immediate effects for industrial relations than foreign trade.

Econometrics indicates that FDI explains up to three quarters of economic growth in Central and Eastern Europe (Ferrazzi and Revoltella 2008). Yet these studies (mostly sponsored by western financial institutions) do not dispose of historical counterfactuals on policy alternatives and are therefore not fully convincing. But even if there is little doubt about a significant contribution to capital formation, technology and growth, question marks remain with regard to the quality of growth and change, and to the social effects. Onaran and Stockhammer (2008), analyzing data from Czech Republic, Hungary, Poland, Slovakia, and Slovenia between 2000 and 2004, found that FDI, in the medium term, has a negative effects on wages. The direction of the causal link is unclear: it might be that FDI prefers countries with low wage growth, rather than that low wage growth follows FDI. In either case, however, a growth pattern based on FDI inflows, and competition for those inflows, should not be taken as inherently good for society. The evidence is, rather, that it involves a worsening relative situation for employees, economically and politically: wage growth falls behind productivity growth, and political influence is undermined by the subordination of political and social policies to the preferences of prospective foreign investors.

In Poland, the 'Working Poles' survey shows that employees of large multinationals are the employees most satisfied with material working conditions (technology, training), but also, paradoxically, the most dissatisfied with work organization issues: management fairness, trust between management and employees, employee influence on their work, intra employee relations (Czrazasty 2009, 398–399).[1] Those working in medium-size MNCs (94.1%) and of those working in large MNCs (92.7%) declare that 'submission to orders dominates', and 'modern autocracy' emerges as the typical organization culture of MNCs, as distinct from 'participatory-integrative' and 'enlightened paternalism's cultures found in Polish public- or private-owned companies (*ibidem*, 399,407). The survey authors conclude therefore that 'foreign capital is most frequently characterized by opportunistic behavior, rather than participative employment relations' (*ibidem*, 417).

The issue of whether inward investment can help entrenching the 'European Social Model' is complex, because FDI is a very varied phenomenon. A range of contingent and interplaying factors, of economic, social, and institutional nature, need to be considered. The most important are the following (Marginson and Meardi 2006): whether FDI motivation is market or efficiency seeking; whether the factor composition of the activities is capital or labor intensive; whether inward investment entry was through 'brownfield' acquisition or a 'greenfield' start-up; the home country of the MNCs concerned; industrial relations institutions in the host country; and the influence of company-specific transnational institutions. In addition, local linkages and institutions will determine how far inward investment may have indirect or spillover effects on indigenous firms. The two more contested issues are entry motivation and factor composition of FDI.

The entry motivation of FDI into the new member states has gradually shifted from market access to efficiency considerations due to EU integration. The EU is a 'macro-market', where tariff and (most) non-tariff barriers have been dismantled and where internationally integrated production is possible. In addition, the need, by western companies, to eliminate (usually through acquisitions) local market competitors was mostly concluded in the 1990s. After accession, only service providers and some specific manufacturing companies still need a local presence for market reasons—for the others it may be cheaper to export. By contrast, local production for re-export becomes more attractive. In fact, in the 1990s MNCs imported into new member states much more than they exported, therefore protecting rather than eliminating jobs at sites in the West. By 2004, however, they exported more than they imported (with the exception of the 'bubble economy' Baltic states), and mostly back to western Europe. This is most visible in the automotive sector, where many final producers already in 2004 re-exported to Western Europe around 90% of their production (Pedersini 2004).

Differences among sectors are important in shaping the evolving pattern. At the time of enlargement, investors and experts' surveys (UNCTAD-DITE 2004; Tholen and Hemmer 2004) expected FDI inflows to increase in food and beverages, motor vehicles, other transport equipment, and, to a lesser extent, publishing and media, and electrical and electronics equipment. By contrast, FDI in low-wage sectors like textiles and clothing is not expected to grow. Improved prospects for FDI in the services sector focused on non-tradable services (e.g. construction, retail and wholesale trade, business services). The FDI flows were polarizing between expanding service sectors, where market-access is the main motivation and certain manufacturing sectors, where efficiency considerations dominate.

Contrary to expectations about conforming to local practices, market-seeking investment can involve dramatic change. Much inward investment into retail, hospitality, food and beverages, and business services has provided, by introducing new products and forms of service, the most visible examples of westernization. As far as labor conditions are concerned, considerable attention has focused on foreign hypermarket chains, for example in Poland (PIP 2005) where systematic violations of the Labor Code have been detected by the Polish Labor Inspectorate and on meat production (e.g. Kennedy 2003). Such instances profoundly influence popular representations of foreign investors.

An additional important distinction, in the new member states, occurs within the broad efficiency-seeking category of FDI, between so-called first generation (until the late 1990s), 'outward processing' operations and second-generation operations, which are integrated within a cross-border production network (Fichter 2003; Radosevic *et al.* 2003). Outward processing involves re-location to new member states of labor-intensive, low value-added activities by MNCs, either on a sub-contract or wholly-owned basis. The emphasis is on taking advantage of significantly lower labor costs and weaker labor protection. Such investment can be regarded as escaping the requirements that the 'European Social Model' places on employment practice, and its governance, in Western Europe. Its prevalence in the mid-1990s even resembled the *maquiladora* phenomenon at the Mexico-US border (Ellingstad 1997), which has been shown not to benefit working conditions (e.g. Bacon 2004). First-generation efficiency-seeking FDI had its dominant period in the early 1990s under the EU's special tariff regime for Outward Processing Traffic in the (then) associate countries (Pellegrin 2001). Enduring longer than expected, it eventually declined in the face of the gradual reduction of overall tariffs and a slow but steady increase in labor costs. It only gained a significant presence in Hungary, which initially attracted most FDI. Not surprisingly its influence on industrial relations was assessed as largely negative (Makó and Novoszáth 1995).

Efficiency-seeking inward investment of the second generation (since the late 1990s, when EU accession became a clear prospect) tends to be implanted in an international production network (already well-established in Western Europe). The emphasis is on comparative advantage in unit labor costs (i.e. the combination of labor costs, labor quality, and labor productivity), but with the focus shifted from wages to productivity. Insofar as institutions and conventions governing employment practice in Western Europe are seen as potentially contributing to such comparative advantage, inwards transfer seems more likely. The structural change towards this second generation in the late 1990s opened a period characterized by a fast increase in productivity (faster than wages), linked to technological and infrastructural upgrade (Galgóczi 2003). Since MNCs are the main source of productivity improvements in the new member states (Barrer and Holland 2000), their unit labor costs have probably declined much faster than for the aggregate economy. The upgrade of production in Central and Eastern Europe is a continuous process, which in turn affects MNCs' employment practices. The cases of a German-owned investor in Hungary and Fiat in Poland (Meardi and Tóth 2006) demonstrate this: after an initial period of direct, one-to-one transfer of practices, which led to a number of difficulties, the central European sites developed into innovative model plants, and settlements of industrial relations were achieved, which no longer reflect the original model.

A related and equally important distinction is between labor-intensive and capital-intensive activities. Bohle and Greskovits (2006) contend that in general, labor-intensive export industries such as electronics, clothing and footwear, and furniture, have become the leading sectors in new member states. There are differences among countries. In the Visegrád countries (Czech Republic, Slovakia, Hungary, and, to a lesser extent, Poland), skilled-labor intensive industries are prominent, whereas in the Baltic countries, Romania, and Bulgaria unskilled-labor intensive industries prevail (but in Romania FDI in skilled-labor production has been increasing). In more capital-intensive industries the activities which have been located in new member states tend to be those which require a relatively high labor input, such as car assembly and automotive parts manufacture. Most exports from the new member states to the EU15 are of low or medium-low technological content (even if there has been an increase in high and medium-high tech exports), and FDI has played an important role in this process of international specialization (OECD 2009). Critics, such as Hardy (2009), stress that the positive effect of FDI is limited by the low investment in research and development and the enduring specialization in lower technological segments. While low- and mid-skilled sectors in the new member states have benefited, high added-value ones have not: the Central Eastern European machinery production industry is a loser of economic integration (Jürgens and Krzywdzinski 2010).

According to Bohle and Greskovits (*ibidem*), the implications of this profile for the successful implantation of the 'European Social Model' are unpropitious. The socio-economic basis of the compromise between capital and labor in Western Europe reflects—they argue—a combination of employer preparedness to accommodate to labor's demands and a labor movement strong enough to secure, and maintain, such an accommodation. This compromise stemmed from conditions prevailing in leading sectors, which in the instance of (North) Western Europe were capital goods and capital-intensive consumer goods industries. In these sectors, relatively skilled labor represented a crucial (not easily replaceable) factor of production and labor organizations' capacity for disruptive action was strong. In addition to these potentially coercive influences on employers, business had an interest in labor as an important source of direct and indirect (in the case of capital goods sectors) demand—and hence in improved standards of living. However, in the labor-intensive industries, which tend to be the lead sectors in the new member states, none of these conditions apply with sufficient strength. Indeed the obverse pertains: relatively unskilled labor is more easily replaced, labor organization is weak, and, given the export orientation of much production, business interest in labor as a source of local demand for products is diminished. Bohle and Greskovits' stark conclusion is that in the new member states the socio-economic basis for the 'European Social Model' does not exist.

Yet FDI is more than the actual investment. Its centrality in economic and political discourse goes beyond the amount of investment MNCs decide to do. Competition for investment puts in place broader social and economic change, even if the investment does not happen. The negotiation power unbalance can be easily abused in the absence of careful strategies by host countries authorities and trade unions. Hungary was the most enthusiastic promoter of FDI immediately after 1989 (Stark and Bruszt 1998), but the other countries of the region followed its example in rather similar ways. Their one-sided view of FDI as an inherently good thing, however, contrasts with ILO and OECD studies underlining that FDI may often have substitution, rather than positive, effects on employment and that if it occurs through mergers and acquisition it is frequently associated with job losses (Kim 2006; Molnar *et al.* 2008).

As a matter of fact, the largest MNCs were sometimes in a position, when they planned major investments, to play different countries off against each other in offering the best investment conditions. This was most apparent in the cases of Toyota, Peugeot, and Hyundai in 2002–2004, which organized open tenders across several Central European countries, which echoed the popular image of social and tax dumping. Poland lost all three opportunities, which were promising aggregate totals of about 20,000 jobs each: Toyota chose the Czech Republic; Peugeot-Citroën and Hyundai chose Slovakia. Yet the political effect of the process was larger than 20,000 jobs, by impacting on the media and political perception of foreign investment.

These MNCs' strategy of exploiting the competition among the countries of the region through a slow and gradual decision process was comparable to a beauty contest: initially, localization offers are collected from all countries; then, two or three countries are 'short-listed' and negotiations are undertaken with local authorities, in order to bargain the best possible offers in terms of tax exemptions, public infrastructure support, etc.; finally, the decision is taken but without declaring the reasons of the choice, therefore, leaving local actors in the dark as to how to negotiate more effectively with them. This is particularly relevant for employment issues. There is no evidence that labor costs and industrial relations—as opposed to, above all, infrastructure—played a decisive role in these three localization decisions: labor costs are actually higher in the Czech Republic, and unionization rates are actually higher in Slovakia and Czech Republic; moreover, pay-rolls make up a tiny part of production costs in the region. However, it was the labor issue to be strongly stressed in the media, in political debates and even by the authorities. A statement by the Polish Agency for Foreign Investment on the day of Hyundai's decision stressed that 'during the negotiations we have been repeatedly pointed to trade unions' activeness and strength', while Economy and Labor Minister Hausner declared that 'surely labor costs have been a problem' (Kubik 2004). In the preceding and following days media repeatedly insisted on labor costs and industrial relations barriers to national competitiveness.

Foreign investors have also largely avoided joining indigenous employers' organizations or created their own (Rugraff 2006). Even in the case of German companies in Slovakia (that is, firms with a home history of strong organization in a host country with relatively strong associations), membership of local Chambers is low (Tholen 2007). In Poland, MNCs took the leading role in the creation of a separate employer confederation (PKPP) in 1998. In Bulgaria, foreign employers organized originally in a separate association (the Bulgarian International Business Association), although this later merged into the Confederation of Bulgarian Employers. In Lithuania, a new MNC-dominated business association (IF) has been created. The MNCs in the region also have the frequent tendency to join national employer federations, but not their sector organizations, as it has happened in Bulgaria, the Czech Republic, and Poland.

The knock-on effect of FDI is visible in the activity of local foreign investment agencies, revealing how far governments in the regions treat labor considerations as an important asset in an open competition with their neighbors. These agencies' websites (www.sario.sk; www.czechinvest.com; www.paiz.gov.pl; www.itdh.hu; all websites accessed in July 2006) were outspoken: the Slovaks stressed low overall labor costs and the World Bank title of most flexible labor market in Europe; the Czechs highlighted low indirect labor costs, that 'there is no history of large-scale strikes', and that union membership had fallen from 2,292,000 to 610,000 (11% density) between 1995 and 2005; the Poles were proud of having the longest working hours in Europe; and the Hungarians argued that they had the lowest earnings for the highest productivity in the region.

By contrast, the positive knock-on, or spillover, effects are hard to detect and seem highly doubtful, as pointed by studies already before the enlargement (Radosevic *et al.* 2003; Ladó 2001). No evidence to the contrary has emerged after EU accession, with the isolated exception of some working time arrangements, as we will see.

A survey of EU countries' national observatories on MNCs and collective bargaining for the European Industrial Relations Observatory in 2009 adds some more information on the role of MNCs in the region (Marginson and Meardi 2009). In most new member states, collective bargaining appears to be higher in MNCs than in national companies but only because MNCs tend to be larger employers (unfortunately, the available information does not allow to test for size systematically). In some countries (Poland and Hungary, plus Romania and Slovenia where coverage is close to 100% for the whole economy) there is no difference—and therefore no positive effect—between MNCs and national employers. Worst of all, in Estonia and Latvia collective bargaining coverage is reported to be lower in MNCs than in the rest of the economy. In these two Baltic countries FDI tends to be concentrated in lower-skill, lower-value added sectors and may follow a similar low-cost, labor intensification logic to the well-known *maquiladora* investments on the US-Mexico border.

So far we have reviewed the available, but very partial, statistical and national-level information on FDI. For a better understanding of its effects, it is best to look at in-depth case studies.

EVIDENCE FROM MULTINATIONALS' SHOP FLOOR, 2004–2005

To assess more closely the effect of the EU in this regard, I will now present the results of two research projects comparing German (and Austrian) employers with US and UK ones, with regard to the industrial relations models followed in their Central Eastern European sites. This will help to understand whether the employers from the core countries of the 'European Social Model' have any distinctive effect, as compared to the Anglo American ones.

The US-Germany comparisons in industrial relations have a long tradition and include different views as to whether German companies are still distinctive. American and German companies have been frequently contrasted (e.g. Lawrence 1991; Stewart *et al.* 1994; Wever 1995) and their HRM styles compared. The latter is generally described as a 'collaborative' system, while in the former 'firms are islands of authoritative control and order amidst market disorder' (Whitley 1999, 43). However stylized this distinction may be, the empirical validity of such a dichotomy has been demonstrated in comparisons between British and German firms (Ebster-Grosz and Pugh 1996; Lane 1998). Moreover, such comparison is of theoretical relevance, for the two business systems differ notably on the decisive variable of employer-employee relations and on the nature of flexibility (Streeck 1987): the US model is based more on the principle of 'contract' (on the assumption of 'exit' implicit in the American idea of 'employment at will') while the German on that of 'status' (which includes the right of 'voice').

Some have expressed skepticism, however, as to the endurance of the German variant of the continental model, when faced by global capital (Altvater and Mahnkopf 1997; Streeck 1997; 2009), and others have noted that German companies are eager to learn from practice in Anglophone countries (Ferner and Varul 2000). Global 'best practices'—whether inspired by 'dominance effects' of US hegemony (Smith and Meiksins 1995) or strategically chosen (Taylor *et al.*1996)—will then prevail in the employment practices of MNCs.

In fact, while American MNCs' specificities are illustrated by recent studies of employment relations in their European subsidiaries (Almond and Ferner 2006), the case of German companies is somewhat different. Since the German business system relies more heavily on domestic associations and public institutions, it is more difficult for German-based MNCs to export their practices abroad. Hence, attention has been paid to the limits of practice transfers by German companies abroad. Transfer may occur more in style than substance (Ferner and Varul 2000; Tüselmann *et al.* 2008), be conditioned by practice-specific cost considerations (Rosenzweig and Nohria 1994), or be modified by local functional equivalent (Meardi and Tóth 2006).

Nonetheless, the German model is still seen by some as transferable: 'the German system of co-participation is stable and recognized (. . .) [and] radiates in the European Works Councils at the EU level' (Pries 2004, 95). Some (positive) 'German' specificity in terms of social dialog was detected in the region, especially by Galgóczi (2003) in Hungary and by Jürgens and Krzywdzinski (2010) and Bluhm's (2001) in Poland and Czech Republic— although Bluhm herself would subsequently revise her evaluation downwards (Bluhm 2007). One clear example of German influence of industrial relations is the increasing popularity of 'working time' accounts, in collective agreements and in legislation, in Czech Republic, Slovakia, and Poland, three countries with a strong presence of Volkswagen, a promoter of this form of working time flexibility. While negotiated working time flexibility might be an important area for implementing participative industrial relations; however, it is debatable whether its implementation in the new member states is sufficiently well-balanced between employees and employers.

Others have questioned the presumption about the specificity of MNCs from continental Europe with regard to their operations in Central Eastern Europe. Dörrenbächer (2002), Rugraff (2006), and, lately, Bluhm (2007) contend that it is equally plausible that German MNCs are looking to escape certain features of the domestic institutional landscape, including Germany's robust system of co-determination and consultation and its sector-level collective bargaining arrangements. Further, there may be important 'intra-national' variations in the sector- and company-specific expressions of national institutional models: concerning Germany, Bluhm (2007) points to differences between large and medium-sized companies, which reflect also different ownership structures.

The research I conducted in 2004–2005, with an international team of colleagues from Britain, Germany, Poland, Hungary, and Slovenia, tried to shed more light on this unsolved issue. The research was based on a sample of 12 subsidiaries of German and US companies in the components sub-sector of the automotive industry in Poland, Hungary, and Slovenia, preceded by an exploratory study of the sector in each host country. Two companies from each country of origin were selected in each of the three Central Eastern European countries, as a two-by-three comparison allows for greater generalization (see the Annex for details and names of the case studies).

The automotive industry was chosen because of its high level of internationalization and its importance for FDI in Central Eastern European economies (UNCTAD 2005). The FDI in the component sub-sector is particularly dictated by efficiency considerations, as 90% of the production is for export, unlike vehicle final assembly which is more market-oriented and therefore somewhat less prone to direct cross-border efficiency comparisons (see Chapter 8).

The initial mapping of the population of foreign investors in the sector revealed, counter-intuitively, the lower unionization in German than American companies in Poland (the country with the highest number of foreign companies), even controlling for size and mode of entry (Table 3.1)—already an important blow to the expectation of German companies transferring participation and representation practices. The low number of cases requires caution: the results contradict the thesis of German investors being more pro-unions than the American, without being significant enough to conclude that they are less so. They suggest that many German companies are fleeing, rather than transferring, the German model.

Table 3.1 Union Presence in German and US-owned Automotive Component Companies, Poland

Entry	Tot	Greenfield				Brownfield			
Size		≤300	301–1,000	>1,000	Tot (%)	≤300	301–1,000	>1,000	Tot
German	35%	0/4	1/6	2/2	25%	0/0	3/4	0/1	60%
US	77%	0/1	1/2	3/3	67%	1/1	2/3	3/3	86%
Tot (%)	53%	0%	25%	100%	39%	100%	71%	75%	75%

After the mapping, a sample for case studies was constructed according to theoretical significance: market leaders, high-technology, and high-quality companies, which are economically successful and not affected by specific crises, were identified. The selection of successful companies, where transfer of practice is unlikely to have been inhibited by business failure, provides a robust test of the institutionalist approach, according to which the 'social model' of companies is an intrinsic, complementary dimension of their 'productive model'. In addition, one more low-wage, low-cost segment company in each of the host countries was included. Without distorting the overall picture, it provided some variation as to the boundaries of the 'high road' to competitiveness in the region.

The analysis focused on six dimensions of employment practices, where the academic literature has detected systematic differences between German and US model (Table 3.2): employee participation; numerical flexibility; pay flexibility; working time; skills and training; diversity management.

The overall findings with reference to the comparative analytical grid are presented in Table 3.3 (removing Slovenia, which is less 'permissive' in terms of employment practices, and where two plants had had both American and German ownership in the past). German companies tended to rely more on functional flexibility in the form of multi-skilling, job rotation, and internal mobility. Their preferred form of working time flexibility was the

Table 3.2   German and US MNCs Ideal Types

	German	US
Employee participation	Indirect: regular consultation of works councils and/or trade unions	Direct: individualized HRM, quality circles, suggestion schemes, direct communication
Numerical flexibility	Permanent contracts, reluctance to resort to compulsory redundancies	Temporary contracts, use of agency workers, 'hire & fire' approach
Pay flexibility	Variable pay <10%, subject to standard, objective rules and indicators	Variable pay >10%, subject to individual performance appraisals by supervisors
Functional flexibility	High: multitasking, long multifunctional training, job rotation	Low: training 'on the job' reduces internal mobility
Working-time flexibility	High, annualization of working hours (constant pay), subject to joint rules	High, in the form of unilaterally managed overtime
Diversity management	Weak: no specific attention to specific groups' needs	Strong: programs for effectively including women and minorities

Table 3.3 Employment Practices of Multinational Companies in Hungary and Poland

	German companies (N: 4)	American companies (N: 4)
Participation	One company transfer elements of employee participation	All companies transfer anti-unionism
Numerical flexibility	Three companies have low numerical flexibility	One company has high numerical flexibility
Pay flexibility	One company has low pay flexibility	Two companies have high pay flexibility
Functional flexibility	Three companies have high functional flexibility	One company has high functional flexibility
Working time flexibility	Two companies have annualized hours	All companies have unilateral working time flexibility
Diversity management	No company has a diversity management policy	Two companies have a diversity management policy

annualization of working hours. By contrast, US companies tended to rely less on functional flexibility and to achieve working time flexibility through unilateral imposition of overtime and flexible patterns of shiftwork.

On the other dimensions, it was hard to detect any systematic variation according to home country. Diversity management was, as expected, completely absent from German-owned operations (where questions on the topic were hardly understood at all), but its practice at the two US sites where it was found was ad hoc. German companies made more generalized use of open-ended rather than temporary contracts but their overall numerical flexibility was high nonetheless.

Most important for the discussion of the 'European Social Model' were the results with regard to employee participation. There was no systematic variation according to home country; German companies were not more likely than American ones to embrace indirect employee participation through either trade unions or works councils, corroborating Table 3.1's finding on Poland; at the same time, they were not less likely to use direct participation mechanisms. Only one German company had a high degree of conformity with its ideal type, and the specific reasons for this are explored below. The other companies both departed from the home-country model, and varied in the ways they depart from it.

To understand why German companies actually differ in their employment practices it is useful to look more in detail at the German companies in Poland and in Hungary (indicated by the acronyms Gp1, Gp2, Gh1 and Gh2). I omit Slovenia here because the country is less 'open' to foreign influence and because one of the 'German' companies actually had a history of mixed foreign influences.

Gp1, which most fully follows a German model, is part of a large company with a distinctive system of corporate governance allowing a greater-than-usual voice to stakeholders, such as the local authority and workforce. It also has a specific industrial relations tradition and has been in the vanguard in elaborating international systems of employee consultation and information. Such features are evident in the company's corporate culture and are referred to in Poland. This Polish greenfield site was built in 1998 in an area with high structural unemployment. It employs about 1,000 people, with plans for further expansion. The company has steadily increased production and employment in Central Eastern Europe, while downsizing has been prefigured in Germany. The importance of the home country corporate culture is apparent from the status of the German language (commonly used for training and important for career progression). German expatriates are prominent in foreign subsidiaries although their number and role diminishes gradually. For six years the personnel manager was a German expatriate, eventually replaced by a native Pole.

During the research, the German production model was clearly visible in the amount of training and the form that it takes (including co-operation with local schools), in work organization (with elected team leaders and daily team meetings), and in industrial relations. In a country where union density was about 15% (and lower at greenfield sites and among younger employees) Gp1 had 76% unionization, a detailed collective agreement (albeit one that follows Polish patterns) and a sophisticated system of consultation: the latter extended to representation on the EWC. The union also had de facto veto power on the appointment of team leaders. Interviews in both Poland and Germany indicated that the role of German managers and trade unions in establishing such a system had been considerable. Interestingly, Polish managers were less enthusiastic than German ones about extensive social dialog, seeing it as compromising their status and slowing down decision-making. The most direct example of the transfer of home country model was working time. With minor adjustments due to different legal regulations, the same system of working time flexibility operating in Germany was introduced in Poland, through a collective agreement.

Gp1 has been able to be highly selective in recruiting its workforce: production employees are all men, highly qualified and aged under 32 at time of recruitment (the current average is 26), while administrative employees are of both genders, almost all with university education, and aged under 35 at time of recruitment. This age and gender composition is different from that of the company plants in Germany, and reflects the imbalance in the local labor market and also lack of concern with diversity management.

The dimension on which the company sharply departs from German practice (and, conversely, conforms to Polish reality) is pay, which was much more variable than in Germany. Rather than through bonuses (5–15% of earnings), variation was achieved through a system of bi-dimensional classification of jobs, which expanded the pay fork (7.5 times between best and worst paid, and two times among workers on the same production line) and accorded discretionary power to foremen on how to classify employees and their jobs. As a result, the pay system had been strongly criticized by the trade union.

The situation was very different at Gp2, an investor in the same region with a comparable factory (600 employees, built in 2002) and whose German parent had similar traditions, size, and market power to those of Gp1. This corporate group is more internationalized: turnover and employment in foreign subsidiaries exceed that in Germany. In recent years, employment at German sites has been repeatedly reduced, and the headquarters of some divisions have been moved outside Germany. References to the company tradition and to its social responsibility notwithstanding, corporate culture was less clearly German than in Gp1, with more stress on change. Expatriates were less prominent and more international in their experience. Gp2's business language is English and contrary to practices in Gp1, local managers are not expected to learn German, while German managers are required to learn Polish during their secondment.

In terms of industrial relations, the trade unions blamed the company for undercutting previously achieved standards of social dialog. While there had been no strikes in recent years, collective bargaining over pay had been fraught, and Solidarity had refused to sign the most recent agreement. The other main trade union, post-communist OPZZ (slightly larger than Solidarity), had a more co-operative standpoint. Yet at all levels in the plant, from collective bargaining to shop floor teams, relations were more adversarial than at Gp1. Moreover, there was still no integration of the plant into the European Works Council.

A peculiarity of human resources at Gp2 was the deep segmentation of the workforce, between a majority of core older, experienced skilled (male) workers, a layer of younger and/or female workers, and a marginal but important layer of contract workers, 'leased' from job agencies. The company showed commitment to its core workers when it relocated the factory from the previous site to a brand new one 40 km away and organized transportation of its existing employees instead of rejuvenating the workforce. While the German plants also have a marginal layer of the workforce to facilitate flexibility, at Gp2 this layer was significantly larger and was not covered by union representation. Unlike Gp1 (which immediately offered permanent contracts to new employees), Gp2 imposed two prior steps of agency work and then temporary contracts for up to two years (a common practice among Polish employers). Such practice was perceived negatively by both trade unions and employees, even if the treatment of such employees had improved after a change in Polish law banning differences in pay, social security, and working conditions.

More typically German in nature was the organization of production, with an emphasis on multi-skilling and training including co-operation with local schools through apprenticeships, the form of working time flexibility (although with more overtime than at Gp1) and also, unlike Gp1, the pay structure.

Moderating factors can explain the differences between these two German case studies. First is the different mode of entry: greenfield as against brownfield. Implementation of a home-country model might have been more possible at Gp1 because it was less constrained by pre-existing practices and arrangements. Yet Gp2 is not exactly a brownfield case, as the factory is entirely new and 40 km from the previous one. The transfer of the majority of the workforce was a company choice, not a necessity. Another possibility is that differences between Gp1 and Gp2 reflect differences at home between the parent companies. As noted above, the governance arrangements of Gp1's parent company are a distinctive variant of the German model, which does not correspond to general practice. This was confirmed by respondents at parent headquarters, who confirmed that Gp1 strategies corresponded to company idiosyncratic practices: 'it is our company model, not the German one', interviewees repeated with pride. Substantial elements of this model have been transferred to Gp1. In contrast, a central works council official at the head office of Gp2 in Germany indicated that the company had been departing from the traditional German model, through the internationalization of its structure and corporate culture, the building of non-union sites abroad (although not in western Europe) and extended use of contract workers. In this case, the whole corporation, not just the Central Eastern European subsidiaries, have changed: the German works council leader was irritated by the suggestion that Polish employees might be more flexible than the Germans: 'we work seven days a week, 24 hours a day; I don't think the Poles themselves can do more'.

The differences between the two parent companies, which share a similar past as showcases for the German model, relates to the nature of the company, its strategy and labor market power. The organization of production seems important in accounting for the different strategies of the two parent companies. Gp1 is much more closely integrated with the operations at other company sites in different countries than is the case at Gp2. As a result, there are spillover effects at Gp1 arising from the cross-border standardization of employment practices, which include cross-border work-related contacts. The degree of internationalization is also different. Home country operations are still pivotal to the European business of Gp1's parent company, reflecting strong home-country location advantages (corporate structure, public support, reputation, knowledge). As noted earlier, the German operations of Gp2's parent are no longer as central as they were. Gp2 is a specialist factory, in competition for production mandates with other European plants. Its production is not integrated with other plants belonging to the parent company, including those in Germany, and its business headquarters are located in France. Even the central company works council in Germany has little interest in what happens in the Polish factory.

These two factors—technological and international—interact: growing international competition exacerbates differences among German employers, as visible in their attitudes to sector-level wage settlements (Fichter 2005; Doellgast and Greer 2007). When combined, these factors explain the differences of the two companies within the same home-country. While Gp1 seems to aim at a revisited 'German revival' model, Gp2 represents a form of 'globalised German model', to an extent that, in the industrial relations area, it may be even be defined as a 'German capitulation' model.

Disintegration within the German model is confirmed by the two case studies in Hungary. Both Gh1 and Gh2 resisted employee organization and participation rights, rather than promoting them. While Gh2 is in a low-skill segment, a factor that may itself explain low interest in employee participation, the case of Gh1 is particularly illuminating. This company is controlled by the parent company of Gp1. Yet, there were deep differences between the home country model and employment relations at Gp1, especially on industrial relations. A large factory with 5,000 employees, the Hungarian plant was used for experimenting with new practices rather than to transfer a successful home model. It was even conceived as a non-union plant, and union recognition occurred only after seven years of conflict, pressure from IG Metall in Germany and a change of management. Subsequently, an elaborate system of consultation was implemented, but this (as we will see in Chapter 7), far from being the investor's original aim, was the result of a compromise following changes in the local labor market situation (with shortages and high turnover) and the socio-political one (anti-labor economic policies, which previously prevailed were replaced by a more conciliatory stance since the late 1990s in Hungary). Gp1 and Gh1, and their related factories in Germany, correspond then to different production strategies even within the same corporate group. While Gp1 continually works with German counterparts (an integrated internationalization process), once the German-specific production had been relocated to Gh1, this plant was free to depart from German practices (a vertically and horizontally disintegrated form of international reorganization).

The overall lesson from these case studies is twofold. On one side, Gp1 demonstrates that it is possible to successfully implement high-road, high involvement employment relations in Central Eastern Europe. There is no cultural incompatibility between post-communist societies and the 'European Social Model', in particular in its German variant. But on the other hand, it is clear that Gp1 is the exception, not the rule. The other German investors have preferred to avoid employee representation. Moreover, at the time of the research (2005), it seemed to have been possible to implement extremely efficient production in new member states despite the absence of those social components (employee participation, self-managed teamwork, negotiated flexibility) previously seen as integral to the German 'national business' and 'production' model.

The outcome is a new, emerging production regime in the region, with some specific features. Labor flexibility is high on all dimensions, despite new EU regulations. Sunday work is commonplace in all three countries. And, as some respondents observed, flexibility in post-communist countries is attitudinal rather than regulatory: even though legal curbs on dismissals may appear analogous to the Western European ones, employees are constantly aware that they should not take their jobs for granted. Both the experience of the transformation crisis in the early 1990s (particularly profound in Poland) and current labor market conditions affect the contemporary power balance in workplaces.

Besides being more flexible than their western counterparts, the factories investigated have rapidly achieved world class productivity and quality. They cannot be considered as backwards or marginal: indeed some of these factories have become benchmarks for western plants (as a telling example, Polish workers at Gp1 were proud of having overtaken the German plants in the internal comparison of '*Ordnung and Sauberkeit*', i.e. order and cleanness). But at the same time, mechanisms for employee representation lag far behind western European practice. MNCs had been looking creatively for functional equivalents of western institutions, and had reproduced work organization principles without other institutional elements. In the case of German companies, it was the industrial relations pillar of the productive model which in general was not transferred (with the notable exception of Gp1), and when it was, only under host-country pressure and as a compromise (as at Gh1 and Gh2). By contrast, a consistently distinctive element of German companies, as compared to American, was their approach to functional flexibility and skill creation. While both American and German employers make considerable efforts in training, it was the German companies that invested strongly in the development of transferable skills, promoted employees' further education, and established strong co-operation links with local schools and universities. This takes place differently than in Germany, however, where vocational education has a strong associational character through the co-operation between Chambers of Commerce, unions, and public authorities. In Central Eastern Europe the associational pillar is missing (although to different degrees: more in Poland and less in Slovenia), and there is no evidence of German companies promoting its creation.

In Central Eastern Europe, especially in the 1990s, weak labor markets, shortage of domestic capital, and weak labor organizations have given foreign investors large margins for maneuver, including the diversification of practice across countries (Kahancová 2010). Deregulation and international capital mobility following integration into the EU may even have increased such space in the short term. German MNCs could find 'creaming off' workers through higher wages a simpler and cheaper alternative to codetermination.

EVIDENCE FROM MULTINATIONALS' SHOP FLOOR, 2007–2008

The regime emerging from the case studies of 2004–2005 looked successful, but at the same time it begged the question of whether such an unbalanced model (state-of-the-art technology and organization without employee participation) was socially sustainable in the long term. With this question in mind, I embarked in a new series of similar comparative case studies in the Czech Republic in 2007–2008, led by Franz Traxler of the University of Vienna. In this case, the research by-passed cross-country comparisons by selecting only the Czech Republic (the economically most advanced and the most 'western' of the Visegrád countries) and narrowed down the focus to, among employment practices, employee participation, but introduced a cross-sector dimension. The research design focused on a comparison of transfers in the automotive component sector, where FDI is particularly efficiency-oriented (as we will discuss in Chapter 8), and in the finance sector, where FDI is more market-oriented. We investigated whether in services, where international cost competition pressures are less relevant, there was more space for transferring and developing employment participation mechanisms.

Table 3.4 shows the general picture across the 12 case studies in terms of industrial relations transfers and outcomes. Industrial relations transfers are overall very low, especially in the automotive sector. Once we look at the details of the specific IR practices, it is clear that automotive companies predominantly perceive their home country IR arrangements as costs, rather than advantages. Therefore, non-transfer, rather than transfer, is a symptom of the relevance of international competition. This is in particular the case of employee representation and collective bargaining. By contrast, the two finance companies with a medium-high degree of transfers (US-BAN and UK-FIN) are from Anglophone countries and transfer exactly the opposite kinds of practices, i.e. anti-unionism and union-substituting forms of direct participation (surveys, meetings, employee interviews, suggestion schemes) as well as one case of indirect participation (an Employee Forum).

International competition considerations imply that automotive MNCs *do not* want to transfer those home country operations that are perceived as disadvantages and additional costs and prefer to benefit from the looser

Table 3.4   Employee Participation in MNCs in the Czech Republic

Company	IR transfers	Labor relations	Indirect participation	Direct participation
D-INS1 Greenfield	Avoided	Paternalistic, individualized, anti-union	Employee reps (managers) in supervisory board	Workshops on strategy and corporate culture
D-INS2 Greenfield	Minor	Individualized, participative, information-sharing	None	HR department pretends to have a Works Council role (advice, mediation, discussion)
A-BAN1 Brownfield/ Greenfield	Avoided	Individualized, participative	Union, in brownfield part	Employee survey
A-BAN2 Greenfield	Avoided	Individualized, Informal	Informal shopfloor spokespersons	Works meeting
US-BAN Brownfield	Partial	Individualized, anti-union	Employee reps in supervisory board, union organizing attempt in progress	Works meeting, employee survey, appraisal interviews
UK-FIN Greenfield	Partial	Individualized, strict control	Non-statutory Employee Forum, but not re-elected	Engagement survey
D-CAR1 Greenfield/ Brownfie Minorld	Minor	Information-sharing, some consultation/ negotiation	Union at three out of four sites (low membership)	Teams (Continuous Improvement Process), suggestion scheme
D-CAR2 Greenfield	Avoided	Paternalist, opposition to works council creation		Manager's bilingual assistant acting as mediator/ rep. Employee participation dialogue, works meetings, petitions, mailbox, suggestion scheme
A-CAR1 Greenfield	Avoided	Unilateral management		Suggestion scheme, employee survey

(continued)

Table 3.4 (continued)

Company	IR transfers	Labor relations	Indirect participation	Direct participation
A-CAR2 Greenfield	Avoided	Unilateral management, opposition to works council creation		Informal workshop spokes-persons
UK-CAR Brownfield	Avoided	Pluralist negotiations	Union (55% density)	Works meetings, job satisfaction interviews and surveys
US-CAR Brownfield	Avoided	Collaborative industrial relations	Union (40% density)	Works meetings, employee survey and feedback

regulations of the Czech Republic. At D-CAR2 a German manager justifies such choice through an alleged fragmented nature of Czech unions, even though these are in fact as unitary as the German ones.

> I am actually a friend of co-determination, and this is always a feature of our company . . . we actually want co-determination, but already structured and representative of the majority of the workforce . . . Here, five people are enough to create a union and represent their group's interest, and then yet another union can be built. Obviously, we try to avoid this. (German plant manager, D-CAR2)

By contrast, finance companies, while still not interested in full transfers, engage in exporting those company-specific HRM and industrial relations practices (pay systems, direct communication), which are seen as valuable assets to face the competition they meet within the host country, or to move within it as product innovators with a first-mover advantage. Overall, such process results in a very pragmatic, or even opportunistic, approach to employment relations in the host country. And one that works against the transfer of the 'European Social Model'.

The outcome (Table 3.4) is that in only four of the 12 case studies (and only two of the eight German or Austrian ones), there are trade unions, and in none there is a works council (despite the Directive on Information and Consultation of Employees). In five companies, among which are four Germanic ones, anti-unionism and unilateralism are explicit. By contrast, and this is a new development in comparison to the previous study of 2004–2005, there is a clear effort towards direct participation. Such effort is particularly developed and sophisticated in the Anglo American companies, which often draw on solutions from the countries of origin. Particularly popular are individual interviews and job satisfaction surveys. The same direct participation methods reveal however limitations and a social demand for more information, which at US-CAR has translated in broader scope for trade unions (see Chapter 7). In this company, employee surveys revealed dissatisfaction with the existing degree of information, while at UK-CAR, the union complains for the poor quality of information.

> It would have been sufficient if the new management team had organized a meeting to introduce themselves. (. . .) Instead of negotiating, they order things (. . .) Management promised a meeting with the employees in March: we are in June and still no meeting. (Union Representative, UK-CAR)

In the finance sector of Anglo American companies, the preference for direct participation is even clearer. US-BAN explicitly rejects trade unions and advocates a direct unitaristic relationship between employer and employees.

> We have a very proactive approach to employment relations. Instead of involving a 3rd party (unions), we prefer direct communication. Unions and collective bargaining exist in some places, depending on the size of the subsidiary and on the country. Overall, we are less likely to be unionized than a similar company in a given country. We are not actively anti-union, but we do look for better alternatives where possible. (Headquarter Personnel Manager, US-BAN)

Its 3,000 Czech employees have no form of collective representation besides the statutory elected representative in the supervisory board, who is a manager. Interestingly, this elected representative tells that he has been asked by employees to demand higher salaries and therefore to play a collective bargaining role, which apparently, to a small extent, he does play. UK-FIN introduced a works-council like 'Employee Forum' in most of its European operations. Interestingly, this was first experimented in Poland and then introduced back in the UK and in other countries, including the Czech Republic. In spite of the big importance given to these bodies, their actual working is questionable: in the Czech Republic, its mandate had expired two years before our research visit, all representatives had left the company since, and no new elections had been yet organized because management prioritized the conduction of an employee survey, a more important direct communication tool.

Similar limits are apparent in the case of direct participation tools in German or Austrian-owned companies. Sections of management (at D-CAR2 and D-INS2) are requested to play representative and mediation functions. The suggestion scheme at D-CAR1 is run in a more management-led way than in Germany. In most companies, employees do not participate actively in works meetings.

Although the Czech operations of these companies are overall success-ful, the prevalence of direct participation does not seem to have avoided a 'representation gap' and a demand for collective services in the workplaces, in a situation similar to that of the US (Freeman *et al.* 2007). Direct par-ticipation, when introduced, is management-led and conditional—and not sufficient to prevent employee turnover, even though the Czech Republic is often considered as the most successful of all new member states.

CONCLUSION

The results of a large set of case studies leads me to strongly qualify the view of those researchers who had detected some positive effect of Ger-man investors in industrial relations in the new member states (Jürgens and Krzywdziński 2009; 2010; Tholen 2007; Bluhm 2007). These positive cases are not just contingent and partial, as their authors concede. They are so rare to be the exceptions to the rule, like Gp1. The research by Jür-gens and Krzywdziński (2009) is more systematic in terms of coverage of kinds of companies, but it is still restricted to the automotive sector; there-fore, their argument that foreign MNCs follow a 'limited high-road' model is not entirely convincing, as in this sector a core skilled and committed workforce is always needed, and a pure 'low road' path is unviable. Their findings actually confirm a substantial departure from western models, in terms of not just industrial relations (frequent anti-unionism, no works councils), but also more extensive use of agency work, temporary contracts, unilateral restructuring; moreover, the only systematic difference between the German investors and the other companies seems to be in the skill cre-ation area, as in my research.

Overall, my case studies confirm the lack of interest, by western employ-ers, in transferring any form of employee representation, which has been noticed also among Norwegian (Kvinge and Rezanow Ulrichsen 2008) and Dutch (Kahancová 2010) employers. By contrast, in the service sector there is transfer of direct participation techniques meant to actually prevent or bypass employee organization. Our first set of case studies dismantled the hopes in German investors. Our second set dismantled the hopes that the situation could be better in the service sector. Actually, the radical MNC-led restructuring of the (mostly new) service sector in post-communist coun-tries is often very heavy on employees—the Polish retail sector described by Hardy (2009) and Czarzasty (2010) is one extreme example.

Expectations that Western European investors might have transferred a culture of participation and social dialog proved to be even more naïve than the expectations towards the EU I criticized in Chapters 1 and 2. Anna Lewandoska, a Polish employee representative in the works council of Austrian company TU Compensa, offers a graphic tale of the confusion raised by such expectations:

> In our company there are no trade unions. The owner is a firm from Austria—that is from a country where there is a long tradition of social dialog. Hence the feeling that works councils' prerogatives and competences should be well known to the employer. In conformity to the law, the employer organized the elections and the first meeting of the council. After that we heard: 'we have organized you, the rest depends on you, we'll wait for the effects of your activity'. We asked ourselves what's this council for at all, because the employees imagine that we are some sort of social affairs commission, while the employer treats us as—even if they don't say so openly—rather an opponent, than a consultant or partner. Basically we appear as a body that threatens complaints. We can't fulfill the expectations of either side, because in practice we have no powers that would allow us to do it. (Dołowska 2007)

The MNCs, rather than offer opportunities for organizing industrial relations, have been a centrifugal force for further disorganized decentralization. As Rugraff put it, 'by their weight in the economy and their determinant role in the co-ordination of these countries' economies, MNCs impede the emergence of organized industrial relations' (2006, 455). This happens even if most of them come from continental Europe, the cradle of the 'European Social Model'.

This chapter then corroborates the previous two in showing that there has been no institutional transfer of the 'European Social Model' eastwards, neither through EU policies, nor through multinational companies. The main impact of the EU on new member states' politicians has been through the single market and the competition for foreign direct investment, exacerbated by 'beauty contests' organized by large multinational companies such as Hyundai in 2004. The new member states (especially Hungary, Czech Republic, and Estonia so far—but the others wish to follow) are heavily dependent on FDI for capital formation. As documented by Neumann (Neumann 2007) in Hungary, labor relations come to be perceived as a competitiveness issue, favoring deregulation. The overall effect therefore confirms the fears of the more pessimistic forecasts (Langewiesche and Tóth 2003; Clarke 2005). As its pressure for competitiveness is so much stronger than its whisper of a social dimension, the EU is not currently promoting social dialog in the new member states—if anything, it is *undermining* it.

Part II
Exit

4   Migration

The free movement of workers between old and new member states of the
European Union does not correspond to classic views and definitions of
migration, starting with the fact that most of these mobile workers, by staying abroad less than a year, do not even qualify for the technical definition
of migration. But there are other specificities that make this phenomenon
a crucial test for the nature of European labor markets and possibly their
approximation to the long-invoked American model.

The matching, within an area of free movement and low transport costs,
of a large supply of disaffected workers 'exiting' their local disappointing employment conditions and a structural demand for extremely flexible
workforces, has led to an interesting social experiment, which is testing
new boundaries of social sustainability. The global recession that started in
2009 exacerbates the test.

FREEDOM OF MOVEMENT OF WORKERS
AFTER THE ENLARGEMENT

The size and nature of East-West migration after enlargement contradicted
institutional predictions, which only demonstrates how little consideration
and analysis had been devoted to social issues in the pre-accession period.
The most authoritative forecasts from before 2004 proved grossly inaccu-
rate. The 'optimistic' official view foresaw a much smaller influx than the
actual one. Boeri and Brücker (2001), in a study for the European Commission, had estimated an influx of citizens from all 10 Central Eastern
European accession countries (including Bulgaria and Romania) of about
1 million in the first four years after the introduction of freedom of movement, on the hypothesis that it would occur in 2002. Although freedom
of movement was introduced only to few countries, only since May 2004
(giving therefore more time for economic convergence), and with the exclusion of Romania and Bulgaria, the influx in the first four years eventually
was, according to the probably conservative Eurostat data (EC 2009), of
1.1 million from the A8 (the eight Central and Eastern European countries

that entered the EU in 2004) and 0.9 million from Bulgaria and Romania—that is twice as large. Even more macroscopically wrong were the predictions of the UK government, which open the borders expecting 10–20,000 migrants per year (Dustmann *et al.* 2003), but received 812,000 in the first four years, according to the Worker Registration Scheme (WRS), 67% of whom from Poland[1].

Boeri and Brücker (2001) mistook the trend as well: they expected an immediate decrease after the first year, while the flow actually kept increasing until 2006. After 2007, migration from the A8 started declining, mostly for demographic reasons (decline in the number of new 'potential' migrants, which is going to fall faster due to the dramatic birth rate fall after 1989 in transition countries). Only the sudden economic crisis and exchange rate trends (the Polish złoty having gained nearly 40% against the British pound between 2004 and 2008) led to a clear decline, but still not exhaustion, of the flux.

On the other side, the 'pessimistic' forecasts were equally wrong. Sinn and Ochel (2003), who influenced the German decision of closing the borders, had expected movement towards social benefits (so-called 'social raids'), while in reality the flux has been nearly entirely for work. Mobile working-age new member states citizens are in employment 78%, many more than the EU average of 67% (EC 2008c). Not only influx into Sweden, where social benefits are available for newcomers, remained very low, but also demands for benefits did not increase as much as feared in the UK, once the newly arrived workers reached the social security requirement of one-year employment in the country, as I will show. In Ireland, access to social security was particularly restricted (Fanning 2009).

Such gross mistakes shared the same original flaw: foreseeing intra-EU mobility on the basis of extrapolations from previous migration movements (e.g. from Spain and Portugal after EU accession in 1986). In this way, they ignored both the specificity of social problems and expectations in Central Eastern Europe and the novelty of 'transnational' forms of migrations following the 'eroding of distance', that is, the fall of transport and communication costs. It was true, for instance, that geographic mobility of Central Eastern European populations within their own countries was extremely low, as it was stressed by Boeri and Brücker (2001). Yet this neglected both the discontent with national working conditions and the fact that, given the state of transport and housing, moving from Rzeszów in southeast Poland to Warsaw may cost the same as moving from Rzeszów to the East Midlands, as exemplified by Kahanec *et al.* (2009). The new phenomenon emerging from these unique conditions is an unprecedented amount of temporary but not necessarily determined in time and mobility—which has specific effects on the labor market.

While these population movements have raised preoccupation or even outright hostility in some sectors of the population, media, and politics, the European Union's view has remained extremely positive. The EC underlines the positive effects of EU internal mobility, both in its evaluation of the enlargement and in its evaluation of the labor market (EC 2006a, 2006c, 2008c). The free movement of workers has helped GDP growth and inflation control in the host countries and reduced unemployment in the countries of origin, with no particular negative side effect on wages or on the 'brain drain'. The European Commission even designated 2006 as the 'European Year of Workers' Mobility' to promote the idea further.

The early experience of 2004–2006 was seen by the EC (EC 2006c) as evidence of the advantages of opening the borders. The 'transitory periods' selectively applied by some countries have had a strong impact on distorting migration flows, notably replacing Germany and Austria with the British isles as preferred destination countries. Germany and Austria, which until 2004 had hosted the large majority of accession countries migrants and were predicted (Boeri and Brücker 2001) to receive 90% of the new flows, in the two years after the enlargement are estimated to have received only 82,000 and 8,000 new member states' migrants, respectively, against the 265,000 and 63,000 of UK and Ireland, which are also smaller countries (Barrell *et al.* 2007).[2] In the EC's eyes, 'opening' the borders to the new member states' workers is only beneficial: on one side, the transition periods introduced in some countries such as Germany generate illegal employment and pseudo self-employment in the form of service provision. On the other side, a country like the UK has seen extensive complementary migration, leading to increased growth, tax revenue, pension funding, and inflation control.

This experience has contravened another forecast by Boeri and Brücker, after that of limited migration flows: that of a 'race to the top' among countries in restrictive regulations (Boeri and Brücker 2005). Between 2006 and 2009, all EU15 except Austria and Germany quickly lifted the restrictions, whether immediately (Portugal, Spain, Italy, Finland, and Greece) or gradually (Belgium, Denmark, France, Luxembourg, and the Netherlands). Rather than a race to restriction, there has been a race to liberalization— although this stopped to the A8 and did not include the Romanian and Bulgarian workers.

NEW MEMBER STATES' MOBILE WORKERS:
THE ANSWER TO EURO-SCLEROSIS?

These general aggregate positive evaluations by the EU and most EU15 need to be looked at more in detail, given that they are very disproportionately employed in certain sectors and certain professions. Citizens from the new member states constitute, in 2007, 1% of the EU15 population, having risen from 0.4% in 2003, but they account for as many as 1.9% of the employed in elementary occupations and 0.9% of plant machine operators, while they are still an insignificant number (0.1%) in skilled occupations (EC 2008c[3]).

While restrictions have been removed on unskilled labor, in many professions barriers to the recognition of qualifications persist (Currie 2008), implying that the EU15 middle classes benefit most from the new arrangements.

Yet it would be grossly simplistic to see intra-EU mobility as just a strategy, by governments and employers, to lower labor costs, according to the traditional Marxist view of the 'reserve army' (Castles and Kosack 1973). In fact, wages seem to have been affected only marginally in the EU15, including in the sectors with most workers from the new member states such as manufacturing and construction, even if the -0.09% effect estimated by Brücker *et al.* (2009) might be, once again, underestimated and overoptimistic. Sommers and Woolfson (2008) have argued that by recurring to mass migration from the new member states, the EU is aping the growth model followed by the US in the last 30 years, based on mass immigration to provide cheap and flexible labor. But much more than low costs, the specific attractive feature of the new labor supply from the new member states relies exactly in their 'mobility', which offers a corrective to the long-blamed 'sclerosis' of European labor markets.

Migration experts have noticed that the EU has an 'almost desperate structural need, in both demographic and labour force terms, for increased intra-European population movements' (Favell 2008, 704). Geographic mobility is one dimension on which the EU, as a labor market, differs clearly from the US (Krieger and Fernandez 2006), and despite nearly a decade of 'flexicurity' propaganda, labor market flexibility meets, in Europe, clear social, political, and economic barriers. Not only did the governments of France, Italy, and Germany encounter mass protests over their labor market reforms. The financial crisis has demonstrated that labor market uncertainty is a problem for the economy as well, as it inhibits responsible credit and confident consumption and thereby depresses demand (Crouch 2008). In this perspective, intra-EU mobility can appear as the optimal solution within a segmented labor market, where the burden of uncertainty is allocated on workers from the new member states.

From the cynical point of view of the Western European economies, these workers share a number of 'positive' characteristics with non-EU migrants, as described in the founding work by Piore (1979): they are adaptable and mobile; used to long hour and flexible employment regimes; more sensitive to monetary incentives and less sensitive to prestige considerations; and not part of the polity and therefore governments can largely ignore their opinions (they can vote for local and European elections, but this is of little political relevance). They also spend a large part of their income in their country of origin, personally or through remittances, and therefore maintaining their purchase power is not so important for the host countries: if it stops, the problem is of their origin countries that will miss the remittances.

Workers from the new member states have, though, some additional 'assets' in comparison to extra-EU migrants. Even if some racialization has occurred (especially but not only for the Romanians), they appear to cause much less social and political resistance. Because their countries of origin are not too far and provide (also because of the state socialist legacy) better social security than extra-EU low-wage countries, these workers tend to be much more active on the labor market and not to bring their dependants along. In 2007 in the EU15, 78% of working-age people coming from the A10 were in employment, against 67% for the whole EU15 population and 66% for the non-EU born (EC 2008c). These data reveal the difference between A10 mobile workers and other migrants into the EU and make the former similar to foreign-born in the US, who have traditionally had a higher employment rate than the overall population. These mobile workers therefore provide a new valuable productive factor for the EU effort to compete with the US. Not surprisingly, therefore, the EU and the single member states decided, near simultaneously, to open the labor markets to the new member states' citizens, and to elaborate new migration policies with regard to extra-EU countries, by restricting access to unskilled migrants, while promoting the entry of high-skilled ones, through various 'point systems' or 'blue cards'.

So do the new intra-EU migrants offer the flexibility western employers had been desperately looking for? There are, in fact, major questions raised on the social sustainability of migration as a buffer for labor market uncertainty. Migrant segregation is incompatible with two other goals of European countries: good ethnic relations and border controls. A segregated economic position of migrants is likely to lead to ethnic conflicts, and it has been defined as inherently contradictory within democratic countries (Schierup et al. 2006). In fact, it can only be found working in a pure form only in the non-democratic countries of the Persian Gulf, where migrants constitute the majority of the labor force and are excluded from any civil rights. In the EU this would be in clear contradiction with the idea of European citizenship.

If a country wants to avoid reproducing an 'apartheid' system and to integrate migrants socially, automatically those migrants, once integrated, will abandon their 'outsider' acceptance of worse employment conditions and will start claiming equal treatment, thereby making segmentation unworkable. The only solution would be, at that stage, a continuous replacement of old migrant groups—as soon as they 'integrate'—with new ones. Already Piore had argued that capitalist economies require continuous flows of new migrants in order to maintain occupational hierarchies and to provide labor for low-prestigious occupations (marginal jobs): 'it is chiefly the temporary character of the migration stream that makes these migrations (. . .) of value to industrial society' (Piore 1979, 52). In a liberal labor market, without migrants employers would have to pay local workers to take those jobs considerably higher salaries, which, in turn, would have entailed a rise in wage demands from workers in mainstream jobs, who would not accept to be paid as much as those in marginal jobs. But settled migrants are not 'useful': as they gradually socialize into the host society, they adapt their understanding of prestige and their economic demands to the local practices.

This is something countries have tried in the past: Germany's *Gastarbeiter* rotation in 1955–1973 is a famous example. Yet, even in that case, Germany had eventually to face the fact that it is not simple to send migrants home as if they were a disposable production factor. A large number of migrants tend to settle. As Max Frisch famously put it in the Swiss situation, '*Wir riefen Arbeitskräfte und es kamen Menschen*' ('we called labor forces and we got human beings'; 1965, 7). Locally, the same strategy is sometimes still visible: MacKenzie and Forde (2009) describe the case of a British employer continuously replacing marginal labor forces (initially local women, and then in turns Kosovars, Asians, Poles . . .) always in the search of new 'good workers' once the old start demanding too much. Yet what is thinkable for a single employer is not for a government. Unless migrant themselves show a high mobility between host and home country, and especially responsiveness to labor market signals—thereby quitting as soon as market conditions worsen, without needing to be asked (and they cannot be asked, given their EU citizenship). Migrants from outside the EU have a tendency to 'freeze' where they are when they lose their jobs, because if they leave, they do not know if they will ever be allowed to come back—something that explains the failure of various public programs of pay-to-go schemes to subsidize returns, like the Spanish one of 2009 (Martin 2009). By contrast, EU citizens have no such fear. It is this mobility and responsiveness the new attractive feature of workers from the new member states, which the EU hopes to be sustainable—also because forced repatriation of EU citizens is not normally permitted, although France, Italy, and the Czech Republic have tried with Romanians[4].

This issue of integration is not to disregard a second reason of potential social unsustainability, this time not for the countries, but for the migrants themselves. As the European Foundation for the Improvement of Working and Living Conditions has admitted (Krieger and Fernandez 2006), mobility comes at big social costs for the workers themselves and their families. This is a well-known topic in migration studies, even if often forgotten by economic models assuming that migrants benefit from mobility by definition (otherwise, as rational individuals, they would go home). In fact, as Sayad (1999) has convincingly illustrated in the case of Algerians in France, the suffering of the migrant remains mostly silent because it is not socially acceptable in either home or host country—but it is not any less real for this reason.

There are further potential problems with the view of EU mobility as a solution to 'Euro-sclerosis'. Within the EU coexist countries of immigration and emigration, and the positive effects for the former may be negative for the latter. A pan-EU policy is not self-evident, therefore. The thesis of a win-win game relies on the assumption that short-term mobility increases the human capital of mobile workers, who, for instance, can learn new languages and skills, and therefore would benefit both countries of origin and destination. While this is certainly true for many young citizens of the new member states, there is also rich evidence of processes of 'brain waste', deskilling and general 'downgrading' of this group of workers (Currie 2008; Dustmann *et al.* 2008), and when segregation occurs, language learning opportunities are also limited, as one can easily detect by visiting Polish clubs in the UK. And there are also broader political consequences. Even if migrants may be net contributors to the welfare state, media distortions about it may undermine public support for social expenditure. In the same way as ethnic diversity in the US has been seen as an obstacle to the creation of a welfare state in their country (because the ethnic majority at any given moment in time feel the minority would benefit disproportionately), it has been long suggested that migration will lead to the Americanization of the European welfare state (Freeman 1986), even if there is still no evidence of links between the two among European countries (Mau and Burkhardt 2009).

Workers from the new member states have occupied marginal and precarious labor market positions in all EU15 countries, not just those that opened the borders immediately like the UK, which I will discuss more in detail later. There are interesting parallels between countries that opened the borders early and those that took advantage of transitory periods for as long as it was possible. The first group of countries corresponds to the most liberal or flexible labor markets, i.e. the Anglophone UK and Ireland but also, if differently, Spain that opened the borders in 2006. Sweden is an exception, insofar as it has a social democratic employment regime, but it opened the borders immediately by accident, rather than by choice: the parliament failed to agree on time what form of restrictions to apply. The countries that kept the borders closed beyond the 'second deadline' of 2009 are Austria and Germany, representative of Central European corporatism but also, as border countries, the most affected by the issue.

Restricting access to job-seeking Central Eastern Europeans had the side effect, for Germany, to distort the employment profile of immigrants from the new member states in that country: contrary to the experience of UK and Ireland, in Germany they exhibit lower employment and activity rates but a pathologically high rate of self-employment (Brenke *et al.* 2009). Transitory periods do not apply to the movement of self-employed, while in Germany and Austria, transitory periods apply to cross-border provision of services with use of own employees but only in some sectors (see Chapter 8). As an effect, self-employment and posting of workers by Central Eastern European agencies are often ways to bypass restrictions. In 2006, according to the—not necessarily reliable as no systematic monitoring exists—EC (EC 2006c), there were 133,000 posted workers from the new member states in Germany, 7,000 in Austria, 26,000 in France (which opened the borders in 2008) but only 5,000 in the UK. An extreme case, highlighted by Polish and German media in 2007, was the extreme exploitation of Polish migrants in the factories of the largest German meat-packing company, Tönnies, (€3.5/hour pay, 84-hour working week), all considered as employees of a Polish contractor. Cases of migrant exploitation and abuse occur often in the food industry in the UK as well, but at least their illegality is easier to prove (Equality and Human Rights Commission 2010). In Germany, even in organized sectors like metalworking, cases of fictitious self-employment or worker posting occurred in areas like maintenance.

The global recession that started in 2008 offers a test case for the hypothesis that migrants from the new member states constitute a labor market buffer and the most precarious employment group. Woolfson and Likic-Brboric (2008) have suggested, in this regard, that these migrants are carrying an unequal burden of 'toxic' risk, in terms of both precarity and dangerous working conditions. As the economic sectors affected most severely by the recession (construction, manufacturing, finance, and travel-related services) employ high numbers of foreigners (although of different skill levels), it is reasonable to expect migrants to pay a higher cost than average (Martin 2009). There still is no systematic evidence on how much this is true, as returns are not counted in the EU but all points to the burden of precarity being carried by migrants. Aggregate Eurostat data show that in the last quarter of 2008 (when the crisis hit) unemployment increased much more sharply among non-EU nationals (two percentage points) than EU nationals (half percentage point), confirming migrants' marginality and precarity. Yet these data do not distinguish by nationality and unemployment figures do not include returns, and all information points to them having increased massively. In the UK, in the same quarter employment fell only marginally among UK nationals (from 75.2 to 74.8%) but much more sharply among nationals of the countries that joined the EU in 2004 (from 84.2 to 81.3%; Office for National Statistics 2009). Ireland, according to the Central Statistics Office (2009), in the 12 months to April 2009 returned to be, after 15 years, an 'emigration' country—but the *Irish Independent* (2009) titled 'Any Sad New Song Should Be, Perhaps, in Polish', as to revert the balance from immigration to emigration was the departure of 30,100 new member states' citizens. Employment data are more telling. In Ireland, workers from the new member states, while being 6% of the workforce, made 24% of the employment losses in the 12 months to June 2009. During 2009 the number of employees from the new member states fell by 21.1%, while that of Irish nationals by 6.7% (Central Statistics Office 2009). This corresponds to sector differences: in the same period, job losses were most frequent in construction and manufacturing (where there are high numbers of foreigners), while there were counter-cyclical job increases in the public sector, mostly reserved to Irish nationals. Workers from the new member states have largely lived up, from the point of view of western economies, to their reputation of being disposable. Nonetheless, even these central European 'ideal mobile workers' have largely settled: in Ireland, a

Qualitative Panel Study on Polish migrants found that there were a number of reasons for a majority of them to remain in the country: from residual employment opportunities, to welfare benefits, to, crucially, non-economic reasons (Krings *et al.* 2009). Conversely, Polish job centers are yet to register any significant number of return migrants. Are mobile Europeans the perfect *homines oeconomici* the EU was looking for?

THE SENDING COUNTRIES: MIGRATION AS 'EXIT'

Piore (1979) argued that emigration can act as a 'safety valve' for the sending countries, externalizing internal tensions that the social and political system cannot manage. This is relevant for the new member states in two regards: ethnic minorities and workers. In both cases, but in different ways, emigration has been, according to Hirschman's typology, an 'exit' response to existing dissatisfaction, following the lack of 'voice' opportunities.

There is particularly true in the case of emigration of the internal minorities from Latvia and Estonia. From these countries, emigration has been overwhelmingly from the Russian-speaking population, even if this was not economically poorer than the ethnic majority. This 'exit' has had some positive effects in raising previously hidden problems to EU attention. The large non-citizen populations of Latvia (about 350,000, 15% of the population) and Estonia (about 100,000, 7% of the population), in spite of having been citizens of the Soviet Republics of Latvia and Estonia until 1991, have no right to vote, and their 'grey passports' gave them no right of international movement. After the first two years of accession, however, Latvia and Estonia had to recognize them as having the status of EU permanent residents, and in 2007, after a European Council's decision, non-citizens were given freedom of movement in the Schengen area just like any other EU citizen. The majority (about two-thirds) of Russian speakers in Latvia and Estonia do have the citizenship of either their country of residence or of Russia (or another post-Soviet Union republic), and many of them have enjoy a privileged economic position inherited from Soviet times, but in any case they are marginalized in the polity and their mobility, whether towards the EU or towards Russia, is a response to this lack of voice, which, in turn, may reinforce the same marginality. However, there are also signs of shift to 'voice': in the European Parliament elections of June 2009, even if non-citizens were still without right of vote, the Russian-minority parties registered a big advance and gained three (up from one in 2004) of the eight Latvian MEPs. More importantly, the EU required Latvia to grant non-citizens the right to vote in local elections, with the immediate effect that Riga elected, in July 2009, its first Russian-speaking mayor since independence.

In Romania, Czech Republic, and to a lesser extent Slovakia and Hungary, emigration has tended to come disproportionately from the Roma minorities. Roma have political rights, but their social situation is one of

extreme marginality. Their 'exit' is sometimes explicitly promoted by political actors: on the eve of the 2010 elections, *The Guardian* (Traynor 2010)
quotes the extreme-right Jobbik leader young leader, Gabor Vona, saying
that for those Roma who do not accept his definition of honest work, two
alternatives remain: 'they can either choose to take advantage of the right
of free movement granted by the European Union, and leave the country,
because we will simply no longer put up with lifestyles dedicated to free-
loading or criminality; or, there is always prison'. Romania, in sociologist Nicola Gheorghe's (2010) words, has tried to 'get rid of the Gypsies'
through emigration.

Roma's new EU mobility has created international visibility and attention for their previously neglected conditions. In 2008, the EC set up a
Roma Action Group and organized the first EU Roma Summit. While
these have remained rather formal, top-down policies, it is remarkable
that for the first time in the history of EU non-discrimination policies,
the EC is considering the viability of positive action for an ethnic minority, given the failure of other policy instruments. In some cases, notably
in Southern Italy and Northern Ireland, Roma mobility has been met
with violence and has thereby reinforced 'exit' in the form of continuous
escape. On the other side, again, there are also some signs of emerging
'voice'. Hungary elected the first Roma MEP, Livia Jaroka, in the history
of the European Parliament in 2004, and Roma NGOs have been increasingly active.

Leaving apart the specific cases of ethnic minorities and going back
to labor market issues, all evidence points to the fact at the majority of
mobile workers from the new member states are pushed by dissatisfaction with working conditions. It is important to notice that few of them
are unemployed, even if there is a correlation between unemployment
and emigration rate. As they are ineligible for social benefits, the unemployed have generally little incentive to move to the West unless they
have very clear job prospects, as they would only lose the little benefits
and social network solidarity they have at home. Migration (as opposed
to mere expressed intention to move), even within the EU, requires generally some entrepreneurship and capital, whether monetary, social, or
human. It is employees and youth in search of their first job that tend
to move.

Only a minority of Central Eastern Europeans were moving for positive
reasons. According to Eurobarometer (Krieger and Fernandez 2006), their
motivations contrast sharply with those of western EU's mobile citizens.
While the latter tend to move for reasons such as better climate, the former
move in search of higher income (59% compared to the EU average of 37%)
and better working conditions (57% compared to the EU average of 36%).
Other surveys, reviewed by Kahanec *et al.* (2009) show that workers in the
new member states are generally more unhappy with their lives, dissatisfied
with their salaries and working conditions, and concerned about the availability of good jobs and insecure about their current jobs, and that these

are the factors pushing them to move abroad (Blanchflower and Lawton 2009; Kadziauskas 2007). The EU accession and freedom of movement have brought to the surface, via migration, dissatisfaction and anger that had largely remained hidden. Kurekova (2010) has detected a strong inverse correlation of migration flows with social citizenship: countries with a worse welfare state, and notably lower social expenditure, worse incapacity and family benefits, and stricter unemployment benefits, are those with the largest migration outflows. The relatively better state of social and political rights explains to a large extent why Slovenians, Czechs, and Hungarians have been relatively reticent to emigrate.

There is an important association between what has happened in terms of migration and what has happened to trade union member-ship, as a form of 'voice' which has been given little effectiveness and power in the new member states. Increase in the former has gone side-by-side with a decrease of the latter. In 2003–2008, while over 1 million workers left the new member states for the EU15, trade unions in the region lost about 1 million members (while membership in the EU15 remained constant, confirming the further divergence between old and new member states). Table 4.1 shows that the countries with the highest number of emigrants have been those with the strongest fall in union membership, especially Slovakia and Lithuania, while those with the lowest migration have also lost less union members, especially the 'devi-ant' Slovenia, but also Hungary and the Czech Republic.[5] Correlation

Table 4.1 Emigration and Fall in Union Membership, 2003–2008

Country	A – Union membership change, 2003–2008 (%)	B – Emigration as % of population, 2003–2007	C – Union membership change, 2003–2008 (000)	D – Population change to emigration, 2003–2007 (000)
Lithuania	–34.1	2.3	–62	–75
Slovakia	–34.1	2.0	–196	–88
Estonia	–18.4	0.8	-8	–10
Bulgaria	–16.2	1.9	–94	–144
Poland	–16.1	1.9	–340	–721
Latvia	–15.8	0.8	–27	–18
Czech Republic	–14.9	0.3	–77	–33
Hungary	–9.3	0.4	–80	–41
Slovenia	+2.6	0.0	+9	0
Romania	+4.2	4.6	+85	–1,000

Correlation between A and B: r = –0.71742.
Data: My own elaborations on Carley (2009) and Brücker et al. (2009).

between union membership change in percentage and emigration in percentage of the populations is high ($r = -0.80$), once the outlier Romania is excluded (Figure 4.1). Romania is an exception insofar as it kept relatively strong unions and collective bargaining survived (Trif 2008) but suffered a major loss of population nonetheless—which can be explained by some functional conservatism of Romanian unions (offering services rather than 'voice', especially at company level) and by the large mobile Roma minority.

Data on migration and union membership are heterogeneous, as the former refer to the whole population and the latter only to the workforce. The association between the two series does not indicate that those who leave the unions and those who leave the country are the same people, and there are unfortunately no data on union membership and migration intentions. What can be said is that (with the notable exception of Romania) union crisis is strongest where emigration is strongest, which means that there is a trade-off, so far, between 'exit' and 'voice'.

Occasional data also point to the fact that EU mobility tends to lower union membership. In the UK West Midlands, for instance, a TUC survey (Anderson *et al.* 2007) showed that among Polish workers, 10% were union members in Poland, but only 3% had joined a trade union in the UK. While these figures are not representative, it is unlikely that the proportions could be much different in the migrant population at large, not because migrants are less prone to unionization, but because of their short stays and their

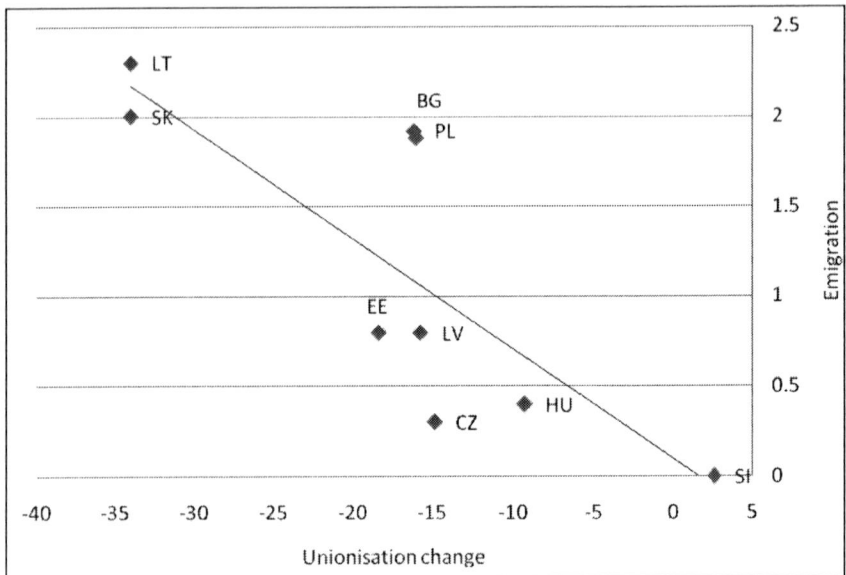

Figure 4.1   Emigration (%) and fall in union membership (%), 2003–08.

concentration in sectors and jobs with low union penetration. Ost (2005) mentions how the experience of temporary and illegal migration from Poland and Yugoslavia to Germany in the 1980s (when travel restrictions had already been eased) instilled among migrants negative perceptions of trade unions, seen as hostile barriers to their earning opportunities. While these phenomena should have been radically reduced by EU accession—and therefore equal rights as the insiders and access to union membership and services -, it seems that the migration process still contributes to weaken worker 'voice' in the new member states.

In sending countries, migration has some positive economic effects: according to Brücker *et al.* (2009), GDP declines, but there are gains for real wages, productivity and GDP per capita. Social and developmental effects are harder to evaluate. Migration numbers as a percentage of the population are much higher in sending than host countries: its effects are therefore more visible in the countries of origin. A precise assessment is impossible because official data from LFS and the EC tend to grossly underestimate flows by missing all short-term movement. In the first three years after EU accession, 2.5% of active Poles, 2.4% of active Slovaks, 3.1% of active Latvians, and 4% of active Lithuanians had registered for work in the UK only, with numbers being much lower for the other new member states (Home Office 2009). If one includes similar data from other countries with high immigration flows (Ireland, Norway, Spain), the total share of workers who have chosen to 'exit' their countries, at least temporarily, after 2004 may be over 10% in the case of the Baltic States and Romania and only slightly less in that of Poland and Slovakia. This contrasts with the old Member States, where mobility since the creation of the European Economic Community only affected less than 2% of the workforce. Many more are interested in leaving: in Poland, in 2007 (despite economic growth in the country at the time) 10.5% of employed people expressed a wish to leave, and 23.1% declared that they could not leave, but they would like to (Gardawski 2009b, 40).

Such massive exit affects the balance of power in employment relations in the home countries. Both real and potential worker mobility (the right to legal employment in other EU states) after 2004 affects employers less than capital mobility affects employees, as capital remains inherently more mobile than labor. Still, by 2007 labor shortages were complained of in all new member states, and employer organizations were requesting the easing of migration barriers to workers from their eastern neighbors (Belarus, Russia, and Ukraine). The exit threat also forced employers and governments to make concessions they had been unwilling to make before. Wages increasing fast between 2004 and 2006, even if less than productivity and therefore without damaging the competitiveness of these countries: by 50.6% in Poland, 59.3% in Lithuania, 60.4% in the Czech Republic, 88.9% in Slovakia, 97.8% in Hungary, 100.4% in Estonia, and 118.3% in Latvia, as against 26.3% in the Euro area (Eurostat 2007). However, inflation was marginally higher, and productivity increased much higher in the new member states. This means that actually there was much more wage moderation in the new member states than in Western Europe (Van Gyes *et al.* 2007). Interestingly, these figures are roughly inversely correlated to collective bargaining coverage (higher in Poland and Slovakia than in the Baltic countries), and wage drift (the difference between actual pay and collectively agreed pay) is greater than in Western Europe. This means that formal industrial relations were not the driving force behind them.

Wage increases were granted not because of union power, but because of exit threats: not surprisingly, they were most generous in sectors such as construction and transport, where employees were most mobile. Polish media reported, during the summer of 2007, how waitresses in the Baltic sea resorts, until then one of the least organized and most vulnerable categories of employees (informal employment, very long flexible hours, pay often only by tips, risk of abuse) started claiming more by sharing the news of their friends who had gone abroad and threatening 'to go to the West', leading to serious disruptions in the middle of the peak season ('Aksamit', 2007).

National and regional governments also needed to take measures against emigration. Apart from easing immigration from eastern neighbors, they proposed a number of disparate incentives and policies to 'bring people back'. For instance, the Polish government promised graduates a two-year exemption from social contributions and 20,000 Polish zlotys (PLN; about 5,000 euro) in grants to set up companies.

An extreme case is that of Latvia, from which perhaps 50,000–100,000 people emigrated in the two years since EU accession. Sommers and Woolfson (2008) argue that the number of emigrants now exceeds the number of Latvians deported under Stalin in the 1940s and that while new Latvian émigrés were not removed by force, poverty has given them few other options. They also report a Latvian State Employment Agency representative confirming that it is employment conditions in their countries that push workers to leave: '[E]mployers in Latvia are not ready to motivate their employees and give them good working conditions. This is the main reason why our citizens are looking for jobs in other European countries' (Sommers and Woolfson 2008, 65). Latvia is also a country that followed the neoliberal creed most closely, introducing the flat tax, a conservative flagship measure, already in 1995 (one year after Estonia). When eventually the financial crisis hit the Latvian bubble in 2008, sending the country into near bankruptcy and the heaviest recession in Europe (an estimated –18% of the GDP in 2009), a further market experiment followed. The government and national bank, tied to international financial orthodoxy, refused to devalue the lat, prioritizing fixed exchange rate with the euro. They opted for major cuts in nominal wages—thereby concentrating all losses on labor rather than spreading them to the whole of the economy, including foreign banks. While real wages happen to fall quite often around the world, cuts in nominal wages are very rare, and even neoclassical economists accept that, for social and psychological reasons, wages are too 'sticky' for being elastic downwards. The Baltic states are different: already during the Russian crisis of 1998 they had demonstrated their peculiar allowance for downward flexibility of nominal wages, with major cuts in construction, fishing, agriculture, hotels, and restaurants (Eamets 2009). In 2009, the Latvian government, with the active support of the IMF, confirmed its commitment to the elasticity of any price, including labor, by cutting state sector wages by 15–27%. The weakness of trade unions allowed this to happen despite protests, but as an effect, it has given a new boost to emigration, testing the limits of social and economic sustainability of the reforms. While overall the global economic crisis (which has hit the favorite host countries of UK and Ireland particularly hard) has reduced propensity to move in the new member states, the opposite has occurred to Latvians. In the first quarter of 2009, the number of Latvians registering for work in the UK increased by 24% in comparison to the first quarter of 2008, while numbers had declined sharply for all other new member states (by 54% for the total of A8 countries).

The large number of young women involved (43% of WRS registrations are of women, and 43% are of under 25), and their strong representation in sectors such as health and hospitality raise further questions for the sending countries. First, it has been argued that deskilling and exploitation of migrants follow gender-specific forms (Kofman *et al.* 2000), and therefore the process of 'brain waste' affects female workers from the new member states more than their male counterparts (Currie 2008). But beside brain drain, female migration (given the overwhelming share of care work provided by women in Europe) also raises the issue of a possible 'care drain' within a 'European care chain', even if most of the personal care sector in Western Europe involves women from outside the EU. Polish media already warn of over 110,000 'Euro-orphans', children left behind by at least one parent moving to Western Europe (Wodecka *et al.* 2008).

In addition, there is the broader issue of migration effects on gender identities and culture, illustrated by Passerini *et al.* (2007) in the case of Hungarian and Bulgarian women migrants. Gender arrangements are in some regards different in the new and old member states, as a legacy of full female employment under communism and traditional values in some countries such as Poland. It may be expected that through migration these different cultures get in contact with potential for change: family culture change in Polish provincial towns following migration has already received considerable media interest (including changes in racial prejudice stemming from Poles coming back with mixed-race children). A sub-question relates to homosexuals, for whom the gap in treatment between old and new member states is wider. It is impossible to produce quantitative estimates, but the phenomenon of homosexual professionals fleeing Poland during the Kaczyńskis' homophobic government reported by the media (Jarkowiec 2007) seems an extreme occurrence of employees 'voting with their feet' when confronted by hostile systems and no space to contest them.

THE HOST COUNTRIES—THE BRITISH EXAMPLE

Until the crisis hit in 2008, the Bank of England, employers, and government were enthusiastic in their assessments of the contribution from these new workers. Net contribution to the public budget, limits to wage inflation and supply of scarce skills were the most advertized benefits.

The positive evaluation stems from the extremely high activity and employment rates of these migrants, and their very young age, which involved very low burdens for the welfare state. There has been indeed an increase in registered workers with dependants in the UK, but the number has remained small: in 2004 only 4.4% of newly registered workers from the A8 had dependants, while in 2008 the number has risen to 10.9%. Successful applications for child benefits from new member states' citizens have increased more than fourfold between 2005 and 2007 (from 10,363 to 44,029), to decline later on with the overall decline of new entries. Successful applications for job seeker allowances were only 18 in 2004 but increased constantly and were 1,671 in the first quarter of 2009. The number of National Insurance Numbers allocated for benefit or tax credit purposes is only 2.2% of the total allocated to new member states' citizens, the remaining being for employment purposes (Home Office 2009).

No particular social problems had arisen, and there was no or little substitution effect on the labor market: unemployment was growing the least where immigration was strongest. Wages were actually rising faster than in 'closed border' Germany (Kahanec 2009), even if Blanchflower and Shadforth (2009) suggest that immigration from the A8 had some negative effect on the relative wages of the least skilled and it induced growing 'fear of unemployment'.

Those positive comments reveal that the scale of migration from the new member states to the UK involved a detectable shift in the power balance of employment relations, as exemplified by the Bank of England's governor's declaration in August 2007 that immigration was limiting wage growth. A Home Office report on the employers' use of migrant labor, besides praising migrants for their prodigious contribution to the British economy, reported among the many employers' tributes to migrants the following: '. . . the more favourable work ethic of migrant workers had the effect of encouraging domestic workers to work harder' (Dench *et al.* 2006, 13)—which sounds as a graphic definition of social dumping.

Despite EU status and higher qualifications than average, new member states' workers occupy the lowest strata in the British labor market (Clark and Drinkwater 2008). Those workers (70%), arriving between April 2007 and March 2008, earned between £4.50 and £5.99 per hour, the minimum wage being £5.52 (£4.60 for the under 22; Home Office 2009). New migrants—of whom the majority comes from the new member states—constitute one of the largest groups of 'vulnerable workers', and the fastest growing one (TUC Commission on Vulnerable Workers 2008). Notably, newly arrived Poles earn several pounds less than immigrants in the same jobs who came to the UK before 2000: a study found that they earned the least among all 26 nationalities examined, including Somalis, Turks, and the Chinese (Drinkwater *et al.* 2009). According to the Labor Force Survey (which tends not to record the newest and most vulnerable migrants), in 2008 35% of workers from the new member states were in elementary occupations, and 20% machine, plant, or process operatives, while the figures for remaining foreigners were 15% and 6% only (Office for National Statistics 2009). One of the main human capital reasons for this disadvantage is the worse knowledge of English than other migrant groups, which, in turn, is frequently perpetuated by employment and housing segregation (Sumption and Somerville 2010). However, given the low-skill jobs these immigrants are called to perform, language appears to be more a pretext for exploitation, than an objective factor of low productivity. The fact that in many cases new EU migrants appear to have replaced, at the bottom of the occupational hierarchy, previous migrant groups, now more integrated, confirms the demand-based, structural interpretation of segmentation employer strategies, frequently substituting workforces in the search for ultimate vulnerability.

From the perspective of labor mobility and flexibility as distinctive feature of this migration wave, the role of temporary work agencies in the UK is central. The issue had important political implication: the designed EU directive on Temporary Agency Work found, interestingly, the united opposition of exactly UK and Poland until a compromise was reached in 2008. Forty percent of A8 migrant workers in the UK registered for work in 'Administration, Business and Management' (ABM; Home Office 2009), but this denomination includes all agency workers regardless of the actual job performed. The data on jobs confirm that only a tiny minority is actually in management or professional business jobs (less than 1%)—the others are employed by agencies, and work in all economic sectors. This contrasts sharply with the situation of UK nationals, of whom only 3% work for temporary work agencies. Moreover, the share of workers in this 'ABM' sector has been constantly increasing: it was not a temporary phenomenon.[6] In terms of contracts, 53% of A8 workers registered for temporary contracts and 44% for permanent (Home Office 2009): again, a sharp contrast with the figures for the whole of the UK workforce, of whom only 6% has fixed-term contracts (even if a higher number had a fixed-term contract for their first job).

Does the fact that over a third of workers from the new member states in the UK receive their first job through agencies stem from choice (flexibility, short-term commitment, cosmopolitanism) or rather from fate, leading to a new form of labor market segmentation? In some sectors, especially local public services but also food industry and manufacturing (media reported of thousands of underpaid agency workers at each of the large companies such as BMW, Coca Cola, Corus), British trade unions point at an 'apartheid' of migrant workers, through their segregation in agency employment. In any city in the UK the number of temporary work agencies has multiplied after 2004, and a tour of those of Coventry in 2007 proved to me that in nearly all of them Polish was spoken, whereas applicants from Western Europe were not considered. The visibility of the link between migration and agency work acted as a catalyst for mobilization and political action on the issue. In 2007 the Trades Union Congress created a Commission for Vulnerable Workers and increased its political pressure over the temporary work agencies issue, obtaining, in May 2008, the government's promise of new legislation giving more rights to agency workers with more than three months employment. Until then, the UK was the EU country with the largest use of temporary work agencies, and the one with the softest regulations and the least employment rights for agency workers (Arrowsmith 2006). Studies have found evidence of misuse of agency employment in the case of migrants (McKay and Markova 2010). Interviews we carried out in 2007 with Polish migrants showed that they perceived agency work (with the reduced rights, security, and pay it entailed) as a form of discrimination, rather than as an opportunity or a 'stepping stone'.

> These agencies are all one big fraud, exploiting people. When there was work, this agency would require 100 people, although it could only employ 20, but with some guarantee of work continuity. And the agency recruited 100, who would compete to work as long as possible, while the agency was only interested in getting the contract as quickly as possible, at the cost of the employees. (Male cleaner, age 34)

> They take the transaction fee from everybody. After 6 months you have to renew the contract and they take the fee again. They also take the first week of salary. Even if it is not actually them who found me the job, they just gave me the information. [. . .] I wanted to leave the agencies; they pay only the minimum wage. (Male waiter, 29)

> These agencies are of no use. [. . .] Any agency you walk into, they just sit and drink coffee. Maybe they have some state subsidies because otherwise they would not survive. I didn't receive any phone call from any agency for six months. (Male kitchen aid, 35)

> Agencies often take on as many people as they can and pay less than the minimum wage or the going rate. I received an offer for £4.47. The agency sacked me when they discovered that I was pregnant. They simply told me that since I am pregnant, I cannot work [. . .] I know that there is a very good protection for pregnant workers with a permanent contract, but nobody cares about those from agencies such as me. Protection for pregnant agency workers simply does not exist. (Female warehouse operative, 21)

These agencies simply make money on us, for as long as 6 months. They take provisions out of our pay. Not just a transaction fee. I don't have a good opinion about them. The worst is, that firms don't want to employ without the intermediation of agencies. It's a self-enforcing business. (Male driver, 40)

Such decisively negative views challenge the argument of deregulated agency work as opening opportunities to, and therefore benefiting, migrants and outsiders: as the quote from the female respondent shows, female migrants suffer even more from agency employment. Although many migrants manage to escape agency work, it is not an easy process and employer preference for it combines probably ethnic prejudice with abuse of flexibility and blackmailing. Other research, as well as the media and social organizations, have documented exploitative practices by some agencies, such as illegal pay deductions under the form of accommodation or other social expenses (e.g. French and Möhrke 2007). This is the extreme form and logical conclusion of the use of mobile workers from the new member states as employment buffer to charge with the maximum burden of flexibility and precarity.

CONCLUSION

The EU-citizen status does not prevent segregation and exploitation. They are already at the bottom of the labor market in terms of pay. As the UK government's immigration policy shifts to requiring an English proficiency test to any prospective migrant from outside the EU (such a requirement would be illegally discriminating against EU citizens), workers from the new member states could become the lowest strata in the British labor market, offering unskilled labor without the language proficiency needed for either developing a career or claiming rights and mobilizing within the local space. Their situation of uncertainty is also one of maximum risk and minimum 'voice'—to the extreme cases of workers whose accommodation is also provided by agencies and therefore dependent on the employer's will. This has led migration experts to warn of the 'risk that a constantly self-replacing stream of A8 workers could fall into the role of semi-exploited (if often compliant) 'underclass', with limited prospects for social mobility and integration' (Sumption and Somerville 2010, 29). The analysis of this chapter suggests that this is not just an unintended consequence of free movement. Rather, it is the coronation of a systematic search for flexibility and mobility, in both host and home countries.

Such a status—particularly 'free' but also often particularly exploited—for so many people is too contradictory not to become a crucial test for EU policies and labor market regulations—even if it seems to make perfect economic sense from the point of view of employers, central banks, and free-market theorists.

5 Political Absenteeism and Populism

Failing to create industrial relations institutions capable to face the increased market disruptions engendered by EU enlargement is not just a labor market issue. What has been lacking in the 'new' Europe, more generally, is the institutionalization of collective voice—which would add a *political* dimension, and when needed correction, to the economic, often socially unsustainable, nature of the labor market. This has been primarily a political failure, and it also has political consequences.

This chapter will discuss the failed creation of political representation of labor in Central and Eastern Europe, linking it to the very high levels of absenteeism and the successes of populist politics.

ELECTORAL ABSTENTION AND THE POLITICAL MARGINALIZATION OF LABOR

On 29–31 August 2005, I attended the official celebrations of 25 years of the formation of Solidarity, the first free trade union in a communist country. Being invited to it was a rather undeserved honor for me, as in 1980 I was finishing primary school in Italy, and in 1989 my role in Poland was that of amused visiting student. A two-day international conference in Warsaw was followed by a day of speeches and commemorations at the shipyard gates in Gdańsk. In three days of scheduled speeches, by a number of professors (Ash, Dahrendorf), presidents and ex-presidents (Havel, Köhler, Yushchenko, Barroso, Wałęsa, and Kwaśniewski, with Bush Sr held in America at the last minute by Hurricane Katrina), political protagonists of various stature (Albright and Baker, alongside John Prescott), labor and unionism were mentioned only once (by John Prescott remembering some union anecdotes related to alcohol consumption). Only one person spoke at length, passionately and in detail of the degrading working conditions in Poland, and the enduring need for fighting for labor dignity just as it was done in 1980. It was Tadeusz Gocłowski, archbishop of Gdańsk, in the homily of the crowded open-air Mass for the people of Gdańsk. While Solidarity, it was repeated many times over the three days, had certainly done much to change Polish and international politics, it was apparent how Polish and international politics had nothing to say to the people who had actually done Solidarity. It looked as if the bishop had not been informed that labor was no longer to be mentioned (Gocłowski was a rather isolated progressive voice within the conservative Polish episcopate, but if the homily had come from a traditionalist voice, such as the one of former Solidarity chaplain Father Henryk Jankowski, it would have probably taken an anti-democratic or even anti-Semitic tone).

That blatant celebration of the marginalization of labor was part of a general process, that had become more manifest with EU accession. The elections to the European Parliament of June 2004, only few weeks after the enlargement, were a warning signal of the weakness of the political representation of labor in the new member states and the overall weakness of the EU political and democratic construction. The turnout across the EU fell to 45%, and the once-dominant socialist group, which is still characterized by strong, if not exclusive, links to European trade unions, emerged seriously weakened. Both developments were driven by the new member states.

All new member states registered extremely low participation rates, which contrasted with the apparent mass enthusiasm of the celebrations of EU accession on 1 May, when millions of people partied in the street with European and national flags. In the new member states only 26% of voters bothered going to the polling station, little more than half the figure of 48% in the old member states. Slovakia had the record of 83% abstention, allowing the ruling Christian Democrats to arrive first by a margin of just 372 votes, and the support of just 2.9% of the electorate (17.1% of the actual voters). In the following European elections of 2009, a strong campaign to remove the shame of being the least-committed voters in Europe slightly improved the participation rate in Poland and Slovakia, but in the other countries little changed: in all new member states except Latvia turnout was lower than in the EU15 (Table 5.1).

The ironic effect of such low participation was that populist parties were defeated, and ruling parties managed to obtain reasonable results even if with ridiculously low support. In the opinion polls published in the weeks before the election, populist parties were clearly ahead in voting intentions, but these failed to materialize in the polling stations. Populists had been a victim of their own success: their discourse against the EU and against democratic representation was so well received, that people rejected the electoral process altogether, including the populists taking part in it. By ridiculing the European Parliament, populist had undermined their own chances to enter it.

Still, populist parties obtained noticeable results and thereby visibility in Strasbourg. In Slovakia, Vladamír Mečiar (who had kept the country at the margins of Europeanization process in the 1990s) obtained 17.1%. In

Poland, with a turnout of 20.9%, the anti-EU Peasant Party Self-Defense obtained 10.8%, and the extreme right League of Polish Families, that had defined the EU as an organization led by pedophiles and sodomites, 16%. The League's MEP Maciej Giertych did not need much time to make himself known in Strasbourg with speeches praising Salazar and pamphlets on the impossibility of integrating Jews and Muslims[1]. The worst populist success was in Latvia, where the For Fatherland and Freedom party, that includes SS apologists, obtained 29.8%.

By contrast, social democratic parties performed very poorly, with the exception of the ephemeral Estonian social democrats' success (37% of the vote, with 27% participation rate, but never repeated). The two Polish social democratic lists obtained 14.8% together, and the Czech social democrats fell to 9%. In Latvia, no social democratic party took part in the elections at all. Parties more to the Left (those united in the European United Left group, that also share some links to the union movement) are virtually non-existent, with the exception of the residual and nostalgic Czech-Moravian Communist Party (which obtained an impressive 21%). The only strong leftist party in post-communist Europe is *die Linke* in Eastern Germany, interestingly enough the former communist country with the most improved living standards, but with a more functional political system. In total, the new member states elected 22.5% of their MEP from left-wing parties (European Socialist Party and European United Left), while the figure was 35.3% for the EU15.

In the 2009 elections, the social democratic crisis continued, although it was now deep in the West, too. The social-democratic share of the vote was 25% across the EU, but below this mark in all new member states except Romania (31.1%) and Slovakia (32%), with record lows in Poland (12.3%), and Estonia (8.7%). And, equally important, as Avdagic (2005) had shown, social-democratic parties in the new member states are characterized by very weak links with trade union constituencies, in spite of some enduring networks with union bureaucracies. As such, they are very little responsive to union (and in generally workers') demands, and offer very little in terms of representation. They also have very few members and no social roots in working class communities. Their post-communist nature (in all new member states but the Czech Republic, Slovakia, and the Baltics) does not help. When the Polish social democrats won the parliamentary elections of 2001, their membership suddenly swelled from 10,000 to 100,000—but the new members were not workers, just former communist party members hoping to regain some of the privileges they used to enjoy until 1989. This membership bubble was the first sign of the corruption scandals that soon hit the party and the government.

Fringe parties' successes in European Parliament elections are not an exclusive feature of the new member states. Actually, even the strongest populist parties in Central Eastern Europe (in 2009, Jobbik in Hungary with 15%, Ataka in Bulgaria with 12%, For Fatherland and Freedom in Latvia with 7%, and Slovak National Party in Slovakia with 6%) remain below the results achieved by their western counterparts United Kingdom Independence Party, Front National, Northern League, or Freiheitliche Partei Österreichs. But Yobbik's impressive 17% in the 2010 Hungarian elections is a sign that EU accession does not stop populism. More importantly, in the new member states the democratic crisis is more pervasive than in the 'old' Europe. Racism and xenophobia are often more outspoken: in February 1999, I witnessed the surreal situation of Italian post-fascist leader Fini (then in opposition) in a controversial visit to Warsaw and Auschwitz, when he felt embarrassed by the level of reactionary bigotry of his hosts from the Confederation of Independent Poland, then in the ruling coalition: in other words, the eastern mainstream Right was more extreme than the western extreme Right. In the eastern part of the EU, extremist parties meet little resistance and easily enter government coalitions (in Poland, Slovakia, Latvia). The populist tone permeates easily more mainstream parties, such as Law and Justice in Poland (which absorbed the League of Polish Families), Fidesz in Hungary (which includes the openly anti-Semite and anti-Roma MP Oszkár Molnár) and Citizens for European Development of Bulgaria. In *The Economist*'s words ('Right on Down', 14 November 2009), in the region 'some far-right ideas have percolated into the mainstream', and 'one reason there are no big Far Right parties in the Baltics is that they have a harder centre-right'. These developments are not just of local importance but affect the EU level, too: it was the accession of Romania in 2007 that allowed the formation of a new, if short-lived, formal group of extreme right parties in the European Parliament. And, again, it was a number of small and big allied in the new member states that allowed the British Conservatives to form a new Euroskeptic, and largely populist, group of MEP after the 2009 elections.

Moreover, abstention is very high in the new member states in the national elections as well: in June 2004, Lithuania held presidential elections on the same day as the European ones, but the majority boycotted the vote even there. The year after, only 40% of Poles took part in their national parliamentary elections. Table 5.1 indicates how turnout in national elections in all new member states is lower than in the EU15. Moreover, it shows a specific negative trend: in all new member states, except Estonia and the Czech Republic (two countries with less emigration than average), after EU accession it has declined more rapidly than in the EU15. The EU seems part of the problem, more than part of the solution.

Given the worsening trend in this regard, it would be wrong to blame any democratic deficit to the communist legacy, which anyway can hardly explain the particularly low participation rate of the new generation, already socialized in the post-communist environment. As with labor

Table 5.1   Turnout in National and European Elections

Country	Year of last election	Turnout	Change from last elections before EU accession	Turnout at European elections, 2009
EU15 (average)		70.9*	−2.4**	52.4
Bulgaria	2009	60.6	−10.0	39.0
Czech Republic	2010	62.6	+4.7	28.2
Estonia	2011	63.5	+5.6	43.9
Latvia	2010	62.0	−9.2	53.7
Lithuania	2008	48.6	−9.6	21.0
Hungary	2010	64.4	−9.1	36.3
Poland	2007	53.9	−7.7	24.5
Romania	2008	39.2	−19.3	27.7
Slovenia	2008	63.1	−7.3	28.3
Slovakia	2010	59.0	−11.1	19.6

Source: Eurostat.
*Average of the last elections until 2010. **Average of the last elections until 2003.

issues, what has happened has been the rapid association of the transition countries with the worst practices and models of the West, adopting that form of democratic distortion through unaccountable economic power that has deserved the definition of 'Post-democracy' (Crouch 2004). Electoral campaigns in the new member states do not resemble the old communist ones anymore, apart from some residual countryside campaign party offering free 'electoral sausages'. They look much more like American elections,[2] dominated by personalities and TV, and without the participation of any strong political party. American campaign and public relations consultants are in high demand in the new member states. A low participation rate is perfectly consistent with such pattern.

Low trust in collective action might be, in part, a cultural legacy of social atomization under the communist system that hampers any democratic process, in the workplace as well as at the national political level. This is a point made by various theories of 'Homo sovieticus', whether in Russia (Levada 2000), in Poland (Tischner 1992), or elsewhere. Some of these theories do have important, if of declining relevance and insights. In the absence of space for a systematic scrutiny of them, I prefer to present them through a sharp real-life comparative anecdote I was told by Hungarian sociologist András Tóth. In Hungary, he explained while standing in a canteen queue, canteen workers tend to serve too little cream (or gravy or poppy seeds) on the plates. Students therefore develop their own individual strategies to befriend canteen servers and obtain more favorable treatment. But, Tóth continued, when he spent some time in a British university, he was surprised to see that the student union had called a meeting to consider action in protest for the insufficient quantity of salad provided in the canteen: collective action instead of individual informal strategies. This argument is exactly the same that is used to explain why in Central Eastern Europe there is high micro-conflict activity but very low association rates (in unions or parties) and formal protests.

There may be some truth in these anecdotes, but culturalist explanations are unconvincing. As Bohle and Greskovits (2006) have argued, there comes a time when you have to stop blaming the past. The disillusion with the democratic process in Central and Eastern Europe is not passively inherited but rooted in the painful experience of democratic reforms in the aftermath 1989 and strengthened by the process of EU accession. The incremental and depoliticized nature of EU accession negotiations has had the direct effect of evading democratic debates and the side-effect of leaving any management of discontent to populist, anti-EU parties (Falkner and Nentwich 2000).

Abstention and populism in the new member states are a cross-class phenomenon with complex cultural and historical roots that vary country by country. Class patterns are however increasingly visible in post-communist Europe, even if not as consistent as in the West (Evans 2006), and it is clear in the whole region that it is the socially most disadvantaged groups, and the least educated, that are most disaffected with the EU and the overall political and economic system. As a result, Eurobarometer surveys consistently show that citizens in the new member states are much less satisfied with their democratic institutions, and in particular their parliaments and political parties, than their western counterparts. By 2009 (EC 2010), only 6% of Latvians, 7% of Lithuanians, 11% of Poles, and 15% of Hungarians and Czechs trusted their parliaments (EU average: 30%). In all new member states, a majority was dissatisfied with their national democracy, while in the EU as a whole, it was the opposite (*ibidem*). Some authors, and especially Greskovits and Ost, have provided useful insights that put together the social and political pieces of the puzzle.

THE ILLIBERAL TURN OF LABOR ANGER

Béla Greskovits, in his comparative study of labor protest in Eastern Europe and Latin America, offers the conceptualization of absenteeism and protest voting as workers' exit strategies (Greskovits 1998). In the 1990s, Greskovits had noted how rather than strikes or riots, Eastern European workers preferred exit from the labor market, protest voting, and rent seeking.

Definitions of which vote is 'protest vote' and a form of 'exit' rather than 'voice' are difficult and always disputable, as no party likes defining itself as protest or populist party (although *populismo* keeps some positive connotation in Latin America). Political scientists offer some definitions. Taguieff defines populism as a 'political style based on the appeal to the people, as well as the cult and defense of the people', which is compatible in principle with all big political ideologies (liberalism, nationalism, socialism, fascism, anarchism) but threatens liberal democracies, because of its inherent ethnonationalist orientation (Taguieff 2004, 17). Hermet goes further in pointing at the specific dialectic fallacy that distinguishes populism: the 'exploitation of the dream of abolishing political reason in its chronological dimension' (2001, 51). Accordingly, it is not the appeal to the people to characterize populism, as this can, or rather should, be shared by democratic movements. It is the oversimplification of representation, whereby the people can be easily reduced to unity bypassing debates among competing ideas and programs. Such unity can take three forms (national, plebian, ethnic), but in each case it excludes adversaries by defining them as outside the people (respectively, foreigners, the 'elite', minorities) and therefore lacking legitimacy and not worth discussing with. The democratic process of competition between programs, ideas, and interests is replaced by opposition between 'people' and 'non people'—be it oligarchs, establishment, conspirators, intellectuals, or ethnic minorities. In this sense, populism is 'exit' and not 'voice'.

These definitions are pertinent to many political forces in Central Eastern Europe, although they are not fixed in terms of time, and certainly not exclusive to them. Parties like Fidesz in Hungary or Law and Justice in Poland have often used strong populist rhetoric, taking on the role of only defenders of the nation against all others, but at other times, and especially while in power, they have mostly behaved as mainstream parties. In Western Europe, populist parties have been even more successful at times: Le Pen reached the second round of the French presidential elections in 2002, while the alliance between Berlusconi, post-fascists and Northern League won three Italian elections. While there is no point here in discussing which party has been populist when in Central Eastern Europe, what matters is the pervasiveness of the populist discourse, which has taken the place of the debate and negotiation of social issues.

David Ost, in his work on Poland, has elaborated most in-depth the link between the failure of labor representation and the emergence of what he calls illiberalism in post-communist Europe (Ost 2005). His argument is that while democratic institutions are well equipped to accommodate, and negotiate, economic conflicts (e.g. between the Right and Left on wages or tax), they cannot accommodate conflicts between essential identities, where the relations between majority and minority cannot be modified through debate and compromise. Drawing on Hirschman's (1977) work on capitalism, anger, passion, and interests but also on Polanyi's concept of 'moral resistance', Ost claims that the ways economic anger (unavoidable under capitalism) is expressed can have different effects for democracy. In the case of Poland, 'by organizing the anger of economic losers along non-economic lines, Polish political and trade union leaders impeded the development of the emerging democratic system' (Ost 2005, 2). This is because in the 1990s successive union leaders (Wałęsa, Lech Kaczyński, Krzaklewski) used the trade union to fight not against capitalism, but against 'untrue Poles', 'communists', or unspecified 'elites'. In 1997, Solidarity was the leading force of the right-wing coalition that went to power with a program based on anticommunism and restoration of Catholic principles, rather than on the defense of labor interests.

The support of capitalism and the avoidance of class discourse were most evident in Solidarity but are visible in the whole of the post-communist world. Weyland (1999) speaks of 'market populism' to refer to the specific form of idealization of a 'good' market that dominated post-communist politics. In this sense, populism is not exclusive to fringe parties but has actually been fostered by mainstream liberal parties pretending that social distinctions do not matter and a 'good' market would benefit each 'good' individual. Karol Modzelewski, a former dissident and left-wing Solidarity officer, made a provocative point, in 2003, when saying that the liberal leader (and future prime minister) Donald Tusk was more populist than the Peasant Adrzej Lepper of Self-Defense, because the latter showed at least some notion of the state and of social responsibility. Market populism was not invented by Central Europeans: it was propagated by Thatcher and Reagan in the years before the fall of communism. What is distinctive to Central Eastern Europe is not its existence or even success, but the fact that, here, it found little or no opposition. As Ost put it, in post-communist countries people were left free to choose parties, but not policies, in a system of electoral accountability without political accountability. A pattern has been frequently observed in Eastern Europe and Latin America: an alternation between two parties, with the ruling party following the neo-liberal policies dictated by international actors and the opposition protesting against it, but as soon as the opposition wins, the roles are swapped, and the government policies never change. Indeed, in Central and Eastern Europe, very rarely have incumbent governments won the elections (never in Poland, despite seven parliamentary elections between 1989 and 2007)—but the overall economic policies have hardly ever changed. 'Right' and 'Left' mean little here, as formally right-wing parties defeated ruling 'leftwing' coalitions in Poland (1997, 2005) and Hungary (1998, 2010) on the basis of social protest against market reforms. Alternation between political parties, which is considered as the ultimate proof of democratic consolidation by those theorists of 'democratization' only concerned with formal procedures, has a much darker side from a perspective that also considers actual policies, especially in the social realm. It reveals the failure of the political system to provide any constructive expression to the discontent that people manifest by constantly voting government parties out of power.

While arguing that the space for populism in Central Eastern Europe was created after 1989, Ost adds that EU accession expanded it. The economic reforms mandated by the EU accession process meant that Polish politicians actually had very little room to maneuver in terms of the policies they could pursue once elected. During the negotiations, accession countries' governments were put in the position of 'penitents' listening to the priest—the European Commission (Jacoby 1999). Given these constraints, Ost, following Grzymala-Busse and Innes (2003), points out that those parties that make the strongest effort to differentiate themselves with nationalist, culturally conservative rhetoric may have an advantage in that they appear to offer a genuine alternative. After Bruszt and Stark (2003), he claims that EU '*normalization*' increases domestic exclusion from political process.

Ost mentions other examples of populist activities beyond Poland. In the Czech Republic, the extreme right obtained 8% in 1996, and an anti-Roma wall was built in Usti nad Labem in 1999; in Hungary, Fidesz turned into a nationalistic, anti-EU party; and Yugoslavia is the most extreme case of economic anger finding non-class articulation. But if populism were only a matter of fringe parties, it would be less serious a threat than in Western Europe.

In fact, even when populist parties are not present, the underlying democratic deficit in the representation of social demands is still there. In Hungary, Tóth and Grajczjar (2007) explained that the lack of electoral success of the extreme right until 2006 was due to the extreme right party MIÉP's misplaced focus on traditionalist/historical right-wing ideology, of declining appeal in today's Hungary, but added, on the basis of in-depth interviews in significant working class milieus, that economic insecurity and powerlessness at work were leading to political frustration. Reality quickly vindicated their view. In 2006, there were nationalist riots in the streets of Budapest, in 2009 the neo-fascist party Jobbik obtained an impressive 14.8% in the European elections, and in 2010 it reached 16.7% in the parliamentary elections.

Riots are indeed another important, if rarer, form of 'exit' from the new political and economic regime. Besides the mentioned Usti nad Lebem in 1999 and Budapest in 2006, large Gypsies' riots took place in Slovakia in 2004 and Russian-speakers' riots invested Tallinn in 2007. The ethno-nationalist nature of these events is important. In those new member states with strong ethnic cleavages (especially the Baltic states with regard to the Russian speakers, but to some extent, at times, also Romania, Slovakia, Czech Republic, and Hungary with regard to the Roma and/or Hungarian minorities), identity politics replaced social issues in the political system. Social cohesion could be achieved there against a minority, rather than through social compromises within the majority. It is not a surprise, then, that the Baltic states have the weakest trade unions and that their social democratic parties are either weakest or least social democratic among the new member states.

Overall, like with abstention, populism cannot be explained just through the past, as it is often done (e.g. Minkenberg 2011). The countries where it has developed most (Poland, Slovakia, Hungary, the Baltics) are exactly those that, at the moment of EU accession, were considered as the best performer in 'transition' and 'transformation'—those that been most committed to free market liberalism. In the 'Transformation Index' of 2003 of the Bartelmann Stiftung (2003), that ranks Western reforms across the world, the first places were for Hungary (first), Slovenia, Czech Republic, Slovakia, Lithuania, and Estonia (joint second), Estonia (sixth), and Poland (seventh; Bertelsmann Stiftung). Latin American countries were well behind: but despite this, and despite not entering the EU, it was them that developed lively democracies in the following decade.

But in Central and Eastern Europe, especially Hungary, Slovakia, Poland, and the Baltics, the oscillation from free market to populist policies has confirmed Polanyi's classic intuition on the double movement between economy and society.

> The victory of fascism was made practically unavoidable by the liberals' obstruction of any reform involving planning, regulation, or control. Freedom's utter frustration in fascism is, indeed the inevitable result of the liberal philosophy, which claims that power and compulsion are evil, that freedom demands their absence from a human community. No such thing is possible; in a complex society this becomes apparent. (Polanyi 1944, 257)

THE STRANGE CASE OF THE KACZYŃSKI BROTHERS

The Polish and Slovak cases are the most telling with regard to the succession of EU-led free-market policy, social discontent, and populism. Here, while populists had already had some success during the 1990s, they went to power *following* EU accession. Ost wrote his book in 2005, before the Polish elections of that year, when populist strengthening was still only a hypothesis. Subsequent events corroborated his view and help explain why the Polish translation of his book, published in 2007, became an influential best seller in Poland. It is therefore worth looking at the Polish case more in depth, in order to elaborate the link between EU, labor, and populism with more insight that Ost could have in 2005.

The Law and Justice (PiS) party that won the Polish elections in 2005 and ruled the countries for two years, led by the Kaczyński twins, became the most visible representative of the populist right in Central Eastern Europe. The populist radical right in Poland—in its different party manifestations—has been well described by Pankowski (2010) in relation to

Polish nationalist traditions. What has been overlooked is, as already mentioned in Chapter 2 with regard to social policies, the link between this party and labor issues. Lech and Jarosław Kaczyński were prominent leaders of Solidarity, the former having been its vice-president in 1990 (and narrowly failing to become its president once Lech Wałęsa left the trade union for the country presidency), and the latter having controlled its weekly, and at that time influential, magazine *Tygodnik Solidarność* after its previous director Tadeusz Mazowiecki became Prime Minister in 1989. After his death in the tragic plane crash of Smolensk in April 2010, the official speech for the funeral of Lech Kaczyński was given by Solidarity's president, Janusz Śniadek.

The link to labor is not just in the biography of the party leaders. In the social and economic field, the program of the party was elaborated by the leading sociologist Jadwiga Staniszkis, who in the West would be considered left-wing and even with neo-Marxist orientations. Staniszkis played a leading role in pushing Solidarity to create the right-wing front Solidarity's Electoral Action (AWS) in 1996,[3] which won the elections the year after. The 2005 program of PiS included defense of the welfare state and dialog with the trade unions (even if it then appeared that dialog was intended only with Solidarity, with the exclusion of the other unions). Lech Kaczyński himself was committed to those ideas. As a university professor of labor law, he was a rather rare example of pro-labor Polish academic and already in the 1990s had taken a prominent role in debates on the new Labor Code, criticizing its liberalization. In 2005, the Kaczyńskis promised that they would not liberalize labor law, and they kept this commitment, unique among all post-1989 Polish governments.

The PiS electoral victory of 2005 was not anticipated. The liberal party Civic Platform (PO) was ahead in the polls and the two parties were expected to form a liberal-moderate coalition. The triumph of PiS was precipitated by two separate events at the beginning of September, a couple of weeks before the parliamentary elections and a month before the presidential ones. First, the social-democratic (post-communist) candidate Cimoszewicz, a target of growing corruption allegations in the media (then proved unfounded), decided to withdraw from the presidential race. The disappearance of the Left allowed PiS to take on the role of only defenders of social justice.

The second event was an extremely successful TV advertisement by PiS, reacting to the liberals' manifesto including a 'flat tax' that would have reduced income and capital tax and increased value-added tax (VAT; especially on those goods that benefited from reduced VAT), bringing them to the same level. The advert portrayed an average working family, in their typical little flat, experiencing the sudden vanishing of medicines, children's toys, milk, and the fading away of electric light. The advertisement concluded explaining that these would be the effects of VAT increases and that the elections' choice was between a 'solidaristic' (PiS) Poland, and a 'liberal' (PO) one. Socio-economic issues, generally neglected in Central

Eastern European politics, became the center of the campaign and allowed PiS to win with a message which, in the West, would have been clearly marked as 'leftwing'.

After the elections, which created a lasting hostility and bitterness between PiS and PO, the Kaczyńskis, who had no absolute majority in the Parliament, decided to form a coalition with two populist and strongly anti-EU parties: the Peasant Self-Defense party, whose leader Lepper had declared that in the EU Poles would become 'slaves', and the ultra-traditionalist League of Polish Family (LPR), linked to the anti-Semitic broadcaster Radio Maryja and frequently defined the EU as a new USSR defending pedophiles.

The coalition's nature obscured the local social roots of PiS and high-lighted its international isolation and cultural conservatism. Social issues took a national and cultural dimension. The PiS adopts a strongly anti-German stance, with Lech Kaczyński cancelling a meeting with the German president in 2006 and arriving to ask German authorities to take action against the newspaper *Tageszeitung*, guilty of publishing a satirical piece against him and his brother. Lech, as mayor of Warsaw, had already notoriously banned gay demonstrations in the capital city, and in December 2005, soon after his presidential investiture, the police brutally repressed a pacific demonstration of homosexuals in Poznań. The new education minister Roman Giertych, leader of the LPR, proposed the introduction of Polish history as a separate subject from history and distributed in all schools a brochure explaining that homosexuals are handicapped with criminal tendencies and short life expectancy. During the papal visit in May 2006, neo-Nazi skinheads attacked the chief rabbi of Warsaw, and while Kaczyński condemned the act strongly and immediately, the feeling was that extreme right activists felt legitimated by the new authorities (the LPR, in particular, included paramilitary youth organizations). Anti-semitic violence and discourse remained marginal, but racist attacks on immigrants kept increasing.

The PiS government took on a EU-skeptic stance as well, although it must be remembered that the liberals of PO had played the same card in 2003 with their surreal slogan against the proposed constitutional treaty 'Nice Treaty or Death'. Kaczyński (alongside the UK, and later Czech president Klaus) rejected the Charter of Fundamental Rights of the EU and delayed his signature of the Lisbon Treaty.

As it happens most often to populist governments, the PiS—Self-Defense—LPR coalition was quickly undermined by its own contradictions and lost the snap elections of 2007 badly. Yet, it remains that social demands are more likely, in Central Eastern Europe, to be expressed in illiberal and EU-skeptic ways than in labor-based forms. In Hungary, where the ruling Socialist party has moved to free-market economic policies in a similar ways to the Polish social-democrats in 2001–2005, the conservative Fidesz displays strong populist tendencies. Already in 2002, the

Fidesz government had conceded unprecedented, and unaffordable, wage increases. In 2004, while in opposition, it campaigned in a referendum against any privatization of the health service. In 2010, it channeled social discontent against foreign banks and foreign companies. In Slovakia, the new left party Smer not only entered a coalition with right-wing nationalists but adopted a nationalist tone itself, ordering in 2010 all schools and town halls to sing the national anthem every week. Social demands, lacking labor voice, exit social negotiations and emerge in other places with different political colors.

It is still to be explained why trade unions, even if weak, do not oppose such trends towards populism. Again, Poland offers the best illustrations. Solidarity promoted the right-wing AWS in 1996 and supported explicitly PiS in 2005. Zygmunt Wrzodak, anti-Semitic leader of Solidarity in the tractor factory of Ursus near Warsaw, was elected to Parliament for the LPR. I had tried to interview Wrzodak in 1998, while researching Polish trade unions. The interview could not take place, he explained to me on the phone with a peculiar logic, because, being a foreigner, I could be a spy. This seemed a missed opportunity, but it was actually a sufficiently robust answer to the research question on whether Polish extreme nationalism has a paranoid element: on that, he gave me the information I needed. Yet it was possible for me to interview unionists from the other trade union in the factory, as well as Ursus Solidarity members during street demonstrations. While Ursus demonstrations often displayed intolerant (anti-EU and antisemitic) tones, and occasionally minor vandalism, those interviews with Ursus workers unveiled a very rational and instrumental attitude. With slightly embarrassed smiles, respondents conceded that Wrzodak was a joke but also pointed at the large presence of journalists and at the government's willingness to engage in negotiations—all effects of Wrzodak's visibility. Most of Solidarity initiatives at Ursus, on privatization and restructuring, were socially and economically sound, as even the neo-liberal economic journalist of *Gazeta Wyborcza*, Witold Gadomski, generally a critic of trade unions, conceded. Workers' support to Wrzodak was a form of rational 'political exchange': left without institutional representation and collective bargaining, workers used political disturbance as last resource.

Even more compelling evidence of the links between nationalism and frustrated unionism comes from the small, but very active, Silesian trade union Sierpień 80 (August 80). Created in the early 1990s as a breakup of Solidarity 80 (itself a breakup of Solidarity in 1989), this union was particularly active in mines and in the Fiat car factory of Tychy. As I described in detail on the Fiat case (Meardi 2000; Meardi and Tóth 2006), this trade union expressed, not just in its name but also in its workplace activity, the purest continuity with the working class roots of the Solidarity movement. Yet its political isolation, and the extreme hostility from the media, pushed it in the early 2000s towards not just opposition to the EU but also extreme right fellow travellers and even to support the authoritarian General Wilecki (known for his appreciation of Hitler's social and economic policies) in the presidential elections of 2000. It would have been easy, then, to dismiss this organization as just regurgitation of historic nationalist extremism. Yet this is to forget that Polish socialism, especially in Silesia, has been, historically, repeatedly associated with nationalism. This is not unusual in countries and regions fighting for independence, in the East as well as in the West and in dependent countries around the world. But even more importantly, behind that unattractive political façade, August 80 was a real trade union of 100,000 members, very engaged in everyday shop floor action and starting to organize also in new workplaces, such as retail chains. Its leader Daniel Podrzycki, and most of its activists, while admiring the national traditions of Polish socialism (as about the only positive identity references for a labor movement in Poland, after the negative experience of communism), declared themselves as 'obviously' left-wing.[4] Behind populist 'exit', there are genuine worker demands.

CONCLUSION

The failed construction of forms of 'voice', as institutional collective representation, for workers in the new member states affects not just the industrial relations sphere but also the political one. The weakness of social democratic and left-wing parties and their weak link and responsiveness to workers are striking. Moreover, this weakness is now spreading to the EU as a whole, with social democrats being punished by voters for their ritual pro-Europeanism and the European Commission turning decisively to the Right after the enlargement of 2004.

Worker grievances that do not find space through trade unions or left-wing parties emerge, as it has been described by Ost on the Polish case, to illiberal forms that 'exit' the normal political process: abstention and populism. This problem has not taken really dangerous forms just because so far abstention has been stronger than populism: this has allowed mainstream parties to generally win the elections even if with very small support in terms of popular vote. Yet in situations in which half of the population, and often the majority of workers and unemployed, do not vote, political stability is jeopardized. Instead of smugly celebrating their supposed economic success, EU governments would then be better advised to consider their social and political failures more seriously and provide channels to social demands to be expressed and taken seriously, before their repressed energy undermines the foundations of the building they sit in.

6   Organizational Exit and Misbehavior

Besides 'exit' from the country and from its political process, organizational exit is an additional option for workers. This may be of two different kinds: job separation (quitting) or, counter-intuitively, 'internal' exit through organizational disloyalty and misbehavior within the workplace. Employment turnover is the typical form of 'exit' contrasted to 'voice' in industrial relations studies (Freeman and Medoff 1984). Organizational misbehavior is a more recent area of research in labor studies, which has emerged from the observation of increasing opportunities for 'recalcitrant employees' despite the apparent decline of formal forms of resistance (Ackroyd and Thompson 1999)[1]. While this area of study has developed in the Anglo-Saxon world and is often associated with Western post-industrial or even post-modern capitalism, it is highly relevant to the post-communist and EU accession context. In communist times (as also in Nazi Germany), the concept of 'internal migration' was elaborated by intellectuals to describe the frequent social experience of those unable to emigrate but who tried to isolate themselves from the surrounding system. One particular evocative image is the idea of 'Švejkism', recently rediscovered by organizational scholars to describe a form of resistance based on passive ritualism (Fleming and Sewell 2002). This is rooted in central European social imaginary, the literary good soldier Švejk created by Hašek (1923) being a Czech soldier in Austro-Hungarian times, to which later periods of foreign dependence resemble—possibly including the current economic dependence on international capitalism. Burawoy, in his pioneering study of the state socialist labor process in 1980s Hungary, described similar forms of superficial compliance, defined as 'painting socialism' (Burawoy and Lukacs 1985).

Both job and internal exit are difficult to measure and interpret. This chapter will review available evidence of low organizational loyalty and commitment and informal resistance, in Central Eastern European workplaces, including a look at the plants of foreign companies.

THE TURNOVER PROBLEM

Ironically for supposedly planned economies, communist countries experienced high employee turnover, arising from labor shortages, in the period before the transition (Cazes and Nesperova 2001). Turnover was voluntary: at that time, 'exit' compensated for the lack of 'voice'. Labor markets, both on pay and employment, displayed surprising flexibility, bringing Burawoy to theorize that communism involved the market in the workplace and hierarchy in the relations among companies, to the exact contrary of American capitalism (Burawoy and Lukacs 1985). After the transition, crisis and restructuring made turnover suddenly involuntary. During the 1990s, employee turnover in Central Eastern Europe followed different paths than in the West. While in the West job tenure is generally pro-cyclical, according to employee (supply) rational behavior, in the East it was counter-cyclical and demand driven. This suggests a deeper feeling of job insecurity after the experience of the transition shock (Cazes and Nesporova 2007). In other words, while in the West, turnover is a response to improved opportunities, in the East, it is rather a response to increased pressure. Both the 1980s and 1990s, in different ways, saw turnover become the main form of labor market adaptation, in contrast to change in the workplace.

In the 2000s, with EU accession, the situation stabilized but that behavior pattern remained. According to existing statistical evidence (EC 2009), excess turnover (that is, total number of appointments and separations minus the net job creation) in the new member states is slightly below EU average, although it is, unsurprisingly, higher in the hyper-liberal Baltic states, which match the record levels of UK and Denmark. Aggregate data for the whole economy, however, can be distorted by different sector composition. The new member states are characterized by a higher share of employment in manufacturing and especially heavy manufacturing, which everywhere displays longer job tenure (Vandenbrande 2006): this explains particularly low overall turnover rates for Czech Republic and Slovakia. Also, they are likely to present very deep differences between private, state, and privatized sectors, with relatively high tenure for older generations and the residual state sector hiding the very low security and tenure in the new private one. And very importantly, actual mobility in the new member states is forcedly restricted by very low geographic mobility within the country, due to housing shortages and lower availability of private transport. An indication of the differential nature of turnover comes from gender disaggregation of data. While in Western Europe, turnover is higher for women than for men (due to typically female career interruptions), in the new member states, there is almost no difference (EC 2009). The relatively high turnover for men in the new member states may indicate that separations, in the East of the EU, affect more frequently the core of the labor market.

Even more importantly, it is the nature and reasons of employment separations, as well as the frequency of separation threats, rather than the total number, that provide information about the nature and strength of the employment relationship. This is revealed by the different nature of expected mobility, as measured by Eurobarometer data in 2005 (Vandenbrande 2006). Employees in the new member states apparently show a similar level of expectation of changing their jobs in the next five years as the EU average (again, a higher level in the Baltic states and lower in former Czechoslovakia, while Romania and Bulgaria were not included in the survey). However, the reported reasons for expected mobility are very different: a much smaller share of respondents, in the new member states mentions 'neutral reasons' (i.e. impersonal, structural employment, or business change), while many more report intentional change, whether 'voluntary' (employee led), or 'forced' (employer led). Eighty-six percent of Latvian workers, 81% of Estonian, 74% Lithuanians, 73% of Poles, and 69% of Czechs expect to voluntarily change their job, as against a 64% EU average; 38% of Poles, 31% of Slovaks, and 28% of Czech expect to be forced out of their jobs, as against 23% EU average. Job change as a voluntary 'exit' from the employment situation, whether by the employee to improve their situation, or by the employer through dismissals, is perceived as more likely in the new member states than in the old ones.[2]

NON-COMMITMENT EMPLOYMENT RELATIONS

In some new member states, the nature of the employment relationship as a long-term relationship based on status and commitment, and not just on contract and market (Streeck 1987), has been undermined. Formally, Employment Protection Law levels are similar to those in the West. In 2008, among the Central Eastern European OECD members the Employment Protection Law Index was not far below the levels of Western European countries (Table I.1). The trend after EU accession had been one of slight increase in strictness (except in Slovakia). But what matters is that poor law enforcement and weak institutions, together with low collective bargaining coverage, create much higher real levels of flexibility and insecurity. Contrary to the theories of labor market deregulation promoters, among the new member states the Employment Protection Law Index appears to be positively correlated ($r = 0.61$) with the employment rate, which is lowest (56.7%) in Hungary, the country with the lowest Employment Protection Law Index but high (68.6%) in Slovenia, the most restrictive country. Lower protection, rather than creating jobs as liberals believe, scares people and keeps them out of the labor market. A similar pattern of flexibilization occurs on wages, exacerbating the feelings of insecurity (Tonin 2007). In this regard, the continuous process of employment liberalization and weakening of labor market institutions and employee representation has not simply been socially damaging but also economically counterproductive.

An extreme aspect is the extensive use of fictitious self-employment and of 'civil contracts' rather than employment contracts. This happens predominantly for tax reasons but also demonstrates the permeation of the market logic in what has been considered, under capitalism, as the realm of hierarchy and organization. Fixed-term employment was particularly strongly promoted in Poland in the period before accession, with fixed-term employment jumping from 5.8 to 22.7% between 2000 and 2004 (Cazes and Nesperova 2007). The EU-accession did not stop the trend, and the share of fixed-term contracts kept increasing up to 28.2% in 2007 (OECD 2010a). Self-employment has declined but remains high in some countries: in 2008, 23% of total employment in Poland, 26% in Bulgaria, and 30% in Romania, against a 15.7% average for the EU (Eurostat 2010). I have seen personally how in Poland, in the late 1990s and early 2000s, it was commonplace for secretaries and clerical staff of large foreign companies to be employed on the basis of civil contracts, with no employment rights whatsoever, as if they were occasional consultants rather than calling at work every morning. The flexibility ideology promoted at the time by the Polish government and by the EU alike suggested that this was in the interest of the workers themselves, who could benefit from more opportunities and choice. Yet the 'Working Poles' survey of 2007 reveals how workers on civil contracts or self-employed have mostly negative opinions about their contractual arrangements: the majority rather endures than choosing such precarious condition (Męcina 2009a). These practices are not limited to the private sector: in Hungary, a senior public officer candidly confessed to me that he commonly employed fictitious self-employees. Fictitious self-employment is not disappearing with EU integration: the Czech Republic and Slovakia were the countries where it was increasing fastest, together with Germany, a country which, interestingly, has a large number of Central Eastern European self-employed workers (OECD 2008).

The same 'Working Poles' survey provides some information also on the turnover threat. While 58.4% of workers declared to be proud of the company they worked for, 47.9% added that they would change job (an increase from 43.7% in 2005). Even more tellingly on the degree of labor marketization, as many as 61.7% (and therefore many of those who proclaimed 'pride' or their employer) would not reject alternative offers for better money, while only 18.7% would reject it (Męcina 2009b, 328).

Actual commitment to the employer is therefore very rare and contrasts with the Western European tendency to commit to a job not merely for monetary gain but also for social identity reasons. In the West, it is odd to declare willingness to change employer for only a few euros more. In Central Eastern Europe (where there is not such a thing, culturally, as wage confidentiality and details about each other's wages are a common talking point), this is perfectly normal. Disclosing and discussing wages is a natural response to employers' over-secrecy. A comparison of job vacancy ads in the press of the new member states with those in the Western liberal countries reveals an evident contrast: in the new member states, wage details are never provided, neither for professional nor for the most menial jobs; the most information one can find is 'wages subject to negotiation'. Employers, in other terms, try to profit from individual negotiation in a situation of heavily unbalanced information and power. Sharing information among employees is an understandable response to such unbalance and in a way is consistent with the idea of an efficient (and therefore informed) market, even if it can be considered misbehavior from the employer point of view. It corresponds to the 'exit' pattern, promoted by reformers and employers and now adopted by employees.

Most of the time, trade unions cannot but sit and observe how employees pass by, without the time to organizing. Wanda Stróżyk, Solidarity leader at the Polish Fiat factory of Bielsko-Biała, in summer 2009 commented on the news of new recruitment as follows: 'great, that we employ new people, but many will quickly quit for better-paid jobs; unfortunately managers don't see this, or they don't want to see it' (Głogowski 2009). Jürgens and Krzywdziński (2009) report actual cases of very high turnover across the Polish automotive sector in 2005–2007, including a level of 20–30% in the company most famous for its commitment to lifelong employment, Toyota.

These survey figures and quotes point to the perpetuation of market instrumentality and organizational disloyalty following EU accession. This reflects improved labor market conditions and increased opportunities, even if not yet for all: in Poland, in 2007, 22.3% respondents were ready to take an undeclared job, down from 38.2% in 2005, but still an impressive number (Męcina 2009b, 328). Central Eastern European labor markets after EU accession have actually experienced an increase in vulnerability, despite economic improvements (Eyraud and Vaughan-Whitehead 2007). Overall, contrary to the argument that Poland would need more flexibility, Poles emerge from surveys as characterized by high potential mobility, adaptability, and disposition to change (Męcina 2009b, 327).

A related issue is absence from work, a classic indicator of informal labor conflict. Unfortunately, there are no comparable statistics on this phenomenon across Europe, and national statistics are incomplete (Edwards and Greasley 2010). We can infer that absence constitutes a growing concern for employers in Central Eastern Europe, though, from the fact that in all eight new member states, there have been recently strong shifts towards tighter controls on sick absence and on reduced sickness benefits; the only old member state to have followed the same route is Luxembourg (*ibidem*). This is a strong indicator of a very low trust employment regime developing in the new member states, and it has also raised concern for the risk of 'presenteeism' (that is, employees calling for work even when actually ill, at serious cost for their own health and for organization's performance) the new rules create.

In addition to turnover, there has been massive 'exit' from the labor market altogether, whether into the informal economy, including subsistence farming, or into benefits. The informal economy accounts for a larger share of the GDP in all new member states except the Czech and Slovak Republics, than in the West. As mentioned in Chapter 2, it is estimated that the informal economy accounts for around 30% of the GDP in most new member states, as against around 15% for most of the EU15, and there is no sign of the gap being closed (Schneider and Buehn 2007).

A major role in 'exiting' workers from the labor market and avoiding protest was played by the welfare state. The strategic nature of selective social policies to avoid political protest in the region has been described by Vanhuysse (2006). After 1989, early retirement programs leading to 'Great Abnormal Pensioner Booms' and a very liberal use of incapacity benefits allowed companies to proceed with major restructuring in a fast and rather unobstructed way in Poland and Hungary (but not in Czechoslovakia and then the Czech Republic, where the government preferred to concentrate on avoiding job losses, deferring company bankruptcies). As a result in these two countries, despite increasing employment rates, activity rates have not increased after 2004, and remain (at 63.8 and 61.5% in 2008) among the lowest in the EU: while this form of exit predates European integration, it has not been reduced by it.

INDIVIDUAL CONFLICT: LEGAL DISPUTES

The existence of a trade-off between collective representation and individual legal disputes has been known to industrial relations for some time. Rogers and Streeck's (1995) comparison of works councils identified an advantage of these institutions in their potential to replace costly and disruptive disputes in the courts with faster and more flexible local negotiations. More recently, in the UK clear competition and tension has emerged between grievances through legal firms and grievances through trade union representation, the latter being more likely to produce sustainable social gains.

Not only are individual disputes frequent in the new member states, something which may be linked to less law-abiding employers, and in particular to late wage payments (EIRO 2004). When disputes happen, they are more difficult to solve than in the West. A recent comparative study of the European Industrial Relations Observatory on the use and development of 'Alternative Dispute Resolution' found a clear divide between two groups of member states: 16 countries where the use of Alternative Dispute Resolution was rare, and 11 where it was frequent (Purcell 2010). All 10 post-communist new member states belonged to the first group. The explanation is directly linked to the low level of trust that individualized employment relations have produced in the new member states: in the absence of social dialog, effective employee representation, and overall legitimacy and recognition of employee voice, neither workers nor employers take the risk of 'speaking' to each other through mediation and conciliation procedures and opt instead for arms-length dispute resolution via the courts. This apparent effect of the insufficient development of 'political', let alone democratic mechanisms in the workplace is particularly evident in the case of Poland.

In Poland, various avenues are open for Alternative Dispute Resolution (ADR)—including out-of-court settlements, court supervised settlements, the use of a mediator, and/or arbitration linked to the court. Despite these arrangements—and while there were about 180,000 labor law cases brought before the civil courts in 2008—'the number of disputes resolved by ADR is negligible; the social partners speak of about a dozen cases a year, the majority of them settled before the conciliation commissions' (Towalski 2010). How can this be explained? The national center suggests that 'the largest obstacle to propagating ADR in Poland is constituted in reluctance on the part of employees, who are unwilling to trust methods other than court proceedings. Trade unions are in favor of ADR, the employers are ambivalent, and the government thinks it has done enough in establishing a mediation council for use in a wide range of civil court cases. In order to bring about change, there will be a need not only for involvement of the social partners but also for a change in the mindsets of employees and employers alike. Such change may be difficult to achieve, given the generally low trust in public institutions among Poles (Purcell 2010, 6).

ORGANIZATIONAL MISBEHAVIOR:
A FORM OF DISLOYALTY?

According to Polish sociologist Gardawski (2009a), Polish workplaces are dominated by a culture of competition, rather than by a culture of dialog. This directly reflects the prevalence of 'exit' and market over politics and 'voice'. A problem Gardawski detects is that such a culture is associated with white-collar crime, as known to Western scholars (Coleman 1995).

There is no sufficient information on workplace crime, and I will resist the temptation to replace it with anecdotes. There has been some research on organizational loyalty, though. An important and useful, if dated, comparative study was carried out by an international team led by British sociologist of work Duncan Gallie in 1994 (Gallie *et al.* 1999). Gallie's team's surveys in the Czech Republic, Slovakia, and Bulgaria found that in all these post-communist countries organizational commitment was lower than in the UK. But most interestingly, this was not simply due to a common and uniform historical legacy. There were differences among the three countries, with organizational commitment being inversely correlated to market reforms: it was lowest in the (already largely privatized) Czech Republic, higher in Meciar's Slovakia, and highest in slowly reforming Bulgaria. The finding suggested that the transition experience and degree of exposure to marketization caused, or at least exacerbated, organizational commitment deficiencies.

Fifteen years on, it is plausible to affirm that Gallie's findings were not restricted to the immediate transition period: there is no evidence of organizational commitment recovering. Marketization and insecurity have actually increased, and, with EU accession, even moved from the national to the international level, adding to employee fears those of direct foreign competition, international financial crisis, and rapid mobility of capital and labor. The Polish surveys mentioned in the previous section are probably not exceptional, and in the other member states the situation might be even worse. In the Baltic states, a survey carried out in 2007 found that 61% employees were committed neither to their employer nor to their work and that only 19% were committed to both (EWCO 2008).

A look at employee commitment and at workplace informality solicits more skepticism about the frequently held view of Central European workers as inherently quiescent. The quiescence thesis is mostly based on the very low strike data in the new member states, nearly 10 times lower than in Western Europe around the time of EU accession. However, strike data are notorious for their unreliability. When Polish official figures report only one strike for the whole of 2002, there are reasons to doubt their coverage. In most post-communist countries (Warneck 2007), industrial conflict regulations are very strict. An extreme case in this regard is Romania, where the relatively recent Law 168 of 1999 imposes on trade unions a social peace clause for the duration of collective agreements, even if the employer does not observe the provisions of the same collective agreements, as it often happens (Vasilescu and Contescu 2003). In such situations, in Romania and elsewhere, many forms of protest fall short of the official (legal) strike definition, whether as undeclared strikes or other forms of action. But most importantly, it is potentially distorting to treat strikes as the only, or principal, indicator of labor resistance.

There are some historical reasons for strike unpopularity in the region. Some view it as a consequence for strike prohibition under state socialism. Such a view is not entirely precise (strikes were not formally forbidden in 'people's democracies', sabotage was) and does not correspond to the full post-socialist reality. Strikes did occasionally occur in the GDR, Romania, USSR, and frequently in Yugoslavia and Poland. Strike restraint seems then linked more to the new system than to the old one, as argued by Bohle and Greskovits (2006): it has strengthened, rather than declined, as capitalism was enforced and consolidated. Possible explanations include ideology, labor market conditions, and regulatory changes. As to the former, the Eurobarometer (a very rough source, but a comparative one) in 2003 showed that in the then-applicant countries, big companies were slightly more trusted than national government, and only slightly less than trade unions: 24% of people trusted big companies and 57% distrusted them, while the figures were, respectively, 23 and 65% for governments and 26 and 52% for trade unions. It was not employers who were loved but rather the trade unions that were mistrusted. Weak collective action does not signify satisfaction. Regulatory changes are also a part of the picture, although not necessarily according to their formal content, in countries where strikes occurred before the regime fall. In-depth research on the Fiat case in Poland provided an example (Meardi 2000). The factory was strike prone before privatization, in the 1980s, and during the privatization process (1992). Yet in following years, in spite of industrial relations remaining for years extremely adversarial and unions exceptionally militant, only one short strike took place (in 1994). Interviews revealed one unglamorous but important reason for workers' disaffection with the strike instrument. Polish workers under state socialism used to see as 'normal' the fact of receiving their pay for strike hours: as strikes were generally not officially recognized but just 'tolerated' when repression was impracticable. When the new law on work conflict, passed in 1991 and gradually implemented in the following years, established alongside the right to strike the principle that strike hours are unpaid, workers saw it as an abnormal violation of their rights, hesitantly tried to protest, and eventually just stopped striking as a reaction. Disaffection with strikes was exacerbated by the experience of some major strike defeats in the 1992–1993 wave. In order to perceive the existence of resistance, we need to shift the attention from formal organizing and protesting to informal action.

INFORMAL RESISTANCE IN MULTINATIONAL COMPANIES

The case studies on multinational companies I introduced in Chapter 3 offer evidence of different forms of employee resistance, even if with no ambitions of comprehensiveness. The purpose of presenting such evidence is different: it is that of demonstrating, against fatalistic views of employee quiescence, the *possibility* of resistance and therefore, regardless of its extension at a given moment, the openness of processes. The fact that the evidence comes from powerful, successful MNCs makes the appearance of resistance all the more significant.

In the Polish automotive plants studied in 2004,[3] employees received good pay by local standards but about five times less than in sister plants across the western Polish border. The plants were developing fast, taking on production from the West. Polish workers had reasons to consider themselves the 'winners' of international restructuring. However, all four companies displayed impressive forms of labor activation, although in different forms—I will now consider the informal ones and present the formal ones in the next chapter.

In Poland, the first of the two German companies considered, Gp1, was, as described in Chapter 3, exceptional in the degree of 'voice' allowed. Unionization was, at about 80%, extremely high by Polish standards (the national average is around 15%). In this greenfield site, there had never been a strike, and union leaders sounded very accommodating. Managerial power was limited by employee information and consultation prerogatives. Polish managers, in the interviews, expressed frustration at such arrangements, which undermined their status in comparison to their peers in other Polish companies, but the relative effectiveness of these mechanisms meant that no particular informal resistance was recorded.

The second German subsidiary in Poland, Gp2, was a 'brownfield' one, with a core old skilled workforce. Resistance to task organization change was a particularly remarkable issue in daily employment relations.

In the first US-owned company in Poland, Ap1, there had been an important conflict in 1995–1996, at the time of foreign investors' entry. Protest by both trade unions operating in the company had led to the replacement of the company manager responsible for industrial relations. Such action corresponded to a form of demonstrative 'founding conflict' that is not infrequent in Poland, through which the local union shows its force in order to ensure a role for itself. The resulting apparent 'social peace' should therefore be seen as a resulting social compromise rather than as simple labor quiescence. In fact, during the research, employees' frustration and lack of commitment emerged continuously in interviews and were recognized by managers as a problem. Dissatisfaction concerned pay, the use of agency workers, but above all, career and development opportunities. In terms of labor process, the established situation defended by the core skilled workforce meant that organization change could be resisted, and work pace could not be dictated. Managers complained that workers had ways to spend long periods of time doing nothing and an attempt to introduce a 'Kaizen' system (continuous improvement) had completely failed due to employees' non-co-operation with the initiative, seen as a unilateral managerial device. A project of introducing lean production was proceeding very slowly and cautiously: in a line manager's words, all management initiatives are seen by employees as just 'more work to do'.

The second US-own company, Ap2, is a case of greenfield investment, in an area of extremely weak trade union presence: in fact, the largest local industrial company had gone bankrupt, according to local views, because of trade union disruptive activity. Union organization was therefore unpopular, and the plant union free. Nonetheless, at one important stage employees were able to obtain the removal of the foreign plant director and secure his replacement with a Polish manager, as well as larger subsidiary discretion. This is one case of instrumental alliance between local managers and employees against the headquarters.

In all four Polish cases, there is a particularity that is worth mentioning. The workforce is predominantly or exclusively male and so is the union leadership; personnel managers, on the other hand, are women. This situation, quite common in Polish manufacturing companies, has some implications for the dynamic of workplace employment relations. Masculinity is, in the Polish society even more than elsewhere thanks to the political representation of miners and steelworkers, an identity resource that both helps unite the industrial workforce and pressure the female managerial side. The exact weight of the gender factor would require more research, but it does seem to be significant. In one of the companies mentioned, before starting an interview in the trade union office, the male union leader phoned a female manager to ask her to arrange tea and coffee for the male researchers.

Two opposite situations of US investors represent the spectrum of employee resistance situations in Hungary. In the first (Ah1), a large factory in Budapest, a noticeable phenomenon is conflict over working time. This was typical for Hungary, a country characterized by very high working time flexibility, with widespread shift work and overtime (Burchell *et al.* 2009). Such form of managerial prerogative seemed however to have reached its structural upper limit: some large foreign employers (e.g. Nokia), in spite of offering higher-than-average wages were meeting serious retention problems due exactly to discontent with shift work. Resistance does not take the organized form of collective dispute but the atomized one of high turnover. In this regard, Hungarian employees are helped by the structure of their labor market, with a very low activity rate and skilled shortages, resulting from the falling popularity of technical education. This results in scarce labor supply and therefore market power, especially for male, younger, and skilled employees in Budapest and the western regions.

Another case of complex resistance is that of Ah2, a plant in an industrially very depressed area in the east of the country, where unemployment reached 25% in the 1990s. Foreign investment has recently taken off, and in the local conditions investors generally offer precarious employment and wages at the legal minimum (around €230 per month), managing to keep their plants union free also with the use of dismissals. In the case study, a greenfield site with a labor intensive but technically very specialized labor process, employees did not tolerate these conditions for long, though. The foreign management team was rejected and replaced by softer local managers, with whom shop floor dialog was possible. Strikes or open conflicts did not take place, but rather everyday shop floor confrontation between skilled workers and management. A peak in employment turnover (18% in a year, before falling to natural levels after the signing of a collective agreement with the new managers) was decisive in forcing management to change approach. In this case, such turning point also involved opportunities for shifting from turnover to 'voice', unionization, and collective bargaining, as we will see in Chapter 7.

Informal protest occurred repeatedly at Gh2: spontaneous (not union-based) protest petition (on wages and on management's authoritarianism), informal work stoppages through 'cigarette breaks' of key employees (on working time), and walk-outs (on the same). No particular occurrence was recorded at Gh1, a company where industrial relations approximate those of Gp1.

The Slovenian case studies are, as it would be expected, different given the relatively strong presence of formal 'voice' channels through trade unions, multi-level collective bargaining, works councils, and formal strikes (frequent also in MNCs such as Renault). Other less publicized aspects of Slovenian industrial relations however resonate with the situation of the other new member states, like work intensification and working time flexibility (Svetlik and Ilič 2005), with the remarkable resistance to Sunday work: as a unique case in the region, Slovenians have also rejected in a referendum the liberalization of shop opening times on Sundays.

Case studies in the automotive sector confirm the existence of institutional or social constraints on foreign investors. A US investor was openly criticized by the Slovenian subsidiary (Ms1), which successfully defended its marketing and product development autonomy. Such resistance was apparently not on class grounds, as it united managers and workers, and trade unions were, in this case, particularly weak. Eventually, Slovenian managers raised the resources to take over the plant and, subsequently, also its foreign sites in US and South Korea. It is telling about the exceptional Slovenian path, where 'exit' is much less common, that Slovenian managers were critical of US and Korean employees, depicted as unreliable and not committed.

A closer look revealed that the 'regulated' nature of workplace relations was not only due to institutional factors. The factory, located in an isolated little town with a mining past, is also constrained by social control of a communitarian nature, whereby the personnel manager is firing averse also because 'otherwise he couldn't enter the local pub'.

Another case (As) sheds more light on the ambiguous nature of Slovenian management in this national system. Here, Slovenian managers were outspokenly critical of their country's strict labor regulations and high taxes and social security costs. At the same time, however, they fiercely defended the subsidiary autonomy and stressed that the plant is Slovenian managed, and not US managed, in spite of strict control from the headquarters. In this context, the country's complex institutional and social regulations become an important resource against headquarters' interference: none from the outside is deemed able to understand Slovenian reality. Against an appearance of social cohesion or even paternalism, then, it seems that the Slovenian 'social compromise' is the outcome of divergent and distinct interests and strategies. Labor power resources are independent and genuine and appear to be 'tolerated' by Slovenian managers for different aims, like defending their position against the headquarters or the shareholders.

To summarize the lesson of the 12 case studies conducted in 2004–2005, in all case studies where no real institutional voice was introduced, informal resistance took place. By real institutional voice, I mean such a right of voice that it actually limits managerial prerogatives, not such that it is in line with managerial wishes. This is the case of the Slovenian companies, as well as Gp1 and Gh1, two German companies which, by introducing strong union rights (Gp1 more consistently, Gh1 more pragmatically), are two exceptions that confirm the rule of Poland and Hungary. As matter of fact, in these two companies, as occasionally in Slovenia too, local managers complain about excessive power being given to employee representatives. In all other six case studies of Hungary and Poland, employee voice is limited, and informal resistance emerges. Resistance, to confirm the rule, has also emerged in one Slovenian company (As1), when American management tried to break away from local traditions.

Similar case studies carried out three years later in the Czech Republic confirmed this picture of multiple under-surface resistance. This is all the more important, that the Czech Republic is, among the post-Soviet bloc new member states, the one with the lowest emigration, share of informal economy, and turnover rates: it might therefore seem that, in this country, 'exit' is not as common and loyalty has been somehow established. The explanation could come from the relatively high level of economic development, the low unemployment rate, and even the political tradition of lowest levels of protest in the region before 1989. Even for the Czechs, however, the picture of loyalty and quiescence is challenged by case studies of multinational companies in the automotive component and banking sectors.

Although the Czech operations of these companies are overall successful, the prevalence of direct participation does not seem to have avoided a 'representation gap' and (apart from the small insurance company D-INS1) a demand for collective services in the workplaces, in a situation similar to that of the US (Freeman *et al.* 2007). The employee representative in the supervisory board of US-BAN is asked to play a collective bargaining role, although this is not part of its role. Even more strange, sections of management (at D-CAR2 and D-INS2) are requested to play representative and mediation functions. At US-BAN, an attempt at creating a trade union occurred (the outcome is still unknown), and at US-CAR employee surveys revealed dissatisfaction with the existing degree of information. Employee demands for more participation might not matter to management, if they were not combined with high and often increasing levels of turnover. Retention is a major preoccupation for all employers researched, reflecting the tight Czech labor market. Managers report that direct participation solutions are a part of their retention strategies: if they appear to be insufficient, more experimentation may follow.

CONCLUSION

The near absence of official strikes in the new member states should not lead to the wrong conclusion. The cases of high turnover and disloyalty that have been detected through case studies are probably only the tip of the iceberg: these are leading companies, offering higher-than-average salaries, in core economic sectors characterized by long job tenure; in the case of the Czech Republic, it is also the country with the lowest mobility. The 12 case studies conducted in Poland, Hungary, and Slovenia show a virtually perfect correlation between absence of genuine institutional voice (as in near all Hungarian and Polish plants, as well as, temporarily, at a Slovenian one) and explosions of informal resistance.

What is striking is the generalized and intensifying concern with employee retention and commitment registered between 2004 and 2008—although this may have diminished with the crisis starting in 2008. An additional expression of such concern is the increasing promotion of 'anti-competition' clauses in employment contracts, forbidding employees to move from a company to their direct competitors—a preoccupation, which seems higher than in Western Europe, even if economic development structure, and therefore the relevance of sensitive information, is lower. Yet employees in the new member states are more likely to 'moonlight' (have double employment) and to look for earning opportunities with competitors. At the state level, tightening of controls on sickness leave reveals a similar concern.

Such a situation is in direct response to the imposition of a flexible employment regime, where opportunistic behavior is explicitly prized. While the institutional settings and regulations vary among the new member states, the general tale of market individualism covers all of them, with only the notable exception of Slovenia. After EU accession, the story has not changed, even if there is some convergence towards the mean: the Baltic states may have slightly moderated their neo-liberal enthusiasm, while Slovenia started departing from its co-ordinated model, under the general pressure that everybody had to imitate Slovakia (an explicit argument used by the Slovenian conservative government of 2004–2008).

The employment relationship has been constituted as short rather than long term, inverting the communist habits very quickly. Baxandall (2004) has shown how easy it was in Hungary, in 1989, to dump nearly overnight the communist ideals of secure employment—together with all other communist symbols and monuments. It is not just a matter of legal framework but rather of the meaning of work. According to the European Working Conditions Survey, in the new member states, as compared to the EU average, paid training is rarer, functional flexibility (in Streeck's terms, a feature of 'status' opposed to the numerical flexibility of 'contract') is lower, and employees have less autonomy (Parent-Thirion *et al.* 2007).

Overt protest against these conditions is difficult in the new member states, given the limited space for institutional 'voice'. Trade unions are weak, and open strikes are rare. Tacit effort bargaining is less feasible than under state socialism, when line managers were very keen on keeping social peace in the workplace, as described by Burawoy and Lukacs (1985). Yet this emerging employment regime does not translate in total control. The frequent demand, detected in the case studies, of replacing foreign managers with local ones reveals the demand to re-open at least some informal channels of communication and bargaining. Still, the bargaining power of employees emerges mostly in tacit forms: turnover, absence, and diffidence towards management initiatives.

Just as happened with the decentralization of pay setting (Chapter 2), having relentlessly promoted labor market flexibility, companies are now facing the costs of their excessive success. The reality of the work-places—in terms of turnover and organizational fluidity—shows signs of excessive flexibility, undermining the manageability of companies as organizations.

Part III
Voice?

7 The Possibilities of Trade Union Revitalization

As is evident from the data reported on the link between union decline and emigration in Chapter 4, trade union density is not recovering in the new member states after EU accession. Its fall may have slowed down, but this is of little consolation: it is simply reaching the bottom and can no longer fall at the rate it did in the 1990s when starting from near 100%. The authorities (with the mentioned temporary exceptions of Poland and Slovakia) are not promoting it either. In Chapter 1, we have seen how the Directive on Information and Consultation of Employees has been used against the unions rather than in support to them. In Chapter 2 we have seen that when social and labor market pressures force them to concede wage increases, governments prefer to do it unilaterally, bypassing unions and collective bargaining (as repeatedly happened in Hungary and in Estonia). In Chapter 3 we have seen how state agencies for the promotion of foreign investment present union weakness as country attractions. Overall, the EU has opened little institutional opportunities for employee voice and employee rights in general.

If we look deeper, however, there are signs that labor market integration, through foreign investment and especially the freedom of movement of workers, is affecting worker propensity to take action.

QUIESCENT LABOR?

Fears of social dumping in the enlarged EU have raised the question of who can defend employees in the new member states. Trade unions have been a significant absence in discussions of capitalist transformation in post-communist countries (Meardi 2006b). It emerged early in the 1990s that despite (or maybe because of) considerable organizational power inherited from the previous system, reconstructed unions were generally unable to affect the transformation process, whether at the political or at the company level. This turned the labor movement in post-communist countries into a merely speculative research issue, a 'negative' problem summarized by the question of why labor does not mobilize in spite of the serious social costs of transformation. A question to which many observers just replied 'why should it?' arguing that what was a constituting institution of Western capitalism in the twentieth century would be a redundant one in the 'new' capitalism of the twenty-first.

Many view Central Eastern European labor as condemned to structural weakness. A particularly structuralist explanation, drawing on Erik O. Wright's neo-Marxist theory of social compromise, has been provided by Bohle and Greskovits (2006) on the grounds of the lack of pre-conditions (political, macroeconomic, and production related) for business's 'accommodating' strategies. An alternative, more Gramscian explanation focusing on hegemony and ideology, has been put forward by Crowley and Ost (2001). In particular, a crucial role is given to the ideological legacy of communism, including acceptance of capitalism and misunderstanding of class divisions. Within an integrated common market, such labor weakness would open up the possibility for a 'race to the bottom' in employment conditions. Whatever the explanation, the evidence put forward for the thesis of labor quiescence is varied and includes political and social aspects (Avdagic 2005; Kubicek 2004). As mentioned in the introduction, in the new member states, as compared to the 'old' ones, union density and especially collective bargaining coverage are much lower. Things are made worse by the extreme concentration of membership (70–80%) in the shrinking public sector and by the rapidity of the decline (from near 100% in 10 years). Nor are trade unions able to mobilize discontent: strike volume in 1998–2002 was 6.5 days/1,000 workers in the EU7 (new member states of 2004 minus Slovenia) as against 57.5 in the EU15 (EC 2004). More structurally, labor is a weak actor in most post-communist countries. The shortage of capital and the high supply of labor (including female labor supply) that characterizes post-communist societies make the balance of power different from that of advanced capitalist countries.

The thesis of Central Eastern European workers as inherently quiescent is not convincing. First, such a view does not cover the whole region. Notably, Stanojević (2003) has powerfully contested Crowley and Ost's view of post-communist labor weakness in the case of former Yugoslavia. Historically, major mobilization has occurred throughout the region, not only in the momentous forms of Poland. Moreover, the idea that quiescence is due to the communist past is challenged by recent observations of labor activism in Russia, China, and Vietnam—where the communist regime has been longer-lived or even harsher (Pringle and Clarke 2010). Second, as discussed in Chapter 6, strike data are notorious for their unreliability. Third, and crucially, it is potentially distorting to treat strikes and union density as the only, or principal, indicator of labor resistance.

STRIKES AND PROTESTS

In fact, there is an increasingly wide range of information suggesting the spreading of employee assertiveness in the region, even if this does not

translate into union density recovery at the macro-level. International statistics on strikes collected by the ILO (2010) are too incomplete to indicate
the trend for the whole region, as there are no complete series arriving to
2008 for any new member state (and no data at all for Bulgaria, Czech
Republic, and Slovenia). Available figures are interesting nonetheless. Some
countries persisted in their virtually strike-free status: only seven strikes
are reported for the whole 2004–2008 period in Slovakia, only one in
Lithuania in 2004–2006, and none in Latvia in 2005–2007. Some awaken-
ing occurred in the latter two countries from 2007–2008, with industrial
action emerging in the public sector (health in Latvia, education in Lithuania against the cuts stemming from the recession). Very few strikes, but
also involving manufacturing and larger numbers of workers, are reported
for Romania. More interesting are the data for Hungary, as they include
days lost per 1,000 employees until 2007, and they show an increase in
strike volume in 2006–2007, especially in manufacturing and transport.

In the largest country, Poland, we can find clearer indications from national-level statistics. Here, strike figures (even if perhaps partially distorted, in
case the problem of under-reporting I mentioned in Chapter 6 is declining)
show a very neat, even geometric increase. According to the General Statistical Office (GUS 2009), the number of days lost in strikes has increased even
more: from 400 in 2004, to 3,300 in 2005, to 31,400 in 2006, to 186,200
in 2007, and to 275,800 in 2008. Interestingly, this increase contrasts with
the trends in Western Europe, where according to ILO data, days lost on
strikes per 1,000 employees constantly declined (from 47 in 2004 to 21 in
2008 on average for the eight countries there are data from). On protest at

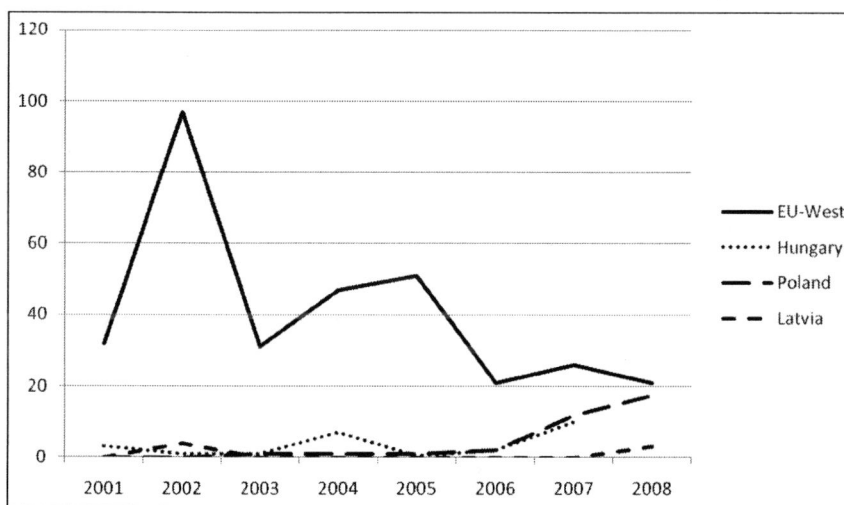

Figure 7.1   Strike volume (days lost per 1,000 employees).

least, workers are starting to bridge the gap between old and new member states (Figure 7.1).

Qualitative information points to the same direction: a systematic review of reports for the European Industrial Relations Observatory (EIRO) reveals a large number of significant events. The EIRO started covering the new member states only shortly before accession, and its reporting system does not follow any systematic criteria. Therefore, reports cannot be turned into quantitative indicators of trends. However, the information provided includes qualitative assessments of their significance and novelty. For instance, the successful union organizing of the Suzuki factory in Hungary in 2006 came after over 10 years of failed attempts (Tóth and Neumann, 2006b). In the first three years after accession (May 2004–April 2007), 73 events involving employee voice in the EU7 have been considered significant by national observers.[1] While we cannot assess their representativeness, we can establish whether they are distributed broadly across sectors, countries, and issues.

The variety and spread of the events is clear. They are not compatible with an image of post-communist workers as quiescent. While pay is the dominant issue, union rights, working time, restructuring, and employment conditions also figure prominently. While the public sector (education, health, railways, and civil service) is over-represented, all emerging private sectors (with the exception of banking and finance) have seen innovative advances as well. Some of them are noteworthy even in a pan-European perspective: the Polish unions, for instance, have recently managed to organize the Lidl retail chain (Czarzasty 2010)—something their German and Austrian counterparts have found very difficult to do (Turner 2009).

While these occurrences of voice are heterogeneous, ranging from strikes to social partnership agreements, mostly they involve an effort in grassroot organizing. The unions are, however, aware of their own limits. One important way in which they are trying, with some success in Czech Republic, Hungary, and Slovakia, to expand social regulation of employment is through collective agreements' extension procedures. Where there is no extension procedure, copycat initiatives fulfill a similar function in socializing collective bargaining gains, as evident in the wave of actions in the various transport companies in Tallinn. Public demonstrations, political lobbying, warning strikes, and stoppages are also more frequent than official strikes, which are subject to strict procedural regulations.

Increased labor assertiveness appears to be in relation with improved labor market conditions following EU integration, through increased foreign investment and emigration, both leading to labor shortages. More noticeable change is to be noticed in those sectors and countries with increased investment (automotive) and with most mobile workforces (transport, construction, health, tourism). Kaminska and Kahancová (2010) have pointed at the case of health sector trade unions: those of Slovakia and Poland have used emigration and the resulting labor shortages as leverage for their negotiations, while those of Hungary, a country with much less emigration, have been less active. The forms of such activation vary country by country:

Polish unions chose industrial action (see also Hardy 2009), while the Slovak ones utilized institutional channels of tripartite negotiation.

It is still early to tell whether such change can reverse the trend towards 'exit' rather than 'voice' described in Chapter 4 for the period 2003–2008. Lasting results are not guaranteed: Polish nurses and doctors obtained important wage increases in 2007 but had little influence on health sector reforms the year after. The authorities may be willing to make wage concessions but resist the establishment of institutional voice. When, few days before the 2007 elections, Polish Prime Minister Jarosław Kaczyński conceded to nurses' demands, he made clear on a televised address that he did not so as a concession to their trade union, but only to keep Polish nurses from leaving the country. Similarly, in the Polish construction sector, affected by simultaneous emigration and increased demand for labor on major EU-funded projects and Euro 2012 stadia, trade unions were unsuccessful in their efforts to negotiate multi-employer collective agreements. The employers preferred to perpetuate an 'exit' regime by facilitating immigration from neighboring countries, rather than engage in negotiations with representatives of their own employees.

UNION REVITALIZATION

Union revitalization has been defined, in a broad way, as a 'variety of attempts to tackle and potentially reverse . . . problems' of membership decline, workplace organization erosion, mobilization weakening, institutional change ,and power loss (Frege and Kelly 2003, 9). The concept does not require the actual reverse of these problems, as these are also dependent on an environment in which unions have little control. It requires the detection of active and creative reaction, which would allow treating unions as 'actors' and not simply as secondary organizations managing their own decline. Whereas this issue has received some interest in the West, there has been little effort in applying the concept to post-communist realities, where the challenges to trade unions are even tougher, but the theoretical possibility of revitalization is there all the same. Revitalization as a concept may sound unsuited to post-communist Europe, where labor still needs to emerge as an independent actor in the first place. In the case of Central Europe, and especially of Poland and Slovenia, labor has historically been a very strong actor in the past, especially since the 1970s. In Hungary it may have been less visible but was effective in defending core workers and had a role in the negotiated transition of the late 1980s. In any case, neither the discussion by Frege and Kelly, nor social movement theory, necessarily requires a 'strong' past as a necessary element of 'revitalization'. We can therefore tentatively apply the concept to Central Eastern European reality. More specifically, we can test the relevance of six main revitalization strategies that have been detected in the West (Frege and Kelly 2003): organizing, organizational restructuring, coalition building, partnership with employers, political action, and international links.

Signs of union revitalization have been reported recently, especially in Poland. The earliest detection was by Gardawski (2001) in case of the organizing efforts by Solidarity and, to a lesser extent, OPZZ. After EU accession these initiatives have gathered more momentum. Some researchers, such as Ost (2009) and more explicitly Krzywdziński (2009), consider revitalization through organizing as exclusive to Solidarity and not shared by other unions either in Poland or in the rest of Central Eastern Europe. Others have detected similar trends in other Polish unions: at the small radical August 80 union (Mrożowicki *et al.* 2009), at OPZZ (Hardy 2009; Ostrowski 2009), at both OPZZ and the new federation FZZ, especially at sector federation level (Gardawski 2009a). Even more innovative are the activities of the new small trade union 'Worker Initiative', that organizes largely through the Internet and conducted protests in important workplaces such as the Polish Post and Volkswagen, as well as in the defense of tenants or against McDonald and Tesco. These trends towards revitalization follow the pattern of unions in 'Liberal Market Economies', where bottom-up organizing rather than reliance on existing institutions is required from trade unions and vindicates the idea that social movement unionism can be appropriate in the region (Meardi 2005; Shlyk 2009), an idea that had been challenged by Ost (2002) himself previously.

These initiatives are not widespread, and indeed revitalization does not necessarily coincide with membership recovery. Yet just by their existence, they prove a possible variety in forms of unionism and the non-ineluctability of union irrelevance in post-communist societies.

There are cases of political, international, and organizational restructuring among unions in post-communist states, but the decentralized nature of industrial relations suggests that revitalization is more likely to appear at the company and workplace level, whether as organizing or as partnership efforts—just like in the Anglophone countries that Central Eastern Europe resembles in many aspects of industrial relations.

EVIDENCE FROM MULTINATIONALS

The MNCs are a privileged field in which to test the possibility of union revitalization in post-communist countries, as they are arguably the front-runners of capitalist restructuring, where the nature of employment relations should be clearer and 'purified' from past state-paternalistic legacies. However, the actual effects of MNCs on unions in post-communist countries are a disputed issue. On one side, some argue that their increased visibility and pressures from both home and host countries push MNCs to upgrade the quality of employment relations, including the possibility of unionization, even if—as we have seen in Chapter 3, foreign direct investment is not a channel for the transfer of the 'European Social Model' at company level. In particular, it has been argued that trade unions in post-communist countries 'target' MNCs for their organizing activities because of the higher expected returns in comparison with organizing in nationally owned private companies. On the other side, however, the economic power of MNCs is often seen as an obstacle to unionization, given the 'exit' threat that MNCs can present. According to Bohle and Greskovits (2006), MNCs are major drivers of the specific form of division of labor within the EU, which, by leaving relatively low-skill operations in the East, hampers social compromises and unionization in Eastern Europe. According to such a view, MNCs and dependent internationalization do not improve unionization, which seems to be confirmed by the increased pace of de-unionization in the second half of the 1990s in spite of fast increasing inflows of foreign investment.

This section will present mixed evidence from the case studies of American and German-based MNCs in Poland, Hungary, and Slovenia, carried out in 2004–2005 and already described in Chapters 3 and 6 with regard, respectively, to management and informal resistance (Table 7.1).[2]

Table 7.1   Trade Union Revitalization in Cases of Multinational Companies

Company	Local unemployed	Work-force % male	Union presence	Sectoral integration	Inter-national integration	Revital-ization
Gp1 Greenfield	15%	1,000 95%	1 union: 75% Negotiation, consultation, some co-determination	Medium	Very strong	Servicing partnership organizing
Gp2 Brownfield	10%	600 80%	3 unions: 40% No collective agreement	Medium	None	No
Ap1 Brownfield	10%	500 90%	2 unions: 60% Declining rolepolitical alignment	Strong	None	No
Ap2 Greenfield	20%	500 60%	No			
Gh1 Greenfield	4%	5,000 90%	2 unions: 40% Conflict, then producer coalition	Weak	Strong	Organizing partnership
Gh2 Greenfield	17%	900 30%	1 union: 75% Conflict, then consultation	Weak	Medium	Organizing
Ah1 Brownfield	3%	2,500 80%	1 union: 85% Negotiation, core work-force defense	None	Medium	Organizing

(continued)

Table 7.1   (continued)

Company	Local unemployed	Work-force % male	Union presence	Sectoral integration	Inter-national integration	Revital-ization
Ah2 Greenfield	20%	260 80%	1 union: 55% Social fringe benefits	Weak	None	Partnership servicing
Gs Brownfield	5%	650 70%	1 union: 50% Consultation, declining	Weak	Weak	No
As Brownfield	10%	900 45%	2 unions: 90% Social fringe benefits, job defense	Medium	Weak	(Organiz-ing) (servicing)
Ms1 Brownfield	15%	900 80%	1 union: 30% No influence	Weak	Weak	No
Ms2 Brownfield	10%	1,200 80%	1 union: 60% Partnership	Weak	None	No

REVITALIZATION THROUGH PARTNERSHIP

Cases of union revitalization are most visible in Hungary, but the single most successful union is in a Polish plant. In Gp1, a German-owned green-field factory, opened in 1998, with around 1,000 workers and an average age of 32, one could expect no union at all for Polish standards. Instead, Solidarity exists as the only trade union in the plant, with 76% member-ship. Solidarity at Gp1 has followed a specific 'partnership' strategy. The corporation's approach was officially to have trade unions in foreign sub-sidiaries, in order to have a social partner. Managers even declared that 'the union has been created to an extent thanks to the employer'. The union confirmed that the director immediately informed workers that the com-pany had no objection to the existence of trade unions, and nobody would be penalized for joining it, which was particularly important in a period when the workforce was already on probation. However, the initiative (in 1999, one year after the factory was opened) came from a small group of workers with union experience in previous jobs, and the union did not go beyond a few dozen members for the first year and a half. It was only after 2001, when the local leadership was replaced and political activity was officially excluded (at the time, the national Solidarity-based government was extremely unpopular and local unionists think that that was the main obstacle to union organizing at the plant level) that the union could start a very impressive growth.

The union at Gp1 does devote large resources to the supply of services to members, from advice to insurance systems, sometimes co-funded by the employer. This is considered as the main reason for such a high level of unionization, corroborating indirectly the thesis of Ost (2002) that Polish labor's weakness stems from its 'social movement' nature, and consequent neglect of servicing functions (and even, to an extent, business functions).

Consultation is regulated by an ad hoc collective agreement and has a large coverage covering also investment plans. It is seen as an active, continuous process, with fortnightly bilateral meetings. No official collective conflicts (in the legal sense) have been recorded, but negotiations are 'real' negotiations (according to managers, they 'can be tough'), which last weeks and where the starting standpoints are clearly apart.

The negotiation and the structure of the first collective agreement were proposed by the union, on the basis of a number of examples from other foreign companies. It includes a complaint procedure, training, discrimination and mobbing, health and safety, information, pay, bonuses, protection for women workers, and working time. The pay structure and the related job classification system have become, over the years, the most disputed area. In any case, the union has made big progress in the negotiation of pay. Initially, only the compensation for inflation was included. More recently, productivity increases, and their sources, are analyzed in details and included in the bargaining agenda, although actual pay increases have so far remained in line with inflation, also because of the labor market situation (unemployment at early 30% in the area). Bargaining is also inspired by some form of indirect co-ordination across the sector on the union side, although there is no formal sector-level collective bargaining. The trade union has also obtained considerable assistance from the corporation's international union structures. The members of the trade union have been thoroughly trained in Germany and take parts in meetings in the headquarters, outside formal EWC (European Works Council) activity (the plant has no EWC representative). International co-operation implies, for instance, the Polish plant's undertaking not to take over the production of plants that are in dispute with the group's management. Interviews even show that plant union representatives are better informed about many corporate issues than middle-level managers are.

Union culture at Gp1 is atypical within Poland. There seems to be a unitaristic approach, whereby when union respondents say 'we' it refers more often to the company than to the union. The union's purpose is above all servicing members and protecting jobs (e.g. an innovative agreement on working hour annualization). As the convener tells: 'I have signed a declaration that if at any time our union activity happens to threaten jobs, I will be the first to disaffiliate from the union'. It would be wrong, however, to consider the union as in some way hetero-directed by the employer. Not only are negotiations 'real', but the union also is accumulating a considerable strike fund 'for the dark times', although it unsurprisingly hopes never to have to use it. The high trust between union and company is exemplified by the fact that the fund is kept in an account of the company's financial branch.

THROUGH ORGANIZING TO PARTNERSHIP

A rather different process has taken place at Gh1, an apparently similar German-owned greenfield plant in Hungary, opened in 1993. Here, teams, not trade unions, were the employer's original preferred form of employee participation. Communication was therefore focused on problem solving, operated in a top-down direction, and excluded company-wide information and wages. The creation of a trade union a year after the opening of the factory was prompted by outside organizers of the Metalworkers Union. The union quickly reached around 50% membership. Union activists were skilled workers with no previous union experience, relying therefore on the expertise of the outside organization. Unlike at Gp1, the union was focused on interest representation (especially pay), with no attention paid to servicing. Surprisingly, management, whilst recognizing the union as required by the Labor Code, refused to negotiate with the newly founded organization and to establish a system of consultation, even after the union obtained 90% of the votes at the first works council elections. Disillusion and disappointment at the lack of tangible results spread quickly within the workforce.

Negotiations on a collective agreement finally started three years after the union had been set up. By then, the discontent with the Metalworkers union had left the space open for the establishment of a new independent, more radical, and militant trade union. Such space was also due to the social discontent with the austerity policies of the socialist government, supported by the Metalworkers. The new independent union set the contribution at a much lower level (one-sixth) than the Metalworkers, and advertised the fact that, the union being independent, all of the membership revenue would remain in the plant organization. Membership soared, and the Metalworkers all but collapsed. Management initially refused to recognize the new union, on the grounds that it had not obtained at least 10% in works council elections (it had not participated in any yet). The independent union took the company to the court and won the case on the grounds of the additional Labor Code provision granting recognition to unions organizing more than two-thirds of the employees at workshop level. Management-union relations took a decidedly adversarial nature.

Change was prompted by labor market considerations: the company intended to expand the investment significantly, while labor shortages were appearing in the region. A good reputation as an employer became essential. At the same time, the German unions also intervened to support the Hungarian counterparts, including training on recruitment, reinforcing the unions' strategic preference for organizing even further. The Metalworkers, in particular, managed to recover from their membership fall. The two unions inaugurated a period of joint activity (under the heading of an Interest Representation Alliance), with even talks of a merger. It took another three years for industrial relations in the company to stabilize. Labor Code amendments had made a collective agreement convenient for the employer, due to the possibility of derogations from statutory working time regulations. Not only an agreement was reached, and was improved in the following years, but a system of consultation was established. Following managers' replacement, the company can now portray itself as an advanced case of social partnership. It should not be forgotten, however, that this was reached after years of intensive organizing from both unions. Union density, after an increase in the workforce, declined to around 40%, but remained high for Hungarian standards, and it may be expected that the newly appointed employees could join the unions in the near future. A new 'union ethos' developed, which combined a productivity coalition with firm negotiations on the sharing of productivity increases.

There are similarities in the other Hungarian plants. At Gh2, another German-owned greenfield plant established in 1992, the union was organized in 1994 in protest against the authoritarian and paternalistic management style, and due to grievances related to working time, wages and commuting support. Unlike at Gh1, in this case the majority of the workforce and of the activists, are women. The union was created in facilities outside the company (a nearby canteen), which shows how autocratic management was. Following the employer's refusal to negotiate, a warning strike was organized and membership increased to 500 (nearly 50%). This wave of militancy led to an agreement on wages and working time but was short-lived. Membership dropped to 30%, and the union did not obtain any stable consultation rights. Employees were, however, still dissatisfied with wage stagnation, work pace, and autocratic management. Three years later, a shop floor revolt took place against production line speeding. The revolt took the form of apparently non-organized work stoppages (in order to reduce the pace to previous practice), but the leaders were union activists. The action was successful on work pace, and this time activists managed to capitalize on the success, organizing a mobilization for a collective agreement including significant wage increases. A strike warning was issued, and the union also managed to have the local press on its side. As a result, the headquarters in Germany had to intervene, remove the plant director, and reach an agreement. A new phase of social dialog then started, similar to the Gh1 case. The union consolidated its strength by winning the works council elections, obtaining a representative on the company supervisory board, and increasing membership to up to 75%, including the near totality of blue-collar workers.

The situation changed again after 2002, with a new change in management and with the plant entering direct competition for production with lower-wage countries, notably Romania. The union initially split over the management-proposed restructuring plan, but after some turbulence social partnership was institutionalized with an elaborated, multi-level system of consultation, which allowed management to implement redundancies with the union's consent but also allowed the union to keep control over working conditions.

Ah2 is a medium-sized greenfield plant with around 260 employees, established in 1999. In spite of the very high-skill nature of the jobs, and the extremely high qualifications of the workforce, the very poor regional labor market conditions and financial pressures due to the labor-intensive nature of production initially kept wages only at minimum wage levels. There was employee dissatisfaction at the lack of the customary social fringe benefits and over the intensive nature of production. This led to the rapid establishment of a trade union, first as a clandestine organization and, after registering in the Labor Court, in the open. Creating a union was facilitated by the strong union traditions in the previously heavily industrialized region, but many private companies in the area are still union free. However, management, as recommended by the headquarters, refused to negotiate with the union, which initially remained very weak. Two years later, improved labor market conditions due to the arrival of new similar investors in the area led to a wave of extremely high turnover that made the management of the plant all but impossible. The expatriate director was replaced by a Hungarian one with the task of stabilizing the situation. The union took the opportunity to establish its role, not by mobilizing the discontent, but by offering the new director a role of social partner for the prevention of shop floor anarchy. Gradually, a system of information and consultation was introduced. Wages were increased up to 20% above the minimum wage (which had increased by nearly 50% itself in two years), and social benefits and programs were introduced as co-managed with the trade union. Servicing became an important activity for the organization, which was joined by 55% of the workforce.

INTERNATIONAL LINKS

In Hungary, we see experiences of union revitalization in American-owned companies as well. Ah1 is a former state-owned factory in the Budapest region, taken over by a large American corporation in 1990. Privatization involved massive redundancies, shrinking the workforce from around 7,500 to approximately 2,500. Nevertheless, there was no industrial dispute. Although the plant later took on more production, its position is still fragile due to competition from lower-wage countries, especially China. The trade union in the company was created as an independent union in 1989, during the negotiated democratic transition. In spite of later establishing loose links with the anti-communist confederation Liga, the union has remained basically a company union, very focused on the job defense of the core workforce and on wage negotiations. The independence of the union from sector or national-level co-operation is particularly visible in its secrecy over pay levels and on the lack of contacts with employee representatives in supplier companies.

The non-involvement with politics allowed the union to gain popularity among workers during the economic crisis of 1995, for which other unions were blamed. Internationally, the union importantly benefited from direct support from American counterparts in the early 1990s, and the plant was included in the European Works Council in 2004.

The rather unilateral management style of the corporation does not leave space for sophisticated forms of social partnership, but management-union relations have overall been rather good. The union leader himself defines industrial relations in the plant as 'American-style' rather than 'European-style': with a clear focus on pay, job defense and productivity, and few broader associational considerations. The union is successful at this game: it controls the works council, and membership is at 85%. It has achieved higher-than-average wages, while it has accepted, as instrumental for productive success, a high level of numerical flexibility for the peripheral workforce (a so-called 20% buffer).

FAILED REVITALIZATION

Unsurprisingly, besides these cases of revitalization and of stronger-than expected union role, there are instances in which unions have failed to strengthen their practice or to innovate.

This is particularly visible in Polish brownfield plants, where unions are still led by the leaders of the 1980s and defined by old political identities rather than current employee defense. At Gp2 (a German-owned plant with around 600 employees), the two main unions, the former-communist Metalowcy and Solidarity (with about 20% membership each) are divided and frequently have different negotiation strategies. Solidarity is more radical, and its opposition has prevented the signing of pay agreements in recent years. Industrial relations are clearly played as a zero-sum game, and trust levels are very low: Management blames union conservatism and lack of understanding of economic change, while the Solidarity leader defines the German industrial relations model as 'maximum exploitation and repatriation of profits'. But most telling is the unionists' nostalgia for industrial relations with the previous employer and belief that any change introduced by management is detrimental to employees. The unions struggle particularly to defend the employees on temporary contracts and the female employees who are mostly concentrated in one workshop.

At Ap1, a US-owned plant with 800 employees, management-union relations have also been adversarial, with an industrial dispute in 1996 over the company's approach to negotiation. They are now better than at Gp2, but the same two unions Solidarity (40% of the workforce) and Metalowcy (20%) are kept apart by political considerations that are made stronger by the Solidarity leader's role as union regional vice president. Interestingly, at both Ap1 and Gp2, the unions have virtually no international contacts, in spite of the plants being in direct competition for production with other sites in Europe.

At Ap2, a greenfield US-owned plant with nearly 500 employees, the unions are even absent. One of the employees remembers that during his job interview, the interviewer told him there were not and would never be trade unions in the plant. Yet, the worker quoted does not perceive the lack of trade unions as a hindrance. Some individuals in the plant had wanted to establish a trade union there but found no support. Among employees, trade unions are often associated with the old system, and a case of a local company that went bankrupt because of allegedly excessive union influence is referred to. Other employees argue that unions are appropriate in rich societies (in the West) but not where unemployment is high: a luxury the Poles cannot afford.

The only representation of staff consists of three representatives elected for a period of five years by the general meeting called by the directors. Participation and information have a direct form but cover only production issues and some social problems, leaving the workforce with no information or voice over the plant economic perspectives and pay policy.

REVITALIZATION BEHIND CONTINUITY
IN THE CZECH UNIONS?

Czech trade unions differ from the Polish, Hungarian, and Slovenian for being unitary and for having kept more organizational resources, although at the cost of more continuity, which can make them less responsive to change (Pollert 1999; Myant 2010). The case studies carried out in the Czech Republic in 2007–2008 in the banking and automotive sectors provide a more mixed picture. The Czech Republic has relatively well-organized trade unions, but on a mostly sector basis, and with relatively little change over time: unlike in the other countries considered here, the heirs of communist-time trade unions are still the dominant organizations, with little or no challenge from outside. As a result, the situation varies by sector and the kind of company. In the brownfield automotive sectors, unions tend to be relatively strong, and indeed, in the Anglo American companies, they appear to be stronger than their British counterparts in terms of prerogatives and actual say in plant matters. The Czech unions, even if heirs of the communist-time ones, have developed strong participation activities, without becoming deferential. At US-CAR, in particular, there have been strike threats in the past, even if not actual strikes. In this company there is a clear case of high turnover being turned into a 'voice' opportunity: the trade union organized its own interviews with leaving employees, which then inform its demands in negotiations with the employer. By contrast, in the greenfield companies, both in the automotive component and finance sectors, unions are absent or very weak. This is where revitalization has some scope, and indeed a strong movement of union organizing was taking place in the Czech banks at the time of the research.

THE SLOVENIAN DOUBLE PARADOX

The case of Slovenia is different from Poland and Hungary in two regards. First, from the general perspective of employment relations, the post-Yugoslavian republic displays a much more organized system of industrial relations and sector-level collective bargaining (notably, with collective bargaining coverage at 100%) and more extensive statutory employee rights. But macro-rigidity through the importance and complexity of local regulations and customs is combined with a very high degree of micro-flexibility (functional, pay, working time) in the workplaces. The statutory right of voice of employees and the degree of information and security seem to have produced a high level of trust and acceptance of change, facilitating the reorganization of production.

Management initiatives that in Poland or Hungary, in spite of the permissive environment, cause protests, turnover, or absenteeism, are successfully implemented in Slovenia within a sort of 'flexicurity' approach (Stanojević 2005). It is not surprising, then, that managers in the Slovenian case studies often express strong appreciation for Slovenian social dialog and express skepticism about current political plans for deregulation.

The second paradox is that while in Slovenia, trade unions are overall relatively strong (union density at 40%, well above the EU average, and above 50% in the metalworking sector); in the multinationals' sites, they do not seem to be particularly so. This contrasts with the Polish and Hungarian situations depicted above, where unions in MNCs are often very strong for the national standards. Moreover, they seem to have little to do with the otherwise powerful industrial federation.

At Ms1 (a German-owned factory now back in Slovenian hands) the union organizes only 30% of the workforce and is particularly weak. The company director does not even know its name or how many unions there are. At Ms2 (a previously Austrian and then British-owned factory) unionization is at 60%, and the union is seen as strong but is also basically a company union, using no services or advice from the industry federation and taking no part in industry-wide industrial actions. At Gs, membership level and union influence have been declining since the time of the German takeover in 1997. Density is still at 50%, and the union role is still important, but if foreign capital has had any influence, it has been a negative one.

The only case of union strength is, paradoxically again, in the American-owned plant where flexibility in employment practices is the highest (As). The majority union organizes 80% of the workforce, and a radical minority union a further 10%. The majority union has been successful in defending jobs and securing fringe benefits, as well as in servicing members. It did participate in two sector-level demonstrations but gave only formal support to the latest industry-wide strike (in the words of an employee, it was a 'psychological strike').

It may be said, then, that while Slovenian unions remain important and are an ingredient of their industry's 'flexible specialization' productive success, their strength was rooted in their national-owned industry. In this case, unlike in the other post-communist new member states, foreign capital is not a promoter of union revitalization, but rather a factor of union weakening. Here too we see the general tendency of industrial relations in multinational companies to depart from the national common practice but in the opposite direction.

Why is the modernizing role of MNCs in Poland and Hungary not met in Slovenia? Not only is here the starting point of union strength much higher and therefore less simple to improve. Above all, foreign companies are less rooted in a specific national system of industrial restructuring that has given a large role to local stakeholders and specifically employee representation. It is telling that in some case studies, it is Slovenian managers who most fiercely defend Slovenian established practices and arrangements from headquarters interference. In the Slovenian case, it may be argued that national ownership of industry has been a factor defending union strength. In Poland and Hungary, by contrast, the explicit political option, since the beginning of transformation, for a most rapid sale of industry to foreign investors has made the consolidation of a national model of social partnership (which might have been feasible given the strength of workplace employee organizations) impossible. A decade was lost, and social dialog has now to re-emerge from the ashes of the former system, on the more insecure and hostile terrain of multinationals' plants.

Reflecting not only the Yugoslavian past, but also the double influence of their different north-western neighbors, Slovenian trade unions have strong protest traditions, and they display, besides an 'Austrian' corporatist side, also an 'Italian' pluralist social movement side, as evident from a book the largest confederation ZSSS published on their street protests (ZSSS 2003). Yet, in spite of this active potential, the liberalization and internationalization fostered by EU accession have had negative effects not only on Slovenian social dialog (see Chapter 2) but also Slovenian unions: some recent data on unionization suggest that they are following their 'reference model' German unions in fast membership decline and institutional crisis (Stanojević 2011).

CONCLUSION

The summary table (Table 7.1) allows us to draw some conclusions about the directions of trade unionism in the new advanced exporting sector of the new EU member states. The case studies are not representatives of the manufacturing sector as a whole, and not even of the automotive sector, but provide a rich, varied picture of union chances in the specific higher segment of the sector.

These case studies, even when atypical, have a major relevance because of the innovative and potentially pattern setting, or at least 'showcase' nature of these plants. Overall, it can be said that unions appear to be much stronger and innovative than the national average in Hungary, very mixed in Poland, slightly below average in the Czech Republic, and even further below average in Slovenia. This national distinction largely overlaps with the distinction in mode of entry: greenfield sites are more open to innovative union practice, even if unionization is more difficult initially. Greenfield investment is the favored mode of entry in Hungary (where an automotive industry did not exist before 1989) and is much less common in Slovenia, where the industrial structure is dominated by the revamping of the former Yugoslavian flagship factories. However, other national differences importantly affect the specific trends in union strength and revitalization, as it will be discussed later.

While the mode of entry is very important in determining the space and nature of trade unions, there seem to be no particular difference, in terms of unionization prospects, between Anglo American and German/Austrian companies, or between male and female majority workforces. There are some qualitative differences, though. In terms of country of origin, more revitalization patterns emerge in the American-owned companies, a possible indirect effect of their home systems. In terms of gender, the only two factories with a female majority in the 2004–2005 study, Gh2 and As, show a distinctive focus on union organizing. The local labor market is an important variable, but unemployment rates are not directly associated with unionization rates. Rather, it is the trends in unemployment (with any temporary labor shortages providing major opportunities for union organizing) and the general psychological perception of job security that matter.

Behind structural constraints, the actual strategic orientations of the unions show interesting national variations. Institutional factors can explain the Hungarian preference for organizing: union recognition and collective bargaining status are conditional on membership thresholds and works council electoral results. Therefore, an organizing effort is indispensable for Hungarian unions. Without both a significant amount of members and large support among the workforce, the employers are unlikely to recognize them. In Poland, by contrast, any union with at least 10 members receives a given amount of rights, and in Slovenia union rights are so strongly rooted that no employer would challenge them; in neither case is member recruitment a high priority or indeed a primary necessity. Union pluralism and competition seems to have a positive effect in motivating unions to innovate in Poland and Hungary, compared to the Czech Republic.

Given employers' predominant anti-unionism, the most frequent mode of revitalization is organizing, most often against management. This is where new techniques are being used by the unions, whether at Suzuki in Hungary or in the Polish retail chains. The viability of partnership strategies, by contrast, is dependent on employers' approaches. These are evolving, though. Case studies show a strong structural systematic evolution of management styles in this sector across Poland, the Czech Republic, and Hungary: initial somewhat casual, trial-and-error and unilateral styles are abandoned once labor management problems emerge, whether in the form of employee mobilization or through high turnover. A high degree of employee participation is very hard to achieve over an extended period without compromises and accommodation with forms of employee representation (the only non-unionized company in the 2004–2005 research was also one of the newest).

A final problem relates to the link between these companies and the broader sector and society. While within these workplaces production considerations allow the establishment of good quality industrial relations, this is not the case in the larger economy (with the partial exception of Slovenia). As a matter of fact, in most case studies unions, even when successful, have little interest in what happens at the sector or the national level. Politics are frequently an obstacle to union organizing, and political neutrality is by contrast a frequent factor of popularity. At the same time, however, national unions try to keep a political role. This opens the risk of a divergence between the 'new unionism' experienced in these innovative workplaces and the one in the rest of the society. National union bodies remain predominantly dominated by state sector unions, and often by elderly officers. The union organizations in our case studies have little to share with them, not only culturally. In multinationals' plants, employees may be able to achieve better wages and work conditions, but their dependence on investment flows may make them suspicious of high taxes. Ost (2009) has labeled this form of specific, narrow company-based unionism emerging in some Polish workplaces as 'Mexican', i.e. a factor of further inequality between advanced and obsolete sectors. According to Bohle and Greskovits (2006), the extreme case of Slovakia (a popular foreign investment destination but because of very low taxation also a home to riots and extreme social exclusion) multinationals' employees and their unions would be improving their conditions at the expense of the broader society. Maintaining and developing organizational links, nationally and internationally, becomes a crucial task for the trade unions to support a balanced and sustainable form of development, as well as to disseminate the emerging positive experiences.

A fair assessment is that union revitalization, in some circumstances, can occur—but that what is occurring is far less than would be needed to reverse the trend of worker marginalization. Which is why in the next two chapters we will look at other possibilities of voice for them.

8   Cross-Border Experiments

The EU enlargement, by merging low- and high-wage countries into a single market, raises problems of transnational union co-operation that are similar to those evoked by the issue of 'globalization'. There has been a growing debate as to whether unions can act 'globally' to match the extending geographic spread of markets and capital. In this regard, the enlarged EU is a starting test for union capacities: here, in comparison to other corners of the world, institutional processes are more visible, and trade unions have more resources. In other words: if trade unions cannot deal with Europeanization, *a fortiori* trade unions should struggle with globalization.

This chapter looks at the possibility of transnational labor solidarity through the analysis of union reactions to the freedom of movement of capital, labor, and services (as contrasted to the more indirect effects of mobility of goods) following EU enlargement eastwards. Through empirical examples from MNCs in the Czech Republic, and secondary information as well as interviews on migration and posted workers, I will show that while cross-border union co-operation in MNCs—and especially the European Works Councils (EWC)—reveal with increasing clarity their notorious limitations in impact and extension, the largely unforeseen wave of migration has triggered more active and innovative reactions from the trade unions. The issue the unions struggle most with, however, is the freedom of movement of services.

Before moving to the analysis of transnational voice, two detours are necessary. First, a theoretical discussion of how transnational union action can be best conceptualized. Second, on the nature of the actual threats that transnational union action should respond to, is something which is best shown through the description of a sector strongly affected by international competition between old and mew member states, the automotive component one.

UNDERSTANDING CROSS-BORDER TRADE UNION ACTIVITIES

As it has been put on the case of European Works Councils (Fitzgerald and Stirling 2004), on cross-border unionism, there is an apparent contrast between pessimistic analytical views and optimistic normative/declarative ones (Ramsey 1999). Analytical skepticism may have been caused by a 'national bias' of industrial relations as a field of inquiry (Giles 2000), which has certainly grown within national research traditions as well as within the trade unions themselves (Hyman 2004; Frege 2007). But it is also based on a representation of trade unions as hierarchical organizations, with 'monopoly' (Freeman and Medoff 1984) as the privileged function—a function that by definition calls for unity. Social movement theorists have been equally skeptical. At the time of the creation of the EU, social movement theorist Tarrow (1994a) argued that European collective action was possible *against* the EU rather than for genuinely positive pan-European goals; additionally, resource mobilization theory would underline the shortage of resources for transnational union activity. Social movement theorists stress the lack of a transnational collective identity as an obstacle for transnational union identity—an issue which has been mentioned often in studies of European trade unionism or of EWCs (Whittall *et al.* 2007), and constitutes a potential barrier between Western and Eastern European trade unions (Meardi 2000).

In short, if one uses national benchmarks for assessing the chances of trade union transnational action, the assessment is likely to be pessimistic. However, studies of transnational phenomena have been growing and theoretical arguments have been suggested to interpret the transnational phenomena through different tools. I shall mention three recent examples. First, federalist theory has been applied in an original way to the analysis of EWCs by Hoffmann (2006) to argue that the co-ordination of different local interests and identities required from a EWC is nothing new. Federal countries have done this for decades and employee representation structures can imitate them: the German *Gesamtbetriebsräte*—or central works councils—in multi-site enterprises have exactly the task of co-ordinating and mediating the interests, activities, and identities of different plant-level works councils.

A second way, in which the obstacle of coordinating and mediating between different identities has been downgraded, is through approaches to new social movements. While the existence of a collective identity was a primary concern in early social movement studies (e.g. Touraine 1966, 1978), later works by Melucci (1996) and by Touraine (1997) himself have stressed how new social movements ('societal movements' for Touraine) can emerge from the recognition and defense of *different* identities: subjectivity and diversity become mobilizing, rather than hampering factors. Similarly, new social movement approaches based on resource mobilization have started underlining the potentials of 'coalition building'. The presence of a 'European', or global, labor identity would therefore no longer be a prerequisite for European or global collective action: a number of other social movements—e.g. in the antiglobalist galaxy—seem to do well without it. This approach has already led to a reformulation of debates on labor in the US, focusing on the interactions with a variety of social actors within the complex urban environments (Turner and Cornfield 2007). Equally, it has changed the theoretical framing of international collective action: the same Tarrow who used to see collective action as mostly constrained by national boundaries (Tarrow 1994b), has since moved to studying the processes of social movement internationalization (Tarrow 2005).

The implications of a new social movement approach are clearest in Gajewska's (2009) strikingly sanguine analysis of transnational labor solidarity in Europe, inspired by micro-mobilization theory and the works of Klandermans, Melucci, and McAdam. Her interpretation may have gone too far, and in fact some of the success cases she reports (construction sector, General Motors) turned out to be much more problematic as soon as the book was published—suggesting that her approach, if useful, is not self-sufficient.

The third recent theoretical development is the application of the sociology of social networks. Martínez Lucio, starting from the observation of how new communication technologies can be used, has discussed networking as a specific form of labor activity (Martínez Lucio and Walker 2005), elaborating ideas suggested already by Waterman (2001) and Hyman (2001, 2005), and especially that 'networking relates to communication rather than institutions' (Waterman 2001, 23). Hennebert (2008) has developed a detailed illustration of how the sociology of networks provides analytical tools for the study of transnational unionism, such as typologies of networks, network boundaries, power relations, and internal exchanges, density, cohesion, and homogeneity.

The application of social network analysis to international trade union activities is indeed complex, but there are some important potential benefits. First, the 'benchmark' against which to evaluate union activities changes substantially from that of a hierarchical/institutional perspective. While most analysis inspired by views of trade unions as 'closed organizations' focus on direct effects of trade union alliances as such (and nearly unavoidably lament their paucity), a study in terms of networks will include indirect effects on the peripheral behavior of the actors involved. For instance, the study of the extension of EWCs to Poland showed that while the EWCs as such remain very unlikely to affect corporate decisions, they may have substantial indirect effects on local industrial relations, where the behavior of local actors is affected by information and resources exchanged within the network (Meardi 2004). Furthermore, a network approach allows to reframe the issues of collective identity and collective action, and especially, by focusing on a 'multiplexity' of relations and exchanges, it overcomes the Olsonian idea of an individual calculus on costs and benefits of collective behavior: joining a network is more complex but easier than joining an organization and can take a variety of forms. Networking is also likely to require fewer resources, also thanks to new technologies (Pulignano 2009).

These three theoretical contributions of federalism, new social movement studies, and social network analysis, stemming from different branches of political science and sociology, converge in overcoming methodological nationalism and offer a critique to bureaucracy and institutions as a privileged lens to analyze international union activities. They separately address the three main reasons of pessimism on transnational unionism: diverging interests, lack of common identity, and institutional/organizational weakness. They may not be well-suited to the analysis of all union actions, and in particular they are missing for the study of the paramount function of collective bargaining. Yet, at the international level, since Levinson's (1972) times, it has been clear that collective bargaining would be the last stage of international unionism in MNCs—therefore not the one to start the analysis with. At the multi-employer level, there are important West European efforts at union collective bargaining co-ordination (Erne 2008; Traxler *et al.* 2008), but they can hardly include the new EU member states where a precondition, that is national multi-employer bargaining, is missing. The study of cross-border unionism between high- and low-wage countries should rather start from the most tangible forms of work internationalization, i.e. MNCs and migration.

THE RELOCATION THREAT: THE AUTOMOTIVE COMPONENT EXAMPLE

Most of the empirical research presented in this book is in the motor industry and for a reason. This is a particularly internationalized sector and one that has been of a major strategic importance in Central Eastern Europe. It is, however, internally diversified. While in the 1990s the focus (of local actors, as well as of my research) was on car assembly (which was being implanted into the region to bypass the remaining tariffs), in the 2000s the most important sub-sector became the component one. This is less frequently in the highlights and its specificity risks being neglected—a reason why it was interesting to choose it for most case studies in 2004–2008. This is particularly relevant for international unionism issues, and the relocation threats. In the aggregated economy, relocations are considered to account for only a negligible part of job losses, maybe 1% (EC 2006a). Of the 2,300,780 job losses arising from company restructurings across Europe documented by the European Restructuring Monitor over the period from 2004 until the end of 2008, 5.9% were attributed to relocation (the figures probably greatly underestimate the overall volume of restructuring activity, but the proportion of those involving cross-border relocation is unlikely to be larger, as these tend to be the cases which attract media interest). Yet even if these aggregate numbers may seem negligible, if one moves to car component plants, the threat of relocation is omnipresent. Moreover, car component workforces tend to have weaker representation and political pressure power, meaning that they are more vulnerable than those of large motor companies. Anner *et al.* (2006) had argued that the automotive sector is characterized by union internationalization through firm-level European works councils—yet this is much less true outside the largest assembly companies.

As a whole, the automotive sector is considered as among the 'winners of globalization', due to its high fixed- and human-capital intensity. Fixed capital means that labor-cost driven relocations are not that viable a short-term option, and high human capital involves space for employee 'voice' and participation, as well as the possibility of defending high wages through high quality and productivity. As an effect, national-level compromises have remained distinct in spite of converging global pressures (Katz and Darbishire 2000.) The opening of global markets and the increase of foreign direct investment reduced neither employment nor relative wages in the triad of core producers (Japan, US, and Western Europe) between the late 1970s and the late 1990s (Spatz and Nunnenkamp 2004). In 2003, the opinion-forming German magazine *der Spiegel* could still headline 'Auto-industrie: die Job-Maschine' (*Spiegel*, 8 September 2003), referring to the major planned investments of Daimler, BMW, Porsche, and Volkswagen within Germany. Such a rosy picture, however, hides important sub-sector and regional differences. Notably, the components sub-sector (whose importance is increasing due to the parallel processes of outsourcing and value chain fragmentation) reacts differently to globalization than vehicle production. The degree of labor intensity differs: in component production labor costs are more important, while transport costs are less. In Germany, the ratio of workers to sales revenue is 2.5 higher in the production of auto-components than in that of automobiles (Spatz and Nunnenkamp 2004).

In the EU's new member states, automotive manufacture is the most important sector for inward FDI, second only to financial services, which is mostly market seeking. Within the sector there has been a clear transition in the nature of inward FDI at the end of the 1990s, which reflects the process of EU integration. In the 1990s, investment was mostly in car assembly using imported parts, for market-access reasons (most Central Eastern European countries still had tariffs on car imports); gradually, investment started to be more efficiency-seeking, and in 1998 German car imports from Central Eastern Europe surpassed exports (VDA 2004). In the 2000s, car components rapidly gained importance and overtook car assembly. This is particularly visible in Poland and the Czech Republic, where the government agency CzechInvest claims that 'nearly every car produced in Europe contains Czech-made components' (as quoted in Sperling 2004: 190). The EU accession, by eliminating the last non-tariff trade barriers, has made cross-border production reorganization extremely easy, and 90% of components—as against 60% of finished cars—produced in Central Eastern Europe are re-exported.

Regional integration involving areas with much lower labor costs changes the employment effects of internationalization. While classic theories of trade assume mutual advantages through specialization, this holds true only between comparably advanced countries. When countries differ strongly in their factor (labor and capital) endowments, while being rather similar in terms of specialization, the adjustment pressure can be much greater. The analysis by Spatz and Nunnenkamp (2004) finds that the negative correlation between share of imports in production and the relative wage of low-skilled workers in Germany is stronger for automotive components than for vehicle assembly. Not all automotive workers are among the 'winners' of globalization, then. Following EU enlargement, and only a year after its above-mentioned confident analysis, the same German magazine had to headline 'Bye-Bye "Made in Germany"' (Spiegel 2004). The employment effects of the enlargement turning point did not take long to become visible: while in 1995–2001 employment in German automotive component production had increased by 40%, it declined by 5% in 2001–2007: in this second period, 27,400 manufacturing jobs yearly were relocated out of Germany, 69% of which low-skilled (Jürgens and Krzywdzinski 2010).

Yet the view—still frequently met among Western experts and employee representatives—of Central Eastern Europe as late industrializing (or even as less developed) countries (and therefore comparable to Mexico within NAFTA) is misplaced. These post-communist countries were heavily industrialized and still have a large pool of skilled workers. Indeed, former Czechoslovakia, Hungary, and Slovenia are, in terms of employment, more industrialized than Germany, and their market share in total OECD manufacturing doubled between 1995 and 2003 (Pilat *et al.* 2006). If in communist-times industry lagged technologically, to compensate for the frequent lack of appropriate tools or parts the shortage economy paradoxically required particularly flexible skills on the part of employees. This has been quickly discovered by foreign investors. Volkswagen, which originally expected the newly acquired Škoda to be a low-segment platform, found that its Czech employees were even better qualified than its German ones; Czech-made cars quickly 'cannibalized' more upmarket Western brands (Sperling 2004). Fiat upgraded its Polish factories to 'models' of innovation for the Italian ones (Meardi and Tóth 2006). Spatz and Nunnenkamp's (2004) expectation that readjustment would concentrate high human capital production in the West applies only to some niches. In the internationalized sub-sectors where investment in technology has taken place, productivity has reached Western levels very quickly, leading to widening gaps in unit labor costs in the period around the enlargement (Dyker 2004).

Employees in component factories are therefore, given the lower impact of fixed and of transport costs, under a greater threat of relocations than those in assembly ones. At the same time, however, their trade unions are less well placed to resist. Keeping in mind Anner *et al.*'s (2006) observation that in the automotive sector cross-border union co-operation takes place at firm level, transnational firm-level representation channels (e.g. EWCs) are less widespread than among the large car makers. An additional difficulty emerges insofar as cross-border restructuring leads to concentration of human-capital intensive production in Western Europe, and of lower skilled production in the cheaper new EU member states. The geographic divide could overlap with professional divides making cross-border understanding more difficult. Fichter *et al.* (2004), studying German FDI in Hungary, noted how international restructuring in some cases changed the nature of the German sites' works councils: from blue-collar to white-collar dominated, leading to a changed union ethos and diminished mobilization capacity. In manufacturing, it has not always been easy for trade unions to combine the representation of production workers and white-collar employees (in some countries these categories are organized in different trade unions.) In an extreme scenario, Western EWC white-collar reps would sit alongside Eastern blue-collar counterparts: they would become less directly competitors but also less able to understand each other on working conditions and employment prospects. The evidence from Central Eastern Europe to date—from the data in this section and the case studies in the next one—mitigates such a radical scenario but does not provide a rosier one: competition is widespread even if not in just one direction or on one dimension.

To summarize, the automotive component sector is particularly interesting for considering intra-EU relocations for several reasons: it is regionalized rather than globalized (90% of production sold in the EU is produced in the EU); both labor skills and labor costs are important (lower capital intensity than car assembly), and human resources in the new EU member states are comparable to the Western European, while much cheaper; foreign investment in this sector is overwhelmingly efficiency-seeking rather than market-seeking (90% of production in Central Eastern Europe is re-exported), more so than final car assembly. This makes this sub-sector different from others, where investment is market-seeking (e.g. food, services) or only labor costs matter (e.g. apparel), and the enlarged Europe different from other regional blocs such as NAFTA, where human resources are less similar. Direct competition between Western and Eastern European sites should be strongest in this sector; therefore, it is a valuable test bed for the possibilities of negotiating and regulating relocation threats.

This is not to forget other, different situations, in which the new member states' locations are more likely to be the 'losers' than the ones in the 'old' EU. Car assemblies, to start with, show a mixed picture, with new member states' plants sometimes suffering from their lower political pressure power in comparison to the western ones. Clear examples came during the crisis of 2008–2009: Romanian and Slovenian Renault workers found themselves under strong pressure when the company was under political pressure to keep production in France, and the same occurred to Polish Fiat workers at the end of 2009; Opel workers feared that the prospected, but then aborted, take-over from Magna in 2009 would have involved a preferential treatment of German production sites (interestingly, in that case Polish Opel unions sided with the British against the Germans). Other sectors show even more striking cases. The steel sector, for instance, has been severely restructured in the new member states as a pre-condition of EU accession, with loss of hundreds of thousands of jobs: in this case, the conflict of interests between the old and new member states was evident (Trappmann 2012), but also, as Bacon and Blyton had observed earlier on, 'solidarity with eastern European steelworkers has been notable for its absence' (1996, 778). This trend endured after EU accession: dominant investor Mittal announced 3,000 job losses in the Czech Republic and 7,000 in Poland in 2005–2006. The same can be said of market-access investment, which is often associated with radical restructuring and divestment and sometimes even relocations westwards (a typical case in the 1990s was that of Gillette taking over the factory of the popular Polsilver razors in Łódź to reduce it to a packaging facility). After EU accession, with the elimination of residual trade barriers, market-seeking investment has become less important, but has not disappeared, and solidarity from Western Europe has remained shallow. A clear example of the latter was provided by the 6,000–10,000 redundancies planned in Poland as a consequence of the HVB-Unicredit bank mega-merger of 2006, when the stronger Austrian, German, and Italian unions remained uninterested and more absorbed in headquarter-level politics. Cases of relocation from the new member states to even cheaper labor locations are also increasingly frequent, e.g. Thomson from Poland to India, Carl Zeiss from Hungary to Mexico, Cartefel from Hungary to North Africa and China, and Boxmark from Slovenia to Croatia. Hungary and Slovenia appear from European Restructuring Monitor data to already have more jobs relocated *from* than *to*. A particularly striking case was that of Dell in Poland, though: in 2008, its relocation from Limerick, Ireland, to Łódź was celebrated as evidence of the 'Slavic Tiger' taking the place of the Celtic one. Only one year later, all production was moved to Taiwan. The promise that open market and flexibility would reward workers of the new member states did not take long to be broken by the common reality of insecurity.

CROSS-BORDER LABOR RESPONSES TO CAPITAL MOBILITY

Studies of EWC and of industrial relations in MNCs tend to concentrate on few large and well-known companies. This leads to some 'self-selection' bias, possibly portraying the general situation as 'better' than it actually is. For instance, Gardawski (2007) found some positive effects of EWCs on social dialog in Poland, but he recognizes that his nine case studies may not be representative.

In the case of MNCs in the new member states, actually, there is a shortage of 'positive' examples even among 'better than average' employers. Tholen's (2007) research on Western (mostly German) companies in

Poland, the Czech Republic, and Slovakia detects the presence of some excellent HRM practices but also very little impact from the EWCs. The review of public cases of transnational restructuring (General Motors, General Electric, and Volkswagen) similarly showed that Volkswagen is a sort of exception with its 'global' industrial relations (Fichter and Meardi 2008). On a more positive side, EWCs have some 'information effect' (Meardi 2004), leading to some mutual learning and approaching between different sites. But this does not translate in European-level action unless in few circumstances. My investigation into 12 American or German-owned companies in Hungary, Poland, and Slovenia in the automotive component production—a sector considered as conducive to company-level labor internationalization (Anner *et al.* 2006)—found only three cases of cross-border union activity on relocation threats: Gh1, Gh2 and Gp1)[1]. In two of them, Gh1 and Gp1, unions benefited from specific conducive situations: very large companies, with strong international integration and relatively low share of labor costs in total production costs. In the other cases, national/local strategies were actually more attractive for trade unions, either in the form of specialized production strategies to isolate plants from competition, or in the form of local political exchange that promised better returns than risky, untested cross-border mobilization; in one case (Ah1) open conflicts between employee representatives of the old and new member states emerged.

The research in the Czech Republic carried out in 2007–2008 confirmed that the company is only rarely a conducive field for Europeanization. The Czech Republic is the geographically most central (a short journey for core industrial regions of Germany and Austria) and economically the most developed among the post-Warsaw Pact new member states, should offer a 'best case scenario' for cross-border union co-operation, but the case studies companies (Table 8.1) indicate the patchy nature of cross-border union co-operation.

In the automotive sector, the two German companies are typical of the large number of German medium-sized companies, which, while being strongly influenced by German culture and German HRM dominant practice, do not transfer dominant German industrial relations practices abroad. Employee representation in Czech sites is inexistent or very weak, and as a consequence, there is no cross-border trade union co-operation either. The Austrian manufacturing companies present an even bleaker picture. They are medium sized, from the border region, and the integration of the neighboring Czech subsidiaries is highest, through intense direct control mechanisms by Austrian managers covering both Austrian and Czech operations. These companies have engaged in radical international division of labor, whereby the Czech subsidiaries play a definite role, i.e. low-cost assembly, with intensive work operations and relatively low qualified workers. Therefore management relies on strict control (as against consent/negotiation), with different

Table 8.1   Case Studies of Foreign Companies and Cross-border Co-operation in the Czech Republic

Company (home country, sector) *Brownfield	Total employment (Czech employment)	Union presence in Czech Republic	EWC and transnational union links
D-CAR1*	9,500 (1,500)	Yes	No, but planned EWC
D-CAR2	1,100 (300)	No	No
D-INS1	3,700 (100)	No	EWC, but no Czech reps
D-INS2	181,000 (700)	No	EWC, but no union Czech rep
A-CAR1	800 (200)	No	No
A-CAR2	1,200 (600)	No	No
A-BAN1*	76,000 (1,600)	Yes	EWC
A-BAN2	300 (200)	No	No
UK-CAR*	6,500 (600)	Yes	EWC, information-only
US-CAR*	21,000 (600)	Yes	EWC, information-only
US-BAN*	60,000 (2,200)	No	No
UK-FIN	8,100 (600)	No	No

management practices from those in the high-skill Austrian operations. The radical international division of labor involves the removal of direct comparability and therefore competition among operations. As an effect, Austrian employee representatives are not particularly concerned with working conditions on the Czech side. In both companies, there are is no Czech employee representation, no EWC, and no transnational union activity. Employee representation is stronger in the Czech sites of the two Anglo American automotive companies, as these are old brownfield sites. The EWCs are not particularly strong, though, reflecting relatively little power and capabilities from the Western employee representatives.

The continuing assistance from the European Metalworker Federation is therefore crucial to keep the EWCs working, in an effort of 'articulated' Europeanization between sector and company level (Pulignano 2007).

In the finance sector, companies differ from the best-known cases of Europeanization regardless of size. In the smaller German and Austrian companies there is a EWC, but the Czech operations are not represented. In the larger companies, the EWC appear to have affected a degree of 'dissemination' of co-determination practices across the European operations. These effects are hardly perceived in the Czech context though, where management refuses to increase employee participation rights above the legal limit, the Czech representatives have no information on the industrial relations practices in other countries and have received no form of assistance or co-operation from their Western counterparts. Interestingly, the Czech EWC representatives believe that there is an interest divergence between Western and Eastern European operations, as the former are confronted with major restructuring plans and job cuts, while the latter are in a safer situation. No union contacts exist outside EWC meetings. The finance sector Anglo American companies are characterized by a strong, explicit preference for direct participation over representative one. The employees of the Czech operations have no form of collective representation. As a consequence, there are no EWCs, nor any other form of cross-border networking among employee representatives. It is not that cross-border union contacts are not needed in finance companies: although there is little internal competition (markets are distinct and services are provided in loco), some areas (Research and Development, Information Technologies, some back-office operations) are affected by relocations, and restructuring and working conditions are subjected to company international benchmarking.

To summarize, in these Czech case studies East-West intra-labor conflicts have been avoided—but little solidarity and networking have emerged. In the manufacturing companies, where cross-border competition is strong, the problem is not—as some western trade unions expected in the past (Meardi 2004)—the quality of union representatives in the new member states: the Czech ones actually emerge as better informed and more active than the British. The obstacles are rather anti-union/works council policies by greenfield investors (especially when segmenting production internationally), and the insufficient employment size of component-producing companies for supporting effective international networks. The well-known EWCs of very large companies cannot be replicated even in medium-large size companies.

The geography of production networks is also important. Multinational companies in the new member states will have different effects depending on how far their other locations are. In companies from remote countries (US, and to some extent UK), foreign investment into the region is dominated by large companies and motivated mostly by market access and therefore involves little or no relocation pressure—transnational union links will exist but with no prominent role. Companies from closer countries with no tariff barriers, such as Germany, are more likely to be motivated by efficiency consideration and tempted by relocations strategies: transnational union activity will be needed but uneasy. Finally, companies from contiguous regions, such as from the Austrian borders, are able not only to relocate, but to completely restructure their production across the border, so that some core activities are kept in Austria, and all labor intensive ones are transferred to facilities in the neighboring countries a few kilometers away. This process reminds the *maquiladora* phenomenon of the Mexico-US borders and involves a deep segregation of activities so that different and incomparable working conditions are introduced on the two sides—with least scope for socialization—in spite of contacts—and transnational union links. In the finance sector, efficiency considerations are less important for investors and cross-border competition is only detectable in two of the case studies, but still cross-border union coordination could be helpful in dealing with major restructuring processes. However, in this case, the weakness, and frequently absence of independent employee representation in the Czech Republic means that more time will be needed.

It is not the country of origin, identity issues or networking costs that explain weak transnational links, but rather, the opportunities for networking. In the Austrian companies for neighboring towns, contacts require no resources, and in the finance companies, they would be easy given IT and English-language knowledge—but it is in these cases that social links, and therefore cross-border unionism, are weakest, due to organizational segregation.

CROSS-BORDER LABOR RESPONSES TO LABOR MOVEMENT

I have described in Chapter 4 the large extent of labor mobility after EU enlargement. Of course, this does not mean that labor mobility is higher than capital mobility. In the case of the latter, potential, or threatened, mobility has more important effects that actual mobility. A number of possible 'indirect relocations' in terms of location decisions over future investments occur besides the relatively rare direct relocations. Also, most migrants' jobs do not substitute locals' so that this is not necessarily an issue of direct competition or zero-sum game between Eastern and Western European workers (Galgóczi *et al.* 2009). Still, the scale of East-West mobility affects the nature of EU labor markets.

Immigration can be a threat to trade unions as much as relocations (Castles and Kosack 1973). In the case of the enlargement, the disruptions for social standards have been noticed not only on working conditions in the receiving states but also in the social conditions in the 'leaving states', in particular in the extreme case of Latvia (Woolfson 2007b).

Despite overall positive social and economic effects (EC 2008d), widespread social fears meant that the risk of conflicts between Eastern and Western trade unions was real, as some tensions during the accession process had indicated (Meardi 2002). The diverging interests between some Western (especially German and Austrian) and Eastern trade unions (Meardi 2002; Menz 2008; Krings 2009; Galgóczi et al. 2009) might turn into a divide between Western and Eastern labor. Indeed, the European Trade Union Confederation elaborated its own policy, against transitional limits to the freedom of movement of workers but without the authority to impose it on its reluctant Austrian and German members (ETUC 2005).

Cases of open confrontation have remained extremely rare, though. More visible have been the organizing efforts by trade unions towards the new migrants, especially in UK and Ireland (Hardy and Fitzgerald 2010; Heyes 2009), which have led to numerous successes and to attention in the media, with even reports of Polish migrants as 'bringing solidarity back in fashion in Britain' (Campbell 2006). These efforts are not always successful and overall membership remains very low, mostly because of the temporary nature of stay and jobs (Anderson et al. 2007). Yet some are striking: in particular the successful organizing by the Unite trade union in the British food packaging industry, where working conditions have been shown by a statutory inquiry to be frequently inhumane and involve frequent racist abuse (Equality and Human Rights Commission 2010). After three years of efforts, including the involvement of Polish organizers and 'flying protests' targeting retail chains, a sufficient pressure was achieved to obtain the conversion of large numbers of agency workers into permanent jobs and a colleactive agreement covering 90% of the employees in the sector (Lawrence 2010).

However, the point is not so much recruitment success (which is not organizationally viable for temporary workers), but the creation of links and policies that prevent a divide between nationals and migrants to emerge, with disruptive effects for national union members too. Organizing migrants in the UK included innovative practices, such as co-operation with ethnic associations (e.g. with the Polish Catholic Association in Birmingham) and setting up Polish-language sections (in Southampton and Glasgow). It focused on two particularly important factors leading to migrants' exploitation: information on employment rights and skills, including qualification recognition and English language. On the former issue, the unions made an effort in information materials publication, and it is now unlikely for any new migrant not to receive some publication on employee rights in their own language. Moreover, the unions reinforced their campaigning on employment rights in Temporary Work Agencies, an important labor market segregating institution: over one-third of new migrants receive their first job from agencies, which in the UK do not guarantee the same rights as direct employees. Such campaign had some success, forcing the government to concede new legislation in 2008 and preparing the ground for EU regulations—even if these have been quickly recognized as insufficient (Countouris and Horton 2009).

From the cross-border co-operation perspective, the most significant activity has been the co-operation with Eastern European trade unions (mostly Polish, given the 'critical mass' of Polish migration), leading to the posting of organizers from Polish trade unions Solidarity and OPZZ to UK and Ireland, which, in turn, facilitated the recruitment of activists and organizers among migrants. Such co-operation is made easier by the frequent 'transnational' nature of intra-EU migration, and it has established inclusion as the dominant union approach towards migrants (Hardy and Fitzgerald 2010). British trade unions have proved to have the strategic capacity of putting migration in the broader context, avoiding the temptations of localized exclusionary conflicts. The Trades Union Congress placed the migration issue within the broader social context of—not exclusively migrant—vulnerable work (TUC Commission on Vulnerable Employment 2008), shifting the focus from migrants to poor employee rights as the problem: the case of Temporary Work Agencies shows clearly that campaigns for migrants can also improve working conditions for large numbers of British workers. The British experience is similar to that of Ireland (Dundon *et al.* 2007) and of construction sector unions in other European countries and especially Switzerland (Erne 2008). Combined together, they represent clear examples of new co-operation between trade unions and other social movements in complex social settings, and not simply in the workplace, something which has received particular attention in the US (Milkman 2006; Turner and Cornfield 2007).

However, in terms of cross-border trade unionism, the focus on the national, political level of trade unionism is limited and leads to the unwarranted conclusion of a gap between the 'openness' of British and Irish trade unions in comparison to their German or Austrian counterparts. Such conclusion is often based on the institutional argument that 'Liberal Market Economy' trade unions are more prone to organizing than those relying on corporatist institutions (Krings 2009). This neglects, behind the idea of encompassing national models, intra-sector differences, and especially the fact that in the low-wage sector the German labor market is actually *less* institutionally protected than the British, due to the lack of a minimum wage: it is therefore in countries like Germany that a migrant organizing effort is more needed, and indeed there is evidence of some movement in that direction (Turner 2009).

Developments on the ground are different from national official policies. In fact, not only, as we have seen, have UK trade unions been active in servicing just as much as in organizing. There have also been a number of campaigns on migration by German trade unions, which not only provide advisory and training services to migrants, but have also reacted politically, notably demanding the introduction of a national minimum wage. German trade unions provide advisory and training services for migrants. Construction and agriculture union IG BAU set up in 2004 a 'European Migrant Workers Union', although the unilateral nature of the initiative encountered criticism from Polish construction unions (the only Eastern European union to endorse it was the Polish agriculture sector union ZZPR), and the organization turned into a servicing center for posted workers, rather than an organizing effort (Lillie and Greer 2007). Developments have occurred in cross-border co-operation too, though, especially in the border regions through the Interregional Trade Union Councils (seven of them involve Austrian or German trade unions and partners from the new member states). In 2006, for instance, DGB (German Confederation of Trade Unions), Ver-di (German service sector union), and Solidarity protested jointly in the border region against a megastore that was violating worker rights (Szewczyk and Unterschütz 2009). In May 2009, a Polish-German trade union forum was launched in Gdańsk. In Austria, trade unions are distinctive in their explicit rejection of special projects geared to migrant workers, on the grounds that all members should be treated equally (Chaloupek and Peyrl 2009), which reflects a different national approach to the issue of diversity (Greene *et al.* 2005). But even there, information initiatives have not been lacking, and it is reported that most people seeking help from the Chambers of Labor have a migrant background (Chaloupek and Peyrl 2009). Interviews with trade union members in Austria and Hungary in 2005 and 2006 have revealed that, on the ground, unionists of both sides involved in cross-border contacts did not consider the issue of transitional periods to be an obstacle to co-operation, and that they easily 'agreed to disagree' on that point while still co-operating on others. German and Austrian trade unions, despite supporting transitional arrangements of the freedom of movement of workers, have been aware that these arrangements would end in 2011, and therefore have had the same need as British trade unions to organize migrants (Donaghey and Teague 2006). At the grassroot level, where socialization occurs between workers, possibilities for transnational co-operation do emerge. If there are limits to German trade union activity on migration, we should not forget that there are limits to the more advertised British action. The UK unions programs of co-operation with Solidarity relied largely on public funding, and some proved not to be self-sustainable once such funding finished. Interestingly, in Poland both Solidarity and OPZZ international affairs officers, as well as Polish construction sector's unionists (Meardi 2009, interviews) consider co-operation with German unions, on the ground, to be easier and more productive than with British trade unions.

Whether in the UK or in Germany and Austria, the overall implication for unionism is that, if from the structural side migrants' unionization remains onerous, from a network and new social movement perspective co-operation on migration issues proves the potential for combining inclusion and dialog *within* trade unions with solidarity and dialog *among* national unions, in the long-term interest of union effectiveness (Hyman 1999; Meardi 2000).

CROSS-BORDER LABOR RESPONSES
TO MOVEMENT OF SERVICES

The freedom of movement of services re-emerged as a contested social issue at the same time as the enlargement, in connection to debates on the so-called 'Bolkestein Directive'. Cross-border provision of services with use of own workers has been subjected to similar transitional restrictions by Germany (in the construction, industrial cleaning, and interior decorating sectors) and Austria (in the same sectors and others, including agriculture). Even if the number of 'posted workers' remains smaller than the number of migrants (who take employment in the host country), it has been rapidly increasing and it has more dangerous potential for labor standards: within existing EU regulations, posted workers are not given all rights of local workers, their employment conditions are more difficult to monitor, and their unionization and social inclusion is much more difficult, if not impossible.

Following protests in the street by European trade unions, the 'No' in the French referendum of 2005 and opposition from the European Parliament, the service Directive was approved in the original Bolkestein text and the 'country of origin' principle—binding service providers to the respect of only their country of origin regulations—was removed. Pan-European union protests were crucial in convincing the initially uninterested socialist MEPs and some European governments to oppose the Directive (Gajewska 2009). Importantly, unions from the new member states took part in the protest, even if with a low profile, despite a strong political pressure in their home country to defend their 'national' companies and their competitiveness abroad. An officer of the International Department of the Polish union OPZZ remembers the media's vehement criticism of the unions as 'national traitors' for opposing the Bolkestein Directive, and that within the union itself many were unconvinced about it (interview, July 2009). From some unions from the new member states, adherence to the ETUC protest was conditional on its concomitant condemnation of transitional arrangements on labor migration, which occurred with the above mentioned resolution of December 2005.

Even if pan-European union protest, in that difficult case, seemed to prevail, much of the 'country of origin' principle was then silently, and undemocratically, reintroduced by the European Court of Justice (ECJ) in its interpretations of the Posted Worker Directive in the Laval, Rüffert, and Luxembourg cases (as well as by the EC in its Communication). As a result, the destabilizing effect of the freedom of movement of services for industrial relations has become apparent (Verschueren 2008).

I will not enter here the legal details of the Laval, Rüffert, and Luxembourg cases, in which the ECJ rules that the freedom of movement of services has the priority over local collective agreements and rights of collective action: the debates and analyses have already been numerous (e.g. Bercusson 2007; Ashiagbor 2009; Blanpain and Świątkowski 2009). The important point here is the political one, or better, the emerging need for a political remedy to the extremist market ideology of the European Court of Justice. As Dølvik and Visser (2009) have argued, the subordination of union rights to 'economic freedom' contradicts the nature itself of continental European labor law, and thereby of the 'European Social Model': union rights come to be subject to extremely strict tests and are likely to be subordinated to the (unquestioned) economic freedoms of employers. Moreover, the specific attack of the ECJ is on labor standards set by collective agreements, as the rulings imply that posted workers are only entitled to the legal minimum standards on few core labor rights (introduced by law or by legally enforceable collective agreements), and any action, by local authorities or unions, to defend higher or wider standards are deemed illegal. Thereby, The ECJ jeopardizes economic democracy—the possibility to collectively negotiate standards of employment—and exactly social dialog, the most frequently mentioned aspect of the 'European Social Model'.

This is in direct relation to EU enlargement. Not only all those cases (and the Viking one) related to companies exploiting the gap in labor standards between old and new member states. The ECJ, and with it the EU, also changed qualitatively. As Dølvik and Visser put it: the ECJ widened 'its membership to lawyers with radically different backgrounds and experiences of labor law', revealing a 'neat division between 'old' and 'new' Member States, thus reflecting a broader conflict of rights and interests running through Europe' (Dølvik and Visser 2009, 492–493). The ECJ does not exist in the vacuum: it corresponds to the institutional traditions of the member states and having integrated new states without—as I discussed in Chapter 1—requiring a commitment to the social dimension has had disruptive effects. Moreover, political balances have also shifted, and the ECJ rulings met no reaction at EU level (apart from a cosmetic Forum to discuss these issues organized in October 2008, with no practical consequences), because even member states in favor of stricter rules fear that a renegotiation of the Posted Worker Directive in the Council of 27 could easily lead to further dilution, rather than strengthening (Dølvik and Visser, 503). Only pressure from the socialist group in the European Parliament forced Barroso to make a commitment to propose amendments to the Posted Worker Directive in September 2009. However, in 2010 further proposed Directives, on seasonal work and on intra-corporate transfers, have raised renewed concerns that new avenues may be open to employers to recruit cheap labor in the poorer member states.

From the point of view of cross-border unionism, Bercusson (2007) raised the risk of an East-West divide emerging on those issues, even if, he argued, it would be in the interest of Eastern posted workers to be granted host-country labor standards. Indeed, this has been a difficult issue for trade unions.

In the Laval case, the Swedish and Latvian employer side tried to organize Latvian workers in Latvian trade unions to bypass and undermine the Swedish ones (Woolfson 2007b), although this was avoided by a immediate initiative of the same Swedish unions (Gajewska 2009). The expansion of fake self-employment and transnational sub-contracting in Germany raised the question of whether the transitional arrangements were backfiring for Western unions, as labor migration took 'grey' forms that more difficult to control and organize. The later Rüffert and Luxembourg cases and ECJ rulings highlighted the disparity between EU-protected economic freedom and national regulations (Dølvik and Visser 2009; Ashiagbor 2009).

Interestingly enough, however, the most visible mobilizations against foreign contract workers occurred not in Germany or Austria, but in the 'open border' Sweden (Laval), Ireland (Irish Ferries), and UK (in construction engineering). The question is whether such mobilizations' nature is nationalistic or not. In the Irish Ferries case, as well as in the Laval one (Gajewska 2009), the Latvian trade unions were involved: these cases do not contradict international union solidarity. The case that rang the alarm bell of nationalism occurred in the UK in January and June 2009 at the Total Lindsey refinery, under the banners 'British jobs for British workers' (Barnard 2009). It did not actually involve workers from the new member states, but contractors from one an oldest, founding member of the EU, Italy—but the case quickly gained national relevance for the issue of foreign contract workers in general, especially from Eastern Europe.

In the Lindsey case, the role of the media was instrumental in depicting the protests against Sicilian contractor IREM as 'xenophobic'and creating tensions between British and Italian unions. The European affairs officers of the largest Italian union, CGIL, Nicolosi and Petrucci, signed a declaration opening with the words 'What's going on in Lincolnshire is one of the ugliest pages in the history of the trade union movement in these globalised times: English workers against Italian workers' (CGIL, 2009). However, if one moves from the official level to the local one, the picture was different. In its home town Syracuse, IREM was known for its anti-union practices and for by-passing of national collective agreements (through the affiliation to the artisans', rather than employers' confederation). Unionists on the ground understood the British protesters for two reasons: protection of collective agreements and defense of employment continuity. In short, as one unionist said, if the same problem with a foreign contractor had occurred in Syracuse, 'we would have done exactly the same' (interviews with CISL and CGIL union officers, February 2009). At Lindsey, at the same time, a question mark on the xenophobic nature of the demonstration is raised by the participation in the protests of locally resident Polish workers.

The Lindsey case demonstrates the disruptive effects of the freedom of movement of services, and the possibility of workers' success only through major political pressure: legally, IREM and Total could have claimed, like Laval, that the protests were illegal (Barnard 2009)—and indeed Total attempted to do so in June but still had to succumb to worker unofficial strikes. The problem is that such political pressure generally requires media attention, and that media attention is easier to gain with xenophobic tones than technical arguments on working conditions. The case confirms the weakness of transnational organization: Italian unionists were only informed of the issue through the Italian media at the end of January, even though British trade unions had started negotiating the issue with Total before Christmas. At no stage there have been direct Italian-British union contacts, also due to the non-union nature of IREM foreign operations. Links through European federations in Brussels proved to be too slow, indirect and easily distorted. British unions GMB and Unite did not start the strike nor officially endorsed it, but local shop stewards were involved in the dispute. They took the role of negotiating (even if not formally) and were careful to avoid anti-foreigner arguments and made sure that the final agreement would not involve firing any Italians or Portuguese, and that the new jobs 'for British workers' would be open to non-UK applicants (Unite's national secretary Derek Simpson was as clear as he could in stating: 'it is a class issue not a race issue', Unite 2009). Like in the manufacturing cases described above, the existence of some sort, even if vague, of common European labor organization and identity has prevented, in spite of strong political and media incentives (members of the far-right British National Party were active on site), the emergence of xenophobic conflicts—even if it has proved too weak to produce any positive, active solidarity.

In the case of the freedom of movement of services, the emergence of transnational networks is more difficult than on migration not only because of the lack of institutional and structural resources (union-unfriendly legislation), but also because of the segregation, in the workplace as well as housing, of foreign contract workers—as the IREM barges symbolize. This situation is confirmed by the developments at similar, if less prominent, protests against Polish contractors in England and Wales in winter and spring 2009 (especially, at Alstom in England and at the South Hook natural gas refinery in Wales). Again, no contacts between Polish and British trade unions were established (even though the Alstom's Polish contractors Remak and ZREW[2] are unionized, while Hertel's Polish workers were not), but nationalistic developments were at least sidelined, and the focus remained on the labor issues of working conditions, respect of collective agreements, and employment security.

CONCLUSION

The assessment of cross-border trade union achievements is often negative. In the case of the difficult test of East-West co-operation within the enlarged EU, successes are still rare, too. However, broader theoretical and empirical horizons may allow a more comprehensive view and a different judgment.

The chapter has first argued that through the theoretical contribution of federalism, new social movements, and social network analysis, it is possible to frame cross-border union networking differently from traditional hierarchical institutional perspectives, unveiling direct and especially indirect effects. Even if the EWCs do not achieve much directly, they often affect peripheral behaviors by increasing information and preventing competition: transnational union contacts are at least allowing unions not to harm each other through concession bargaining, even though they are still too weak to help each other. The negotiation of conflicts between constituencies suggests that some sort of weak federalist thinking is emerging, at company (EWCs) as well as multi-employer level, through for instance debates on minimum wages (Schulten 2008). Similarly, while ETUC policies look ineffective in implementing a common migration policy from above, networks are developing in the border regions as well as in the UK, and involve other social actors. Second, by combining the study of MNCs with that of migration and freedom of movement of services (two phenomena hitherto mostly studied separately), the overall picture becomes more mixed, as slow progress in MNCs (as shown by the Czech MNCs' case studies) is compensated by advances on migration, a fertile terrain for coalitions with other social movements, and unexpected difficulties on the freedom of movement of services. Finally, a focus on the 'transnational', unlike 'methodologically nationalist' analytical frameworks, allows to understand why developments depend not so much on national countries, as it would appear from top-level developments (Krings 2009). They depend rather on the ground: on the degree of broader European socialization and networking resources and opportunities. Therefore, EWCs effects vary depending on the size, geography and organization of the company, and migration offers more opportunities than segregated movement of services. Migration, in particular, seems to make it easier for trade unions to 'humanize' foreign workers and develop solidarities with them, than the simple existence of remote foreign subsidiaries. On the freedom of movement of services, the opportunities for socialization are minimal, and (as in MNCs with segregated subsidiaries) the only positive effects come indirectly from broader European labor socialization, whereby nationalism tends to be sidelined.

The overall picture, summarized in Table 8.2, confirms the role of socialization experiences for transnational labor solidarity to be crucial, if besides institutional factors (Hyman 1999; Gajewska 2009). Only through transnational socialization the transnational labor markets created by EU enlargement can be re-embedded in society.

Table 8.2   Opportunities for Transnational Union Action

Transnational issue	Structural opportunities	Networking opportunities
Freedom of movement of capital (MNCs)	EWC—weak and contingent on size	EWC—contingent on company size, geography, and organizational integration/segregation
Freedom of movement of workers (migration)	ETUC policy co-ordination —ineffective; migrant unionization—onerous	Organizing co-operation, Interregional Trade Union Councils, information exchange
Freedom of movement of services	None, except monitoring of Posted Workers Directive, contingent on national rules	None, but indirect effects of broader European socialization

9   Other Voices

For a number of reasons well addressed by Crowley and Ost (2001) and by Bohle and Greskovits (2006) among others, trade unions are comparatively weak in most new member states. As we have seen in previous chapters, EU accession has not improved things, even if its disruptions have offered some occasions for mobilization and contacts (Chapters 7 and 8). As works councils are rarer and even weaker (Chapter 1), employees are left without the institutional channels for collective independent voice in the workplace and economy. Nor are political parties committed to labor rights strong in the region (Chapter 5). Yet it might be that we have to look elsewhere for employee voice and more in general social protest and activation.

In the West, and especially in the liberal market economies to which the new member states resemble, there has been an increasing interest in 'new actors' in industrial relations, as exemplified by a special issue devoted to them by the *British Journal of Industrial Relations* in 2006 (Heery and Frege 2006) and to 'coalition building' between trade unions and social movements (e.g. Turner and Cornfield 2007). These new actors include community-based organizations, employment right organizations, and other professional organizations. In addition, trade unions have become increasingly permeable to minority organizations, whether on ethnic, age, gender, or sexual-orientation grounds (e.g. Colgan and Ledwith 2002). It is increasingly evident, then, that employee voice does not necessarily take the form of unionism, and it can be hypothesized that, with the decline of traditional working class socialization, it increasingly follows more mediated and diverse paths (Van Gyes *et al.* 2000). This might be even more the case in post-communist societies where the concept of class lost much of its potential for social identity. In this chapter I will look at the available, if limited and unsystematic, evidence of the emergence of such forms of voice.

SOCIAL MOVEMENTS IN THE NEW MEMBER STATES

Post-communist transitions in Central Eastern Europe have been surprising for the lack of protest they have entailed: the previous experience of troubled democratic transitions in Latin America, the social costs of reforms, and the initial presence of large trade unions, had raised expectations for frequent mass protests. Leading social movement scholar Alain Touraine, for instance, in 1990 launched a research program on the anticipated social movements of post-communist societies, research that had then to shift to the absence of weakness of the same movements.[1] Reasons for the weakness of social protest include the relative level of social equality (at least initially), the high legitimacy of economic reforms (again, at least initially), and the various forms of exit (to informality, welfare state, emigration) that I mentioned in Part II, as they have mostly continued after EU accession. Even if some other scholars have detected high mobilization in the early 1990s (Ekiert and Kubik 2001), their evidence is rather frail, as commented by Ost (2005), and in any case it does not go beyond 1993. New social movements such as environmentalism and pacifism have failed to grow. The Greens are a visible political force only in the Czech Republic, and even there, with a more moderate outlook than in the West. On the occasion of the Iraq War of 2003, when most of Central Eastern Europe entered the 'coalition of the willing' (prompting Donald Rumsfeld to juxtapose the 'new Europe' to the 'old one', and Dominique de Villepin to define the latter 'the Trojan donkey' of America in Europe) anti-war demonstrations were much smaller than in the West.

It would be a rushed conclusion, though, to dismiss collective action in the new member states altogether. First, the form of mobilization could be different than in the West, as post-communist societies have not developed the same repertoire of protest: leftist slogans that are common in the West may sound artificial or, worse, as Stalinist reminiscences in post-communist countries—but other forms of action could be more natural. It is not just a matter of different symbolism, which often refers to past anti-communist protest: in the autumn 2007 riots in Budapest, protesters even stole a Soviet tank from a museum and managed (after a fuel refill) to take it into the street against the police, in a sort of 're-enactment' of the 1956 revolution; in Poland, protesters often shout 'ZOMO' (the communist-time anti-protest forces) to the police. It is also and primarily a matter of content: the post-communist specificity is visible, in particular, in neighborhood mobilizations, individual freedom defense, and national/cultural symbols.

In communist societies, not only the workplaces but also the neighborhoods attached to them acted as primary socialization institutions. Communist planning concentrated large numbers of people in similar socio-economic conditions in high-density developments characterized by centralized services. It is not surprising, therefore, that protest movements often combined worker issues with local issues, as has been described in particular in the case of Solidarity. In some cases, economic specialization translated also into broader regional collective identities. After the fall of communism, while worker protest lost its political legitimacy, neighborhood protest remained acceptable. As a result, there have been various forms of local and regional activation—interestingly, also in relation to EU integration. The promotion of 'macro-regions' by the EU led to important administrative reforms in several applicant countries in the late 1980s. In Poland (the largest new member state in terms of surface and population), this involved dissolving the previous 50 voivodships (regions) and re-aggregating them into 16 large regions. In 1998, the reforms provoked large protests in many voivodships that were losing their autonomy, and this was particularly visible in regions with specific industrial and historical specializations (Radom, Toruń, Płock, Częstochowa, and Bielsko-Biała). It is worth noticing, in passing, that that EU-inspired reform, whatever its administrative and economic merits, contributed to the general effect of subordinating democracy and public space to economic imperatives: old small regions that had some forms of identity and offered some public space and local media were replaced by abstract, technocratic macro-regions.

At an even more micro-local level, neighborhood movements have emerged very frequently. They have been neglected only because of their fragmentation and rare national-level relevance, but they are telling with regard to the possibility of collective action. Also, as it happens to neighborhood movements in other parts of the world, a prominent role is played by women (Verschuur 2008). This can combine with labor struggles in different ways. I had observed a prominent case well before EU accession (1998–1999) in the Polish city of Płock, where the female workforce of the textile factory Cotex combined its sit-in strike (called by a fringe nationalist trade union) with the defense of the town's status. The protest's iconography was different from the typical one of the West, Holy Mary images replacing red flags and feminist symbols, but the mobilization was impressive: hundreds of women occupied an unheated factory during the whole winter. Trappmann (2012), in her multi-level and multi-method account of restructuring in the Krakow's steel district of Nowa Huta, found that local non-governmental organizations operating at the level of urban restructuring outside the steelworks gates were more active than the trade unions operating within the gates.

The importance of the local dimension combines with various forms of social movements, from the environment (e.g. against some planned motorways) to defense (e.g. against the proposed US missile shield in the Czech Republic and Poland). These aspects may find a suitable explanatory interpretation in the recent works by labor historian Silver (2003) and by an expert of communist and post-communist labor, Michael Burawoy (2009b). The distinction between Marx-type labor movements, rooted in the growing productive centrality of the working class, and Polanyi-type labor movements, stemming from the protection of social communities from market disruption, is relevant for post-communist Europe and contributes to explaining the mismatch between western expectations and Eastern European reality. Western European understanding of labor movements has been strongly marked by the experience of growing 'Marx-type' movements during the periods of economic growth and industrialization in the twentieth century, especially around 1900 and then in the 1960s and 1970s. But in the twenty-first century, and in a context of globalized, or at least globalizing capitalism, there is no self-evident reason to expect social movements in post-communist countries to follow the same path—a path which western trade unions themselves have largely abandoned. 'Marx-type' labor movements might appear in the new member states in the expanding export-oriented industrial areas, where labor is experiencing fast increasing productivity and may find the assertiveness for claiming a larger share of it. But as Ost (2009) has noted, even if such 'Marx-like' revitalization occurred (and he detected some elements of it, even if before the economic crisis), it would be bound to remain very isolated and patchy, in what he names a 'Mexican' scenario, which is characteristic of uneven development. Bohle and Greskovits (2006) had already remarked, in a Marxist framework, that working-class power in Central Eastern Europe appears only at workplace level but in too few (export-oriented) workplaces to gain a political dimension; moreover, the international nature of markets and the low prices in the new member states mean that most export-oriented employers (especially MNCs) have the relatively cheap option of preventing labor activation by paying a wage premium, which is made affordable by fast increasing productivity.

By contrast, opposition movements can emerge in the new member states, as in most dependent societies, for the defense of local communities against the disruption of globalization. This is not happening in the form of so-called anti-globalization movements, which are very marginal in the region like other leftist movements. It happens rather in a communitarian way which is by nature fragmented and politically ambiguous. But not less significant in terms of the dissatisfaction and fear that the economic transition has induced, and the EU has failed to reduce.

GENDER AND IDENTITY MOVEMENTS

A second important dimension of protest in the new member states relates not to community, in a Polanyi way, but to a very different dimension, the protection of subjectivity. Totalitarianism (or aspirational totalitarianism, as Central Eastern Europe communist regimes rarely reached the extremes of Stalin and Mao) meant that any form of protest involved a reassertion of individual freedom (Meardi 2005). In post-communist times, this sort of protest in defense of subjectivity is less needed and less widespread, but it is still visible in the assertion of identities that have long been devalued or delegitimized. The main examples relate to gender: women's movements (whether adopting the feminist label or not) and sexual orientation minorities.

Women have been major sufferers of the post-communist transitions, for many reasons (Pollert 2003). The massive retrenchment of the welfare state and of childcare meant major losses of jobs in feminized occupations and an increase in housework, resulting in the massive 'exit' of women from the labor market, which was particularly pronounced in Hungary and Poland. The acquired legitimacy and often prominence of the Church and of conservative politics in some countries created a dominant public discourse that was detrimental to women's voice. The new member states are largely characterized by a very low presence of women in politics, in spite of some visible exceptions (Poland and Slovakia have had female prime ministers and Latvia a female president—not to even mention the Eastern German Angela Merkel). In 2009, according to European Commission data, all the new member states were below the EU average (24%) in terms of women's share in national parliaments, the worst cases being Hungary and Romania with only 11% (Hungary was also remarkable for not having any woman in the government). Such weak participation exists also in trade unions, which while being largely feminized in terms of membership because of the over-representation of the public sector, are by large led by men.

Nonetheless, it would be very far from the truth to depict women in the new member states as passive victims. On the contrary, they have been very active, both in individual strategies, from the informal to the knowledge economy, and including migration, and in collective protests. Hardy (2009) draws a link between private (e.g. the 'womb strike' of falling birth rates) and public forms of female resistance to economic restructuring in Poland.

Women's protest also occurs around the workplace: the Cotex case of extreme protest mentioned in the previous section was entirely female in composition, leadership, and identity. It is also worth mentioning an additional case study of a MNC in the automotive component sector, included in the first, exploratory phase of the 2004–2005 study presented in Chapters 3 and 7. While the automotive component sector is mostly male dominated, this case (not included in the final 12 comparative case studies) was of a 90% female US-owned factory in Poland, with a typically low-skill intensive production. Interestingly, despite the workforce composition, the trade union leader was a man. However, a major open conflict emerged around the alleged recurrent sexual harassment of manual workers by a Polish manager. The union reacted and skillfully used international linkages by informing the US headquarters (where sensitivity to such issues is higher than in Poland), which almost immediately, given the risk of negative repercussions, removed the accused manager. Of the 12 case studies we analyzed, two (Gh2, As) had a majority-female workforce: and both were among those with revitalization attempts through organizing.

There is no space here to account for the development of feminist, and more broadly female, protest in the new member states in an exhaustive manner. Protests against the prohibition of abortion were among the largest in Poland in the 1990s, and less macroscopic, but still significant protests continued to occur throughout the region on public services, pension reforms, and sexual violence. In the case of Hungary, this often unnoticed but widespread mobilization has been described particularly well (Fábián 2009), but it is in Poland that it is most significant, given that the objective conditions (conservative Catholic Church, worst childcare provision, collapse of female employment) are the least favorable. Moreover, it is in Poland that the linkage to subjectivity is particularly strong, suggesting that women are the best-placed bearers of new social movements, an argument proposed in different terms also by Touraine (2006) in the West. Malinowska (2001) has detected in a particularly subtle way the link between subjectivity, post-communism and female mobilization. While acknowledging that no component of the Solidarity movement had anything to do with feminism, she crucially argues that 'if considered globally as a social movement, Solidarity created nonetheless also an indispensable ground for the emergence of feminist identity: it raised society's subjectivity, making the individuals aware of the right to define themselves in individual categories, as well as of freely constructing collective identities' (27).

A link between anti-totalitarian subjectivity tradition and new social moments is even clearer in the case of sexual minorities. The International Lesbian and Gay Association reports demonstration for homosexuals' civil rights in all new member states, the most important in Poland, Romania, Hungary, and Latvia. In many cases, protests took place in reaction to anti-gay legislation or to the failed implementation of the EU acquis on non-discrimination (see Chapter 1). Gruszczyńska (2009) reports how the Polish 'Marches of Equality', despite the apparent generational and ideological contrast, referred back to the Solidarity social movement, in both public slogans and participants' individual discourse. It is noticeable that mobilization followed EU accession: in the 1990s, the gay and lesbian movements avoided the public arena, engaging in 'institutionalization without mobilization' (Flam 2001). Yet the EU effect is not simply direct and 'from above', in terms of acquired legitimacy and legislative agenda. It is also, and possibly primarily, an indirect effect through the promotion of transnational socialization. Chapter 4 mentioned reports of homosexual Polish migrants finding public space in London: these reports are not local, but on the Internet, and they find echoes in Poland. More specifically, the homosexual movement is particularly transnational and demonstrations in the new member states attract militants and political figures from the West. Transnational links also involve on these issues trade unions: Polish union OPZZ and the British Confederation TUC started a program of co-operation in 2008, which specifically included GLBT (Gay, Lesbian, Bisexual, and Transgender) issues. The OPZZ officer responsible for these policies was assigned to the UK, to combine protection of Polish migrant workers with the development of new union practices for sexual minorities.

CONCLUSION

If one looks hard, it is possible to detect occurrences of social protest in the new member states following EU enlargement. For instance, in her book on Poland, Hardy (2009) mentions a number of Polish leftist, feminist, and labor movements, to suggest that the new form of capitalism is creating its own gravediggers, or at least that path dependency can be broken by agency. But while these phenomena demonstrate at least the possibility of social mobilization under post-communist conditions, they should not be exaggerated. It is actually telling that the protagonist himself of a development that Hardy finds promising (Stefan Zgliczyski, the publisher of the Polish edition of *Le Monde Diplomatique*), does not share her optimism, and in a joint interview dismisses Hardy's attention to new Polish social movements with a laconic 'there seems not to be the merest hint of this' (Phillips 2010).

In this chapter I have reviewed the social movement literature on the new member states, applying sensitivity to the specificities of post-communist social protest, which have largely kept it under the radars of western observers. Still, even with adapted radars there is relatively little to report, most social movements remaining in the field of subjectivity and minority civil rights, or on local issues. It is noticeable that academic journals on social movements (e.g. Social Movement Studies) have published virtually nothing on these countries in the last decade. The weakness of social protest in the new member states is conspicuous in comparative perspective, both with Western Europe and with other emerging economies. In 2009–2010, the contrast between the large and continuous street protests of Athens and the few timid ones in Riga is striking because the social costs of the crisis have actually been heavier on Latvia than on Greece: but the two societies have reacted differently. More protest was recorded in Lithuania (Woolfson 2010), but even there it was short-lived. Southern European democratization in the 1970s and 1980s was—if not without major flaws—more inclusive and less technocratic than in the 1990s and 2000s. In Latvia, debtors hit by the credit crunch and public sector workers hit by budget cuts made some efforts at organizing, but within a market, business-lobby logic. Market ideology and technocracy have been so prevalent in the economic transition and EU integration that even anger against their effects takes on quite naturally the same forms and language.

The North African revolutions of 2011 are a reminder of how unpredictable social movements can be. Yet so far, in the new member states, 'voice' is generally weak, in spite of visible dissatisfaction. Exits still prevail.

Conclusion

Over nine chapters, the discussion of the labor issues associated with EU enlargement has detected social failures behind the economic successes and thereby demystified the myth of a socially cohesive Europe included in the EU's Lisbon strategy. It has also detected emerging trends in terms of employee voice.

The shallowness of the social EU myth is proven not simply by the 'extra-softness' and even distortion of EU policies, whether 'hard' (Chapter 1) or 'soft' (Chapter 2), or by the opportunistically selective transfer of employment practices by the MNCs that benefit from the free movement of capitals and goods in the enlarged EU (Chapter 3). It is manifest in the fact that millions of new EU citizenship have quit their countries, rather than staying at home enjoying the newly acquired EU status (Chapter 4). And this has gone hand-in-hand with other forms of exit, at the political (Chapter 5) and organizational (Chapter 6) levels. 'Exit' signifies the elevation of opportunistic market behavior as the standard in EU labor markets, and the parallel demise of 'voice' and political and democratic processes to regulate the EU economy.

These findings are qualified, of course. Some EU policies, for instance on equal opportunities, have had positive effects on the new member states. Some form of social dialog has taken place in the new member states, if mostly in the form of concession bargaining over the crisis and with subsequent increased problems of legitimacy. Some isolated MNCs have transferred social practices from the West involving employee participation, and some EWCs have constrained the worst consequences of restructuring. Migration, if massive, is obviously not generalized, and the social and political systems of some countries (Czech Republic, Hungary, and Slovenia) have been more resilient than others in maintaining their workforces loyal. Turnover and organizational commitment emerge but are not so generalized, and while electoral abstention is massive, populism is actually below the levels of some western member states. Still, if individual processes are not necessarily devastating, the combined effect of all of them is quite clear: the new member states are not becoming like the old ones in terms of labor standards, and they present competition threats that destabilize social and political cohesion across the EU, in both East and West. The market has progressed, quite successfully—but by cannibalizing the social capital of European societies. Enlargement has been a prominent part of the attack by the European Commission and the ECJ on the institutions of 'organized capitalism' (Höpner and Schäfer 2007). The resulting 'disembedded' market may not be socially sustainable in the long run.

The third part of the book has raised an important open question: is a countermovement, in terms of re-politicization of labor questions, emerging? An empirically grounded conclusive answer is still premature. Trade union revitalization (Chapter 7) is possible, but not frequent. Idem for transnational labor responses (Chapter 8): they are emerging, whether through the EWCs or on migration but still limited in their effectiveness. There are examples, throughout Western Europe, of migrant organizing, and in Central and Eastern Europe, of employees using the migration threat to claim better conditions: these are examples of workers taking on 'vocal exit' strategies reminiscent of MNCs relocation threats, but overall labor has not risen to the challenge. And other social movements (Chapter 9) are if anything even weaker, although there is an interesting dynamism on issues of individual and minority rights.

The question of a 'voice' reaction can be approached through the 'countermovement' idea of Karl Polanyi (1944), according to which the disembedding and disruptive movement of marketization is followed by the countermovement of social protection and vice versa. Polanyi's framework has been effectively applied to the understanding of post-communist transformation (Bryant and Mokrzycki 1994), EU integration (Caporaso and Tarrow 2008), EU enlargement (Bohle 2009) and the globalization of work (Standing 2009; Webster *et al.* 2008). An important point of Polanyi's framework is that its social protection countermovement is not necessarily of a democratic nature: actually, Polanyi was writing during World War II, and the countermovements he had under his eyes were of a totalitarian kind. This means that even if one accepts Polanyi's interpretation of the 'ineluctable necessity' of a countermovement does not necessarily imply 'voice': it could also involve populist or nationalist responses, and there are examples already in Poland, Hungary, and Slovakia. Just like Marx before him, Polanyi should not be used to make predictions on the immediate future but to understand the underlying and politically undetermined processes. There are however elective similarities between the Polanyi's movements and the 'exit' and 'voice' dichotomy, as suggested by Hirschman's own idea of 'shifting involvements' (Hirschman 1982). Another important qualification is that Polanyi actually did not believe that the market could really be disembedded: the self-adjusting market is seen as a utopia because in any case market implies society. In such framework, the movements are not between embeddedness and disembeddedess but rather between forms of embeddedness. Within the EU, the two opposing movements are those of EU market-making regulations (the huge quantity of them shows how far from the self-adjusting utopia the single market is) and social protection, whether transnational or national.

Where and how can a European countermovement emerge? Caporaso and Tarrow (2008) perceive in ECJ rulings a countermovement function in the EU. This appears strikingly misplaced. Their paper was written in 2007 and does not cover the effects of the enlargement. Had they waited until December of that year, with the Laval and Viking rulings, they would have had to revise their argument. Even if those judicial rulings may be seen as going in the direction of harmonizing labor law across Europe, it is in the direction of negative harmonization. Rarely a judicial decision has so violently tried to tear up economic freedom from local social ties (such as Swedish collective bargaining or Finnish right of industrial action). If the ECJ had been known to deliver socially progressive rulings, it was largely on issues in which these were consistent with the overarching idea of liberalization: non-discrimination and free movement of workers. It was not in the direction of social protection. Bohle (2009) is more convincing in arguing than nowadays, with a weakened industrial working class, a countermovement is more likely to occur in a spontaneous, possibly individualized, and informal way, rather than in an organized one.

The specific contribution of this book lies in the connection between 'exit' and 'voice', and between them and the Polanyi's pendulum. To understand 'voice' we need to understand 'exit'. In Central Eastern Europe, 'exit', in both the forms of migration and turnover, has become a social problem, proving that a liberalized labor market is an impossibility. In particular, the new employment regimes, combining high flexibility with poor right of voice for employees, imposed by MNCs emerge as unstable (Chapters 3, 6, and 7). In spite of initial successes, they tend to produce protest and resistance, whether informally or through union organizing attempts, which look like turning points of a 'counter-movement' nature—exemplified by cases when foreign managers are replaced by local, 'embedded' managers, with whom employees can at least hope to start a dialog. American investors, in particular, fail to fully transfer important elements of their 'contract' approach, in particular some flexible practices and unilateral management, and are forced to respect some local conventions. Their solution of using union-replacing direct participation mechanisms tends to be short-lived. Even if employers are not interested in social compromise at the macro level, in manufacturing they do need worker active cooperation (Bohle and Greskovits 2006), given that in some manufacturing sectors of Central Europe the skill and technology content is already higher than in many Western European countries (Pilat *et al.* 2006).

In the new member states pure 'contract' systems appear then to be as unstable as ever, and to meet resistance, which translates into management problems for companies requiring high world standards—and more loyalty and productivity than 'exit' can produce. In the same way, labor shortages and economic crisis have forced national governments to offer some social responses in the last few years. Yet this countermovement is still isolated and does not extend much beyond the gates of companies requiring high-quality employee involvement in their labor process. Employers still do not search for labor involvement, unless forced by 'beneficial constraints'. According to the European Working Conditions Survey, in the new member states, as compared to the EU average, paid training is rarer, functional flexibility (in Streeck's terms, a feature of 'status' opposed to the numerical flexibility of 'contract') is lower, and employees have less autonomy, even if consultation levels appear to be the same (Parent-Thirion *et al.* 2007)—but will 'consultation' mean the same?

An extension of social compromises outside the 'privileged' workplaces would require more social and cultural driving forces, as the economic ones are weak. The new member states societies are in a doubly ambiguous position, which makes defining such forces difficult: with a flourishing manufacturing sector, but already dominated by the service sector and therefore 'post-industrial'; peripheral and post-communist, but part of the European Union. Silver's (2003) thesis that, with globalization, labor movements may follow the industrial working classes towards newly industrialized countries, does not fit precisely with the new member states, which are not, technically, newly industrialized countries. Yet her second idea, that labor movements can shift from assertive, economic 'Marx-type' ones to socially defensive 'Polanyi' ones may be relevant and suggests that outside those 'privileged' workplaces that may afford 'Marx-type' labor movements, at least 'Polanyi-type' movements may emerge. Chapter 9 has discussed the occurrence and further possibilities of such reactions in defense of local communities disrupted by market forces.

The trends are not yet definite and their understanding calls for a better conceptualization of the relationship between voice and exit. How do these strategies change over time? Hirschman himself addressed the issue of the 'shifting involvements' in private and public concerns (Hirschman 1982). He developed the 'rebound effect of disappointment' concept to explain choices, which are different from the continuous utility curves theorized by classic economists. Both the pursuit of private concerns (manifest in individual 'exit') and that of public concerns (manifest in collective 'voice') are shown to be inherently unsatisfactory in the long term, and therefore, the more they are pursued, the more they accumulate dissatisfaction, which over time, will push to the opposite involvement with symmetric strength. Hirschman's concepts and examples allow formulating a theoretical relationship between voice and exit. At a given moment in time, the two options are alternative (although their combined intensity is not fixed: it will depend on the amount of discontent and of 'labor problems', and on the available options), which confirms Piore's (1979) interpretation of emigration as a political 'safety valve' that reduces protest and displaces social problems. However, in a dynamic perspective, they are complementary or mutually re-enforcing: strong exit at a given moment will lead to strong voice at a later stage (or vice versa, in the case of thriving 'voice' being obstructed, e.g. following revolution-type periods such as Hungary 1956, Czechoslovakia 1968, and Poland 1968 or 1980). Emigration itself may, with time, foster 'voice': by exposing population to foreign standards, it can generate more political aspirations (Piore 1979, 128).

Hirschman provided a graphic example on the fall of communism: while under the GDR regime, neither voice nor exit were possible; in 1989 it was massive 'exit' in the summer (through escapes to the West via Hungary) that led to massive 'voice' in the anti-regime demonstrations of the autumn (Hirschman 1993). An even clearer illustration was provided by the North African revolutions of 2011, which followed the draconian tightening of the opportunities to migrate to Southern Europe: the closure of the 'safety valve' prepared the atmosphere for the explosion of 'voice'.

While social sciences do not have the capacity to predict how long one should wait for a 'shift' in involvement, it is possible to express the factors behind it. According to Hirschman, the shift in public concerns will not stem, rationally, from a cost-benefit analysis at a given moment. It will rather originate in the moment when expectations will be disappointed, that is, when they will have grown to an unsustainable level, which is bound to decline, even if the returns of that option are still positive, or even if they had been negative all along. Crouch (1995) has offered a reformulation and application to industrial relations that tries to avoid the excessively mechanistic image of Hirschman's (and Polanyi's) pendulum: voice flourishes when exit opportunities are 'sticky', that is, less viable, not when they are absent, and vice versa, exit can become popular if existing voice becomes 'sticky' (e.g. bureaucratized).

Historically, a number of social scientists have noticed that voice emerges in a cyclical way. Some have tried to explain this from a structural-economic perspective, relating to long-term economic cycles (Kelly 1998). Other social scientists have attempted an endogenous explanation, whereby one wave explains the emergence of a counter-wave, starting from Polanyi's own study of the sequence between social paternalism and commodification (Polanyi 1944), and arriving to Schmitter and his 'Corporatist Sisyphus' (Grote and Schmitter 1997).

The main historical example Hirschman refers to is the unexpected wave of social movements in 1968, after a long period of individualization and economic growth. Can we compare the Central Europe of 2011 to the Western Europe of 1968? A long period of fast economic growth and high social mobility has occurred in both situations. The opportunities for the new generation are more limited than for the previous one experiencing the postwar reconstruction or the emergence of capitalism. At the same time, 'exit' options become fewer. In the 1960s, large migration waves were coming to an end, and workers realized, in France or Northern Italy, they had no further horizons than improving the situation they were in. In today's new member states, one can expect the informal sector to shrink through modernization and the attractiveness of migration to decline because of the narrowing of the East-West wage gap, the economic crisis, and the realization that migrants' careers are subject to barriers and segregation. Populism also is historically short-lived. All this is making exit more 'sticky', in Crouch's terms. The disappointment with exit may therefore lead to the shift towards voice.

Additionally, this Hirschman-based interpretation converges, in this case, with Kelly's one on 'transition periods' between economic upswings and downswings as those leading to mobilization waves (Kelly 1998). However, this also sheds some doubts on the mechanical aspects of Hirschman's and Polanyi's pendulum, in light of the financial crisis that started in 2008. According to Kelly, labor activism increases during the transition between growth and decline, but a condition for this to happen is that such transition period is long enough: you do not create trade unions and militancy overnight. But while in the late 1960s that so fascinated Hirschman, this transition away from fast growth was slow and gradual, the shift from economic euphoria to crisis in 2008–2009 occurred nearly overnight in the new member states, especially in the Baltics and Romania. So the emerging 'voices' detected in 2007–2008 might have been silenced early on, by the returning fear of unemployment.

Beside structural and economic approaches, which unavoidably tend to fall into determinism, it is also possible to approach these 'oscillations' from a micro, interpretative or phenomenological perspective, through the ideas of 'alternation' and the example of conversion (Berger and Luckmann 1967). I had tested such an interpretative approach on the opposite case of the 'privatization' of working-class consciousness at the end of the communist regime (Meardi 2000), but a conversion in the opposite direction is also possible. Within a constructivist approach, micro-level actor interpretation and structural analysis do not contradict each other, but rather complement each other, preventing the opposite risks of structural determinism and culturalism. In this perspective, the declining self-assuredness of managers and the increasing self-awareness and reflexivity of migrants may have more effects on social trends than mere economics.

Recent global developments confirm this. Only 10 years ago, Latin America was seen as a model of neo-liberalism. The main countries were ruled by likes of Fujimori, Menem, and Cardoso. The political Left and organized labor appeared in definitive disarray. Bolivia and Chile were the best examples of World Bank's policies implementation. None seems interested in politics—workers who wanted to improve their lot were better advised to migrate towards the North or engage in the informal economy. But in a relatively short time, following the Argentinean and other shocks, Latin America has nearly entirely shifted to the Left (whether radical or moderate), and the continent now presents the most innovative forms of social organization and protection, such as for a right to basic income (Standing 2009; Fraile 2009). Argentina's experience is particularly telling. While in the 1990s neo-liberal, deregulated labor markets under the 'Washington consensus' dictate had produced mass unemployment, democratic re-regulation in the 2000s reduced it: a clear victory of the logic of the polity over the logic of the market. In 2011, it has been the round of North Africa to repudiate regimes that had been 'best followers' of American recommendations (Tunisia and Egypt) but had actually promoted informality, oligarchy, and emigration. Both the Latin American and the North African cases prove that rather a sudden countermovement is possible and free-market enthusiasm is temporary.

One should not make the mistake of interpreting Hirschman's oscillation as repetition, just as one should not conceive industrial relations only in their Western European classic form. Nor can Polanyi be used to make concrete predictions, as the emerging field of global labor studies is realizing (Burawoy 2010). The new member states will never 'ape' Western European, Latin American, or North African predecessors. Unlike them, they are ageing societies, with less space for major youth movements. Yet the inherent limits of the 'exit' strategies described in the second part of the book, combined with the irregular blossoming of 'voice' listed in the third part, point to the fact that the social regulation of labor problems, and therefore industrial relations, is going to be an issue in the new member states.

One final factor makes the situation of the enlarged EU unprecedented, though. Cross-border contamination is easier than in the above-mentioned cases of Latin America, North Africa, or 1968, as discussed in Chapter 8. European Works Councils have proved to have the potential for such contamination between East and West at the company level, even if they cover only relatively few workers. Migrants are now more temporary and cosmopolitan, and their work experiences at home and abroad contaminate at the individual level. Some cooperation even appears at the political level, such as in the successful joint campaign by European and Global Union Federations against the Bolkestein and the Ports Directives.

Seven years after EU enlargement, industrial relations developments in the new member states challenge frequent assumptions. First, they challenge the idea that the EU institutionally exerts a positive role in lifting the bottom floor of social rights: the current EU clearly does not and socially progressive initiatives are more likely to come from EU opponents. The failed export of the 'European Social Model' through top-down institutional means suggests that trade unions would be reckless if they relied on the EU for their own protection. The socio-economic path followed by Central Eastern Europe during the whole accession period demonstrates that the current EU is, in the first place, a deregulatory project, whose social regulations are so soft that they can easily be bent in the opposite direction. Given the current political equilibrium in the European Commission and in most EU governments, this is not likely to change in the short term. Support for the EU (as it has happened on the EMU) may alienate unions' constituencies: success and advances are more likely with campaigns against the current

EU policies, as against the Bolkestein Directive or through influence on EU-skeptic but pro-labor governments like in Slovakia in 2006–2010. Nor can trade unions rely on employers' willingness to upgrade employment practices. This happens rarely even within large, mature multinational companies. Organizing, grassroot creative (even informal) mobilization, extension procedures, and political campaigns are among the tools that have been required to counter such unwillingness.

Second, the developments presented in this book challenge the idea of an immutable path dependency and perpetuation of post-communist legacies: the situation is actually dynamic, as it is in other post-communist countries more to the East (Pringle and Clarke 2010). Union organizing in MNCs is possible even in the difficult conditions of Greenfield sites in the new member states. Moreover, migrants from Central Eastern Europe are far from being unorganizable in the host countries, and mutual understanding between unions from the East and the West of the EU is not as difficult as I had myself feared before 2004. The public debt crisis of 2010 in the EU periphery (Greece, Ireland, Portugal, but also some new member states), by leading to a reflection on a need for EU-wide fiscal policy and co-ordinated income policies, is an opportunity for a revival of political initiative.

In the new member states, 'industrial relations' still does not have clear translations into local languages and its study is still rather underdeveloped, despite some isolated excellent cases. In international conferences on industrial relations or sociology of work the new member states are still very underrepresented, which is a side effect of the overall marginalization of labor in the post-communist transition and in EU accession. However, this book has argued that such neglect contrasts with the magnitude of workplace transformation and of its economic and political implications.

If taken in a narrow sense, industrial relations may look obsolete, as trade union density remains low. However, taken in the broader sense of 'an institutional infrastructure that humanizes, stabilizes, professionalizes, democratizes and balances' the labor market (Kaufman 2007, 33), industrial relations actually finds an unexpected confirmation of its relevance. The new member states show that even in the most favorable political conditions—governments committed to extreme neo-liberalism and very weak associations—employment cannot be ruled by pure market principles: 'exit' strategies turn into labor problems (informality, insecurity, inequality, populism, and migration), which, in turn, call for 'voice' solutions. If the EU social dimension emerges as largely fictitious, it is better to remember, with Polanyi, that labor itself is a fictitious commodity.

Annex

Table A.1 Case Study Details

Name/ code	Year	Sector	Country of site	Country of origin	Number of employees	Number of interviews	Mode of entry
Fiat	1995–1999, 2004	Auto	PL	Italy	12,000	32	Brownfield
Lucchini	1996–1999	Steel	PL	Italy	2,500	14	Brownfield
FR1	2001	Machinery	PL	France	2,000	3	Brownfield
FR2	2001	Electronics	PL	France	4,500	3	Brownfield
DK	2001	Metal	PL	Denmark	1,000	4	Brownfield
DE	2001	Construction	PL	Germany	500	3	Brownfield
US1	2001	Energy	PL	US	500	4	Brownfield
US2	2001	Consumer products	PL	US	200	3	Brownfield
Gp1	2004–2005	Auto	PL	Germany	1,000	12	Greenfield
Gp2	2004	Auto	PL	Germany	600	17	Brownfield
Ap1	2004	Auto	PL	US	500	16	Brownfield
Ap2*	2004	Auto	PL	US	500	7	Greenfield
Gh1*	2004–2005	Auto	H	Germany	5,000	10	Greenfield
Gh2*	2004–2005	Auto	H	Germany	900	10	Greenfield
Ah1	2004–2005	Auto	H	US	2,500	15	Brownfield

(continued)

Table A.1   (continued)

Name/ code	Year	Sector	Country of site	Country of origin	Number of employees	Number of inter- views	Mode of entry
Ah2	2004– 2005	Auto	H	US	300	6	Greenfield
Gs*	2004	Auto	SI	Germany	700	6	Brownfield
As	2004	Auto	SI	US	900	8	Brownfield
Ms1*	2004	Auto	SI	Germany	900	9	Brownfield
Ms2	2004	Auto	SI	UK	1,200	7	Brownfield
D-INS1*	2007– 2008	Insurance	CZ	Germany	100	7	Greenfield
D-INS2*	2007	Insurance	CZ	Germany	700	5	Greenfield
D-CAR1*	2007	Auto	CZ	Germany	1,500	6	green/ brown
D-CAR2*	2007	Auto	CZ	Germany	300	7	Greenfield
A-BAN1*	2007– 2008	Bank	CZ	Austria	1,600	5	green/ brown
A-BAN2*	2008	Bank	CZ	Austria	200	5	Greenfield
A-CAR1*	2007	Auto	CZ	Austria	200	5	Greenfield
A-CAR2*	2007	Auto	CZ	Austria	600	5	Greenfield
US-BAN	2007– 2008	Bank	CZ	US	2,000	3	Brownfield
UK-FIN	2007– 2008	Finance	CZ	UK	600	4	Greenfield
UK-CAR	2008	Auto	CZ	UK	600	7	Brownfield
US-CAR	2007	Auto	CZ	US	700	4	Brownfield

*Case studies entirely conducted by research colleagues.

Notes

NOTES TO THE INTRODUCTION

1. By new member states, I refer to the post-communist countries that joined the EU in 2004 (Czech Republic, Estonia, Hungary, Latvia, Lithuania, Poland, Slovakia, and Slovenia) and 2007 (Bulgaria and Romania). The region of the new member states will be called Central Eastern Europe in this book. Even though countries such as Poland, Czech Republic, Hungary, and Slovenia are 'Central European' in all regards (geographic, historical, and cultural), it is necessary to distinguish them, in geopolitical terms, from Western Central European countries such as Germany and Austria. Occasionally, I will also use the technocratic terms EU15 (old member states), A10, A8, and A2 (respectively, the 10 'accession' countries, the eight of 2004, and the two of 2007).

NOTES TO CHAPTER 1

1. Workers, instead, appear to evaluate the Europeanization of Polish labor law positively, according to the 'Working Poles' survey of 2007 (Męcina 2009a, 265). However, this opinion is probably superficial and influenced by the good connotations, with which EU law has been constantly presented in public debates. When a more precise question is asked, only a minority of Polish employees believe that workers have obtained more rights or better pay (Czarzasty 2009, 383).
2. As Woolfson discusses, this may be partly due to low economic activity, and therefore fewer accidents, in 1998 in some new member states due to the Russian crisis; however, a similar overall trend exists if we take a longer (from 1994) or shorter (from 1999) time perspective.

NOTES TO CHAPTER 2

1. This section is based on a paper originally written with Juliusz Gardawski (Gardawski and Meardi 2010).

NOTES TO CHAPTER 3

1. This mixed effect—improvement of the work environment and worsening of organization—was already visible during my fieldwork in Poland in the mid-1990s at Fiat and Danone. A striking illustration came in 1995 from an

employee of the Fiat factory in Bielsko-Biała, privatized three years earlier: 'the new owners made major investments and improvements; for instance they redid restrooms and changing rooms, and they are now at luxury, western standards, never seen before; but before, we had the time to go there' (auhtor's interview, 1995).

NOTES TO CHAPTER 4

1. The data of the WRS include many workers who had arrived before 2004 or who have worked in the UK only for a short term and may have returned to their home countries but do not include self-employed nor informal employment (Home Office 2009). The immigration minister's forecast of 13,000 referred only to 'settling' immigrants and therefore is not comparable with the WRS data, but the gap between the two figures does not merely indicate that the government failed to foresee the amount of short-term mobility. According to WRS data, one quarter of the newly arrived intends to stay for a long term, but many do not know how long they will remain. The Migration Policy Institute estimates that one-third of workers from the new member states do not register under the WRS and that more than a half has left the country: this amounts to an estimate of a total of 1.5 million workers coming to the UK from the new member states until the third quarter of 2009, of whom 700,000 would have remained in the country (Sumption and Somerville 2010).
2. Flows do not only depend on regulations but also on other factors such as proximity, labor market opportunities, networks, and cultural/language proximity. The latter two factors would explain the proportionally much higher inflows in Ireland, and much lower in Sweden, despite these two countries having opened their borders at the same time as the UK.
3. Estimates are based on Labor Force Survey data, which notoriously underestimate the number of foreigners.
4. In some regards intra-EU migration has resemblances with intra-NAFTA one, despite different regulations. Both cases differ from traditional postcolonial, guestworker, and asylum migrations and tend to lead to exploitative dual labor markets (Favell 2008). Different industrialized countries have developed different migration systems but all seem in search of extremely flexible migrant labor: see for instance the interesting case of the Temporary Foreign Worker Program in Canada (Fudge and McPhail 2009).
5. Data on unions include only the largest unions in the case of the Czech Republic. Data on migration do not include short-term movements and therefore grossly underestimate exit. Data on Slovenia are disputed, and I will return to them in Chapter 7.
6. Labor Force Survey data, which include workers taking their subsequent jobs, suggest however that the total share number of workers from the new member states recruited through agencies has declined between 2005–2006 (26%) and 2007–2008 (16%; Sumption and Somerville 2010).

NOTES TO CHAPTER 5

1. M. Giertych, *Wojna cywilizacji w Europie*, 2007 (http://giertych.pl/pliki/ Wojna%20cywilizacji%20w%20Europie.pdf)
2. In the Hungarian case, the adoption of worst practices went as far as imitating Italy: the right-wing leader Orbán modeled its 2002 campaign on that of Berlusconi the year before, including signing on TV a 'contract' with voters.

3. The developments of 1996–1997 are well analyzed by Ost (2005), who, however, overlooks one minor but significant event that indicates the link between the missed opportunities of the Left and the right-wing, populist turn of labor. In 1996, Solidarity invited to the discussion of its electoral plans all (indeed, very numerous) political parties that had their roots in the Solidarity movement, including the left-wing Labor Union (UP), which, after having obtained 7% in the previous elections, was enjoying growing popularity, and whose program was probably the closest to unionists' orientations. The UP declined the invitation, arguing that it had nothing to share with other, clearly right-wing forces that had been invited. It is impossible to know what would have happened, had the UP agreed to take part in the discussion, but the missed encounter between the Left and trade union had momentous consequences: Solidarity fell into the hands of exclusively conservative allied (at the time, all individually weaker than the UP) and turned to the Right, while UP lost social support, very narrowly missed the 5% threshold to stay in parliament the year after, and slowly disappeared from the main political scene.

4. August 80 promoted the creation of a left-wing coalition called the Polish Labor Party, with which Podrzycki run for presidency in 2005—but he was dramatically killed in an unexplained road accident two days before voting day.

NOTES TO CHAPTER 6

1. It is important to note that organizational misbehavior is not a prerogative of employees but of managers as well.
2. Hungary is atypical in this regard: higher past mobility but lower expected mobility than in the other Visegrád countries.
3. See the Annex for details on the case studies and their coding.

NOTES TO CHAPTER 7

1. For a full list, see Meardi (2007).
2. See the Annex for details of the case studies.

NOTES TO CHAPTER 8

1. For details on the case studies, see the Annex.
2. In a parallel case in France (another country that initially had transitional limits on migration), ZREW's Solidarity and Alstom's CGT co-operated in 2005–2006 to campaign against bad treatment of Polish workers in the French site ZREW. The French court condemned ZREW to respect French collective agreements.

NOTES TO CHAPTER 9

1. As a doctoral researcher in Touraine's research center (Centre d'Analyse et d'Intervention Sociologiques) CADIS in 1994–1996, I was personally involved in both the hopes and disillusions of that period.

Bibliography

Ackroyd, Stephen and Thompson, Paul (1999) *Organizational Misbehaviour*. London: Sage.

Aksamit, Bożena (2007) 'Bunt kelnerek nad morzem', *Gazeta Wyborcza*, 10th July.

Allen, Matthew and Tüselmann, Heinz-Josef (2009) 'All Powerful Voice? The Need to Include "Exit", "Loyalty" and "Neglect" in Empirical Studies too', *Employee Relations*, 31, 5, 538–552.

Almond, Phil and Ferner, Anthony (eds) (2006) *American Multinationals in Europe: Managing Employment Relations Across National Borders*. Oxford: Oxford University Press.

Altvater, Elmar and Mahnkopf, Birgit (1997) 'The World Market Unbound', *Review of International Political Economy*, 4, 3, 448–471.

Anacik, Agata, Krupink, Seweryn, Otręba, Agnieszka, Skrzyńska, Joanna, Szklarczyk, Dariusz, and Uhi, Hanna (2009) *Diagnoza stanu rozwoju sektorowego dialogu społecznego w skali ogólnopolskiej*. Krakow: Wyższa Szkoła Europejska im. ks. Józefa Tischnera.

Anderson, Bridget, Clark, Nick, and Parutis, Violetta (2007) *New EU Members? Migrant Workers' Challenges and Opportunities to UK Trades Unions: A Polish and Lithuanian Case Study*. London: Trades Union Congress (http://www.tuc.org.uk/extras/migrantchallenges.pdf).

Anner, Mark, Greer, Ian, Hauptmeier, Marco, Lillie, Nathan, and Winchester, Nicholas (2006) 'The Industrial Determinants of Transnational Solidarity: Global Interunion Politics in Three Sectors', *European Journal of Industrial Relations*, 12, 1, 7–27.

Arrowsmith, James (2006) *Temporary Agency Work in an Enlarged European Union*. Dublin: European Foundation for the Improvement of Working and Living Conditions.

Ashiagbor, Diamond (2009) 'Collective Labor Rights and the European Social Model', *Law and Ethics of Human Rights*, 3, 2, 222–266.

Avdagic, Sabina (2005) 'State-Labor Relations in East-Central Europe: Explaining Variations in Union Effectiveness', *Socio-Economic Review* 3, 25–53.

Avdagic, Sabina (2006) *One Path or Several? Understanding the Varied Enactment of Tripartism in New European Capitalisms*. Cologne: MPIfG Discussion Paper 06/5.

Avdeyeva, Olga (2009) 'Enlarging the Club: When Do Candidate States Enforce Gender Equality Laws?', *Comparative European Politics*, 7, 1, 158–177.

Baccaro, Lucio and Lim, Sang-Hoon (2007) 'Social Pacts as Coalitions of the Weak and Moderate: Ireland, Italy and South Korea in Comparative Perspective', *European Journal of Industrial Relations* 13, 1, 27–46.

Bacon, David (2004) The Children of NAFTA. Labor Wars on the U.S./Mexico Border. Los Angeles: University of California Press.

Bacon, Nick and Blyton, Paul (1996) 'Re-Casting the Politics of Steel in Europe: The Impact on Trade Unions', West European Politics, 19, 4, 770–786.

Bafoil, François (2009) Central and Eastern Europe. Europeanization and Social Change. London: Palgrave.

Barbier, Jean-Claude (2008) La Longue Marche de l'Europe Sociale. Paris: Presses Universitaires de France.

Barnard, Catherine (2009) '"British Jobs for British Workers": The Lindsey Oil Refinery Dispute and the Future of Local Labour Clauses in an Integrated EU Market', Industrial Law Journal 38, 3, 245–277.

Barrell, Ray, Fitzgerald, John, and Riley, Rebecca (2007) EU Enlargement and Migration. Assessing the Macroeconomic Impact. London: NIESR Discussion Paper 292.

Barrer, Ray and Holland, Dawn (2000) 'Foreign Direct Investment and Enterprise Restructuring in Central Europe', Economics of Transition, 8, 2, 477–504.

Bartelmann Stiftung (2003) Bartelmann Transformation Index (http://www.bertelsmann-transformation-index.de/fileadmin/pdf/BERT_Tabelle_ENGL.pdf).

Baxandall, Phineas (2004) Constructing Unemployment. The Politics of Joblessness in East and West. Aldershot: Ashgate.

Bayón, María Cristina (2009) 'Persistence of an Exclusionary Model: Inequality and Segmentation in Mexican Society', International Labour Review, 148, 3, 301–315.

Behrens, Martin (2004) 'New Forms of Employers' Collective Interest Representation', Industrielle Beziehungen, 11, 77–91.

Bélanger, Jacques, Edwards, Paul, and Haiven, Larry (1994) 'Globalisation, National Systems and the Future of Workplace Industrial Relations'. In Workplace Industrial Relations and the Global Challenge, edited by Jacques Bélanger, Paul Edwards, and Larry Haiven, 275–284. Ithaca: ILR Press.

Bennett, James and Kaufmann, Bruce (eds) (2007) What Do Unions Do? A Twenty-Year Perspective. New Brunswick: Transaction.

Bercusson, Brian (2007) 'The Trade Union Movement and the European Union: Judgment Day', European Law Journal, 13, 3, 279–308.

Berger, Peter and Luckmann, Thomas (1967) The Social Construction of Reality. London: Penguin.

Blanchflower, David and Lawton, Helen (2009) 'The Impact of the Expansion of the EU on the British Labor Market'. In EU Labor Markets after Post-Enlargement Migration, edited by Martin Kahanec and Klaus Zimmermann, 181–218. Berlin: Springer.

Blanchflower, David and Shadforth, Chris (2009) 'Fear, Unemployment and Migration', Economic Journal, 119, 136–182.

Blanpain, Roger and Świątkowski, Andrzej (eds) (2009) The Laval and Viking Cases. Alphen aan den Rijn: Kluwer Law International.

Blažiene, Inga (2007) Unions Protest over Low Pay and Plan to Extend Working Hours. (http://www.eurofound.europa.eu/eiro/2006/11/articles/lt0611029i.htm).

Bluhm, Katharina (2001) 'Exporting or Abandoning the German Model? Labor Policies of German Manufacturing Firms in Central Europe', European Journal of Industrial Relations, 7, 2, 153–173.

Bluhm, Katharina (2006) 'Auflösung des Liberalisierungsdilemmas—Arbeitsbeziehungen Mittelosteuropas im Kontext des EU-Beitritts', Berliner Journal für Soziologie, 16, 2, 171–186.

Bluhm, Katharina (2007) Experimentierfeld Ostmitteleuropa? Deutsche Unternehmen in Polen und der Tschechischen Republik. Wiesbaden: VS-Verlag.

Boeri, Tito and Brücker, Herbert (2001) *Eastern Enlargement and EU-Labour Markets: Perceptions, Challenges and Opportunities.* Bonn: IZA Discussion Paper 256.
Boeri, Tito and Brücker, Herbert (2005) *Migration, Co-ordination Failures and EU Enlargement.* Bonn: IZA Discussion Paper 1600.
Bohle, Dorothee (2009) 'Race to the Bottom? Transnational Companies and Reinforced Competition in the Enlarged European Union'. In *Contradictions and Limits of Neoliberal European Governance*, edited by Bastiaan Van Apeldoorn, Jan Drahokoupil and Laura Horn, 143–162. Basingstoke: Palgrave.
Bohle, D. (2010) 'Countries in Distress: Transformation, Transnationalization, and Crisis in Hungary and Latvia', *Emecon: Employment and Economy in Central and Eastern Europe*, 1 (http://www.emecon.eu/fileadmin/articles/1_2010/emecon%201_2010%20Bohle.pdf).
Bohle, Dorothee and Greskovits, Béla (2006) 'Capitalism without Compromise: Strong Business and Weak Labor in Eastern Europe's New Transnational Industries', *Studies in Comparative International Development*, 41, 1, 3–25.
Bohle, Dorothee and Greskovits, Béla (2007) 'Neoliberalism, Embedded Neoliberalism and Neocorporatism: Towards Transnational Capitalism in Central-Eastern Europe', *West European Politics*, 30, 3, 443–466.
Bohle, Dorothee and Greskovits, Béla (2010) 'Slovakia and Hungary: Successful and Failed Euro Entry without Social Pacts'. In *After the Euro and the Enlargement: Social Pacts in the European Union*, edited by Philippe Pochet, Maarten Keune, and David Natali, 345–370. Brussels: European Trade Union Institute.
Brenke, Karl, Yuksel, Mutlu, and Zimmermann, Klaus (2009) 'EU Enlargement under Continued Mobility Restrictions: Consequences for the German Labor Market'. In *EU Labor Markets After Post-Enlargement Migration*, edited by Martin Kahanec and Klaus Zimmermann, 111–130. Berlin: Springer.
Brewster, Chris, Wood, Geoff, Crouchner, Richard, and Brookes, Michael (2007) 'Are Works Councils and Joint Consultative Committees a Threat to Trade Unions? A Comparative Analysis', *Economic and Industrial Democracy*, 28, 1, 49–77.
Brücker, Herbert, Baas, Timo, Bertoli, Simone, and Hauptmann, Andreas (2009) *Labour Mobility within the EU in the Context of Enlargement and the Functioning of the Transitional Arrangements.* Nürnberg: European Integration Consortium.
Bruszt, Laszló and Stark, David (2003) 'Who Counts? Supranational Norms and Societal Needs', *East European Politics and Societies*, 17, 1, 74–82.
Bryant, Christopher and Mokrzycki, Edmund (eds) (1994) *The New Great Transformation? Change and Continuity in East-Central Europe.* London: Routledge.
Burawoy, Michael (2008) 'The Public Turn. From Labor Process to Labor Movement', *Work and Occupations*, 35, 4, 371–387.
Burawoy, Michael (2009a) *The Extended Case Method: Four Countries, Four Decades, Four Great Transformations, and One Theoretical Tradition.* Los Angeles: University of California Press.
Burawoy, Michael (2009b) 'Global Turn. Lessons from Southern Labor Scholars and Their Labor Movements', *Work and Occupations*, 36, 2, 87–95.
Burawoy, Michael (2010) 'From Polanyi to Pollyanna: The False Optimism of Global Labor Studies', *Global Labour Journal*, 1, 2, 301–313.
Burawoy, Michael and Lukacs, János (1985) 'Mythologies of Work: A Comparison of Firms in State Socialism and Advanced Capitalism', *American Sociological Review*, 50, 6, 723–737.
Burchell, Brendan, Cartron, Damien, Csizmadia, Péter, Delcampe, Stanislas, Gollac, Michel, Illéssy, Miklós, Lorenz, Edward, Makó, Csaba, O'Brien,

Catherine, and Valeyre, Antoine (2009) *Working Conditions in the European Union: Working Time and Work Intensity*. Dublin: European Foundation for the Improvement of Working and Living Conditions.

Calmfors, Lars and Driffill, John (1988) 'Bargaining Structure, Corporatism and Macroeconomic Performance', *Economic Policies* 6, 13–61.

Campbell, Duncan (2006) 'Poles are bringing solidarity back into fashion in Britain', *The Guardian*, 6th December.

Caporaso, James and Tarrow, Sydney (2008) *Polanyi in Brussels: European Institutions and the Embedding of Markets in Society*. RECON Online Working Paper 2008/01 (www.reconproject.eu/projectweb/portalproject/RECONWorkingPapers.html).

Carley, Mark (2009) *Trade Union Membership 2003–2008*. (http://www.eurofound.europa.eu/eiro/studies/tn0904019s/tn0904019s.htm).

Carley, Mark and Hall, Mark (2008) *Impact of the Information and Consultation Directive on Industrial Relations*. (http://www.eurofound.europa.eu/eiro/studies/tn0710029s/tn0710029s.htm).

Carpenter, Mick and Jefferys, Steve (2000) *Management, Work and Welfare in Western Europe: A Historical and Contemporary Analysis*. Cheltenham: Elgar.

Casey, Bernard and Gold, Michael (2005) 'Peer Review of Labour Market Policies in the European Union: What Can Countries Really Learn from One Another?' *Journal of European Public Policy*, 12, 1, 23–43.

Castells, Manuel and Henderson, Jeffrey (1987) 'Techno-economic Restructuring, Socio-political Processes and Spatial Transformation: A Global Perspective'. In *Global Restructuring and Territorial Development*, edited by Jeffrey Henderson and Manuel Castells, 1–17. London: Sage.

Castles, Stephen and Kosack, Godula (1973) *Immigrant Workers and Class Structure in Western Europe*. Oxford: Oxford University Press.

Cazes, Sandrine and Nesperova, Alena (2001) 'Labour Market Flexibility in the Transition Countries: How Much Is Too Much?', *International Labour Review*, 140, 3, 293–325.

Cazes, Sandrine and Nesperova, Alena (eds) (2007) *Flexicurity: A Relevant Approach in Central and Eastern Europe*. Geneva: ILO.

Central Statistics Office (2009) *Quarterly National Household Survey*. Dublin: Cantral Statistics Office.

Cerami, Alfio (2009) *Social Policy in Central and Eastern Europe*. Berlin: Lit Verlag.

Cerami, Alfio and Vanhuysse, Pieter (eds) (2009) *Post-Communist Welfare Pathways. Theorizing Social Policy Transformations in Central and Eastern Europe*. Basingstoke: Palgrave.

Chaloupek, Günther and Peyrl, Johannes (2009) 'EU Labour Migration: Government and Social Partner Policies in Austria'. In *EU Labour Migration since Enlargement*, edited by Béla Galgóczi, Janine Leschke, and Andrew Watt, 171–184. Aldershot: Ashgate.

Clark, Ken and Drinkwater, Stephen (2008) 'The Labour-Market Performance of Recent Immigrants', *Oxford Review of Economic Policy*, 24, 3, 495–516.

Clarke, Simon (2005) 'From European Union to European Monetary Union: The New Member States and Accession Countries of Central and Eastern Europe in 2004', *Industrial Relations Journal*, 36, 6, 592–612.

Coleman, James (1995) 'Motivation and Opportunity. Understanding the Causes of White-Collar Crime'. In *White Collar Crime. Classic and Contemporary Views*, edited by Gilbert Geis, Robert F. Meier, and Lawrence M. Salinger, 360–381. New York: Free Press.

Confederazione Generale Italiana del Lavoro (CGIL) (2009) *Pagina nera movimento sindacale nella globalizzazione*. Rome: Comunicato stampa, 2nd February. (http://www.cgil.it/UfficioStampa/ComunicatoPrint.aspx?NewsID=1635).

Countouris, Nicola and Horton, Rachel (2009) 'The Temporary Agency Work Directive: Another Broken Promise?', *Industrial Law Journal*, 38, 3, 329–338.

Cremers, Jan (2011) *In Search of Cheap Labour in Europe. Working and Living Conditions of Posted Workers.* Bruxelles: CLR.

Crouch, Colin (1993) *Industrial Relations and European State Traditions.* Oxford: Oxford University Press.

Crouch, Colin (1995) 'Exit or Voice: Two Paradigms for European Industrial Relations after the Keynesian Welfare State', *European Journal of Industrial Relations*, 1, 1, 63–81.

Crouch, Colin (1999) *Social Change in Western Europe.* Oxford: Oxford University Press.

Crouch, Colin (2004) *Postdemocracy.* Cambridge: Polity

Crouch, Colin (2008) 'What Will Follow the Demise of Privatised Keynesianism?', *Political Quarterly*, 79, 476–486.

Crowley, Stephen and Ost, David (eds) (2001) *Workers After Workers States. Labor and Politics in Postcommunist Eastern Europe.* New York: Rowman and Littlefield.

Currie, Samantha (2008) *Migration, Work and Citizenship in the Enlarged European Union.* Aldershot: Ashgate.

Czarzasty, Jan (2009) 'Warunki pracy i kultura organizacyjna'. In *Polacy pracujący a kryzys fordyzmu*, edited by Juliusz Gardawski, 343–417. Warsaw: Scholar.

Czarzasty, Jan (2010) *Stosunki pracy w handlu wielkopowierzchniowym w Polsce.* Warsaw: Szkoła Główna Handlowa.

Czech Republic (2008) *National Reform Programme of the Czech Republic.* (http://ec.europa.eu/archives/growthandjobs_2009/pdf/member-states-2008–2010-reports/czech_republic_nrp_2008_en.pdf).

Dench, Sally, Hartsfield, Jennifer, Hill, Darcy, and Akroyd, Karen (2006) *Employers' Use of Migrant Labour. Summary Report.* London: Home Office.

Długosz, Dagmir (2005) 'System dialogu społecznego w Polsce w latach 2001–2003. Analiza uczestnika', *Polityka Społeczna*, nr 4 and 5.

Doellgast, Virginia and Greer, Ian (2007) 'Vertical Disintegration and the Disorganization of German Industrial Relations', *British Journal of Industrial Relations*, 45, 1, 55–76.

Dołowska, Alicja (2007) 'Droga przez mękę', *Tygodnik Solidarność*, nr 22.

Dølvik, Jan Erik and Visser, Jelle (2009) 'Free Movement, Equal Treatment and Workers' Rights: Can the European Union Solve its Trilemma of Fundamental Principles?', *Industrial Relations Journal*, 40, 6, 491–509.

Donaghey, James and Teague, Paul (2005) 'The Persistence of Social Pacts in Europe', *Industrial Relations Journal*, 36, 6, 478–493.

Donaghey, James and Teague, Paul (2006) 'The Free Movement of Workers and Social Europe: Maintaining the European Ideal', *Industrial Relations Journal*, 37, 6, 652–666.

Donaghey, James, Cullinane, Niall, Dundon, Tony, and Wilkinson, Adrian (2011) 'Reconceptualising Employee Silence: Problems and Prognosis', *Work, Employment and Society*, 25, 1, 51–67.

Dörrenbächer, Christoph (2002) *National Business Systems and the International Transfer of Industrial Models in Multinational Companies.* Berlin: WZB Discussion Paper FS 1 02–102.

Drinkwater, Stephen, Eade John, and Garapich, Michal (2009) 'Poles Apart? EU Enlargement and the Labour Market Outcomes of Immigrants in the UK', *International Migration*, 47, 1, 161–190.

Dundon, Terry, Gonzalez-Perez, Maria-Alejandra, and McDonough, Terrence (2007) 'Bitten by the Celtic Tiger: Immigrant Workers and Industrial Relations in the New "Glocalised" Ireland', *Economic and Industrial Democracy*, 28, 4, 501–522.

Dustmann, Christian, Casanova, Maria, Preston, Ian, Fertig Michael, and Schmidt, Christoph (2003) *The Impact of EU Enlargement on Migration Flows*, Home Office Online Report.

Dustmann, Christian, Frattini, Tommaso, and Preston, Ian (2008) *The Effect of Immigration on the Distribution of Wages*. London: CReAM Discussion Paper No. 03/08 (http://eprints.ucl.ac.uk/14332/1/14332.pdf).

Dyker, David (2004) 'Closing the Productivity Gap between Eastern and Western Europe: The Role of Foreign Direct Investment', *Science and Public Policy*, 31, 4, 279–287.

Eamets, Raul (2009) 'Flexicurity Specificities in Small and Open Transition Economies. The Baltic States'. In *Reconciling Labour Flexibility with Social Cohesion. The Experiences and Specificities of Central and Eastern Europe*, edited by Council of Europe, 103–133. Strasbourg: Council of Europe Publications.

Eamets, Raul and Philips, Kaia (2004) *Working Time Legislation to be Amended*. (http://www.eurofound.europa.eu/eiro/2004/06/feature/ee0406102f.htm).

Ebster-Grosz, Dagmar and Pugh, Derek (1996) *Anglo-German Business Collaboration. Pitfalls and Potentials*. Basingstoke: Macmillan.

European Commission (EC) (2002) *Report of the High Level Group on Industrial Relations and Change in the European Union*. Brussels: EC.

EC (2004) *Industrial Relations in Europe Report*. Brussels: EC.

EC (2006a) *Enlargement, Two Years After: An Economic Evaluation*. Brussels: Occasional Paper 24.

EC (2006b) *Employment in Europe Report 2006*. Brussels: EC.

EC (2006c) *Report on the Functioning of the Transitional Arrangements Set Out in the 2003 Accession Treaty (Period 1 May 2004–30 April 2006)*. Brussels: EC.

EC (2008a) *Industrial Relations in Europe Report*. Brussels: EC.

EC (2008b) *Communication on the Review of the Application of Directive 2002/14/EC in the EU*. Brussels: EC.

EC (2008c) *Employment in Europe Report 2008*. Brussels: EC.

EC (2008d) *Five years of an enlarged EU—Economic achievements and challenges*. Communication. Brussels: EC.

EC (2009) *Employment in Europe Report 2009*. Brussels: EC.

EC (2010) *Eurobarometer 72*. Brussels: EC.

Economist (2009) 'Right or Down', 14th November.

Edwards, Paul and Greasley, Kay (2010) *Absence from Work*. Dublin: European Foundation for the Improvement of Working and Living Conditions.

Ekiert, Grzegorz and Kubik, Jan (2001) *Rebellious Civil Society: Popular Protest and Democratic Consolidation in Poland 1989–1993*. Ann Arbor: University of Michigan Press.

Ellingstad, Marc (1997) 'The Maquiladora Syndrome: Central European Prospects', *Europe-Asia Studies*, 49, 1, 7–21.

Ellis, Evelyn (1998) *EC Sex Equality Law*. Oxford: Oxford University Press.

Equality and Human Rights Commission (2010) *Inquiry into Recruitment and Employment in the Meat and Poultry Processing Sector*. Manchester: EHRC.

Erne, Roland (2008) *European Unions*. Cornell: ILR Press.

Esping-Andersen, Gosta (1990) *The Three World of Welfare Capitalism*. Princeton: Princeton University Press.

Eurofound (2011) *Fifth European Working Conditions Survey—2010* (http://www.eurofound.europa.eu/surveys/ewcs/2010/index.htm).

European Council (2002) *Presidency Conclusions, Barcelona European Council, 15 and 16 March 2002* (http://www.consilium.europa.eu/uedocs/cms_data/docs/pressdata/en/ec/71025.pdf).

European Industrial Relations Observatory (EIRO) (2004) *Individual Labour/ Employment Disputes and the Courts.* (http://www.eurofound.europa.eu/eiro/thematicfeature7.htm).

European Trade Union Confederation (ETUC) (2005) *Towards Free Movement of Workers in an Enlarged European Union.* Resolution of the ETUC Executive Committee (http://www.etuc.org/a/1898).

European Working Conditions Observatory (EWCO) (2008) *Annual Review of Working Conditions in the EU 2007–2008.* Dublin: European Foundation for the Improvement of Working and Living Conditions.

Eurostat (2007) *Labour Cost Database* (http://epp.eurostat.ec.europa.eu/portal/page/portal/labour_market/labour_costs/database).

Eurostat (2009a) *Social Protection Database* (http://epp.eurostat.ec.europa.eu/portal/page/portal/social_protection/data/database)

Eurostat (2009b) *Income and Living Conditions Database* (http://epp.eurostat.ec.europa.eu/portal/page/portal/income_social_inclusion_living_conditions/data/database)

Eurostat (2010) *Employment and Unemployment* (LFS) (http://epp.eurostat.ec.europa.eu/portal/page/portal/employment_unemployment_lfs/data/database).

Evans, Geoffrey (2006) 'The Social Bases of Political Divisions in Post-Communist Eastern Europe', *Annual Review of Sociology*, 32, 245–270.

Eyraud, François and Vaughan-Whitehead, Daniel (eds) (2007) *The Evolving World of Work in the Enlarged EU. Progress and Vulnerability.* Geneva: ILO.

Fábián, Katalin (2009) *Contemporary Women's Movements in Hungary. Globalization, Democracy, and Gender Equality.* Washington: Woodrow Wilson Press.

Falkner, Gerda and Nentwich, Michael (2000) *Enlarging the European Union: The Short-Term Success of Incrementalism and De-Politicization.* Cologne: MPIfG Working Paper 00/4.

Falkner, Gerda and Treib, Oliver (2008) 'Three Worlds of Compliance or Four? The EU-15 Compared to New Member States', *Journal of Common Market Studies*, 46, 2, 293–313.

Falkner, Gerda, Treib, Oliver, Hartlapp, Miriam, and Leiber, Simone (2005) *Complying with Europe: EU Harmonization and Soft Law in the Member States.* Cambridge: Cambridge University Press.

Fanning, Bryan (2009) *New Guests of the Irish Nation.* Dublin: Irish Academic Press.

Favell, Adrian (2008) 'The New Face of East-West Migration in Europe', *Journal of Ethnic and Migration Studies*, 34, 5, 701–716.

Ferner, Anthony and Varul, Matthias (2000) 'Vanguard Subsidiaries and the Diffusion of New Practices: A Case Study of German Multinationals', *British Journal of Industrial Relations*, 5, 3, 286–306.

Ferrazzi, Matteo and Revoltella, Debora (2009) 'Trade and Foreign Direct Investments: The Point of View of Central Eastern European Countries'. In *The EU and the Economies of the Eastern European Enlargement*, edited by Alberto Quadrio Curzio and Marco Fortis, 167–184. Berlin: Physica-Verlag.

Ferrera, Maurizio (2005) *The Boundaries of Welfare. European Integration and the New Spatial Politics of Social Protection.* Oxford: Oxford University Press.

Ferrera, Maurizio, Hemerijck, Anton, and Rhodes, Martin (2000) *The Future of Social Europe.* Lisbon: Celta Editora.

Fichter, Michael (2003) *Internationalization of Production: Options and Responses.* Washington: AICGS/Daimler-Chrysler Working Paper Series (Johns Hopkins University).

Fichter, Michael (2005) 'The German Way: Still Treading the Path of Institutionalized Labor Relations?'. In *Surviving Globalization*, edited by Stefan Beck, Frank Klobes, and Christoph Scherrer, pp. 93–110. Dordrecht: Springer Verlag.

Fichter, Michael and Meardi, Guglielmo (2008) 'Production Relocation. Impacts on Home, Host and Cross-border Industrial Relations.' In *Restructuring in the New EU Member States: Social Dialogue, Firms Relocation and Social Treatment of Restructuring*, edited by Maria Blas-Lopéz and Marie-Ange Moreau, 135–156. Frankfurt: M: Peter Lang.

Fichter, Michael, Dörrenbächer, Christoph, Neumann, Laszló, and Tóth, András (2004) *Internationalization of Production: Options and Responses. Evidence from German Enterprises in Hungary*. Paper to the IRRA 53rd Meeting, San Diego.

Fitzgerald, Ian and Stirling, John (eds) (2004) *European Works Councils: Pessimism of the Intellect, Optimism of the Will*. London: Routledge.

Flam, Helena (ed) (2001) *Pink, Purple, Green: Women's, Religious, Environmental, and Gay/Lesbian Movements in Central Europe Today*. New York: Columbia University Press.

Fleming, Peter and Sewell, Graham (2002) 'Looking for *The Good Soldier, Švejk*: Alternative Modalities of Resistance in the Contemporary Workplace', *Sociology*, 36, 4, 857–872.

Fraile, Lydia (2009) 'Lessons from Latin America's Neo-liberal Experiment: An Overview of Labour and Social Policies since the 1980s', *International Labour Review*, 148, 3, 216–233.

Freeman, Gary (1986) 'Migration and the Political Economy of the Welfare State', *Annals of the American Academy of Social and Political Sciences*, 485, 1, 51–63.

Freeman, Richard and Medoff, James (1984) *What Do Unions Do?* New York: Basic Books.

Freeman, Richard, Boxall, Peter, and Haynes, Peter (2007) *What Workers Say: Employee Voice in the Anglo-American Workplace*. Ithaca: ILR Press.

Frege, Carola (2007) *Employment Research and State Traditions: A Comparative History of Britain, Germany, and the United States*. Oxford: Oxford University Press.

Frege, Carola and Kelly, John (2003) 'Union Revitalization Strategies in Comparative Perspective', *European Journal of Industrial Relations*, 9, 1, 7–24.

French, Stephen and Möhrke, Jutta (2007) *The Impact of 'New Arrivals' on the North Staffordshire Labour Market*. Report to the Low Pay Commission. Staffordshire: Keele..

Frisch, Max (1965) 'Vorwort'. In *Siamo Italiani. Gespräche mit Italienischen Arbeitern in der Schweiz*, edited by Alexander Seiler, 7–8. Zürich: EVZ.

Fudge, Judith and McPhail, Fiona (2009) 'The Temporary Foreign Worker Program in Canada: Low-Skilled Workers as an Extreme Form of Flexible Labour', *Comparative Labour Law and Policy Journal*, 31, 5, 101–139.

Funk, Lothar (2008) 'European Flexicurity Policies: A Critical Assessment', *International Journal of Comparative Labour Law and Industrial Relations*, 24, 3, 349–384.

Gądecki, Jacek (2009) *Za murami. Osiedla grodzone w Polsce—analiza dyskursu*. Wroclaw: Wydawnicto Uniwersytetu Wroclawckiego.

Gajewska, Katarzyna (2009) *Transnational Labour Solidarity*. London: Routledge.

Galgóczi, Béla (2003) 'The Impact of Multinational Enterprises on the Corporate Culture and on Industrial Relations in Hungary', *South-East Europe Review*, 1, 27–44.

Galgóczi, Béla, Leschke, Janine, and Watt, Andrew (eds) (2009) *EU Labour Migration since Enlargement*. Aldershot: Ashgate.

Gallie, Duncan, Kostova Dobrinka, and Kuchar, Pavel (1999) 'Employment Experience and Organisational Commitment: An East-West Comparison', *Work, Employment and Society*, 13, 4, 621–641.

Gardawski, Juliusz (2001) *Związki zawodowe na rozdrożu*. Warsaw: ISP.

Gardawski, Juliusz (2007) *Korporacje transnarodowe a Europejskie Rady Zakładowe w Polsce*. Warsaw: Szkoła Główna Handlowa.

Gardawski, Juliusz (2009a) 'Ewolucja polskich związków zawodowych'. In *Polacy pracujący a kryzys fordyzmu*, edited by Juliusz Gardawski, 459–532. Warsaw: Scholar.

Gardawski, Juliusz (2009b) 'Wstęp. Omówienie wyników badań'. In *Polacy pracujący a kryzys fordyzmu*, edited by Juliusz Gardawski, 15–50. Warsaw: Scholar.

Gardawski, Juliusz and Meardi, Guglielmo (2010) 'Keep Trying? Polish Failures and Half-Successes in Social Pacting'. In *After the Euro and the Enlargement: Social Pacts in the European Union*, edited by Philippe Pochet, Maarten Keune, and David Natali, 371–394. Brussels: European Trade Union Institute.

Ghellab, Youcef and Vaughan-Whitehead, Daniel (eds) (2003) *Sectoral Social Dialogue in Future EU Member States: The Weakest Link*. Geneva: ILO.

Gheorghe, Nicolae (2010) 'Romania Is Shirking Its Roma Responsibilities', *The Guardian*, 3rd November.

Giles, Anthony (2000) 'Globalisation and Industrial Relations Theory', *Journal of Industrial Relations*, 42, 2, 173–194.

Gładoch, Monika (2008) 'Meandry partycypacji pracowniczej w Polsce', *Dialog. Pismo dialogu społecznego*, 2, 59–64.

Głogowski, Tomasz (2009) 'Wkryzysie Fiat przyjmuje nowych pracowników', *Gazeta Wyborcza*, 20th August.

Główny Urząd Statystyczny (GUS) (2009) *Rocznik Statystyczny Pracy 2009*. Warsaw: Główny Urząd Statystyczny.

Gonser, Monika (2010) 'How Hard a Blow for the Collective Representation of Labour Interests? The Baltic Industrial Relations and the Financial Crisis', *Emecon: Employment and Economy in Central and Eastern Europe*, 1 (http://www.emecon.eu/fileadmin/articles/1_2010/emecon%201_2010%20Gonser.pdf).

Gradev, Gregor (ed) (2001) *CEE Countries in EU Companies' Strategies of Industrial Restructuring and Relocation*. Brussels: ETUI.

Greene, Anne-Marie, Kirton, Jill, and Wrench, John (2005) 'Trade Union Perspectives on Diversity Management: A Comparison of the UK and Denmark', *European Journal of Industrial Relations*, 11, 2, 179–196.

Greskovits, Béla (1998) *The Political Economy of Protest and Patience. East European and Latin American Transformations Compared*. Budapest: Central European University.

Grote, Jürgen and Schmitter, Philippe (1997) *The Corporatist Sisyphus: Past, Present and Future*. Florence: EUI Working Paper SPS 97/4.

Gruszczyńska, Anna (2009) 'Sowing the Seeds of Solidarity in Public Space: Case Study of the Poznan March of Equality', *Sexualities*, 12, 3, 312–333.

Grzymala-Busse, Anna and Innes, Abby (2003) 'Great Expectations: the EU and Domestic Political Competition in East Central Europe', *East European Politics and Societies*, 17, 1, 64–73.

Gwartney, James, Hall, Joshua and Lawson, Robert (2010) *Economic Freedom of the World: 2010 Annual Report*. Vancouver: Fraser Institute.

Habermas, Jürgen (1973) *Legitimationprobleme im Spätkapitalismus*. Frankfurt: Suhrkamp.

Hala, Jaroslav (2007) *Controversy over New Workplace Health and Safety Legislation* (http://www.eurofound.europa.eu/eiro/2006/11/articles/cz0611039i.htm).

Hall, Mark and Purcell, John (2011) *Information and Consultation Practice across Europe Five Years after the EU Directive.* (http://www.eurofound.europa.eu/eiro/studies/tn1009029s/tn1009029s.htm).

Hall, Peter and Soskice, David (eds) (2001) *Varieties of Capitalism: The Institutional Foundations of Comparative Advantage.* Oxford: Oxford University Press.

Hardy, Jane (2009) *Poland's New Capitalism.* London: Pluto Press.

Hardy, Jane and Fitzgerald, Ian (2010) 'Negotiating "Solidarity" and Internationalism: The Response of Polish Trade Unions to Migration', *Industrial Relations Journal,* 41, 4, 351–366.

Hartz, Peter (2007) *Macht und Ohnmacht. Ein Gespräch mit Inge Kloepfer.* Pößneck: Hoffmann und Campe.

Hašek, Jaroslav (1923) *Osudy dobrého vojáka Švejka za světové válki.* Prague: Synek.

Hassel, Anke (2006) *Wage-Setting, Social Pacts and the Euro.* Amsterdam: Amsterdam University Press.

Hassel, Anke (2009) 'Policies and Politics in Social Pacts in Europe', *European Journal of Industrial Relations,* 15, 1, 7–26.

Hausner, Jerzy (2007) *Pętle rozwoju. O polityce gospodarczej lat 2001–2005.* Warsaw: Scholar.

Heery, Edmund and Frege, Carola (2006) 'New Actors in Industrial Relations', *British Journal of Industrial Relations,* 44, 4, 601–604.

Heidenreich, Martin and Zeitlin, Jonathan (eds) (2009) *Changing European Employment and Welfare Regimes: The Influence of the Open Method of Coordination on National Reforms.* London: Routedge.

Hennebert, Marc-Antonin (2008) *De la Transnationalisation de l'Action Syndicale au Sein des Enterprises Multinationals:Une Analyse du "Réseau UNI@ Quebecor World.* Montreal: Thèse de doctorat, Université de Montréal.

Hermet, Guy (2001) *Les Populismes dans le Monde. Une Histoire Sociologique. XIXe–XXe Siècle.* Paris: Fayard.

Heyes, Jason (2009) 'Recruiting and Organising Migrant Workers through Education and Training: A Comparison of Community and the GMB', *Industrial Relations Journal,* 40, 3, 182–197.

Hirschman, Albert (1970) *Exit, Voice and Loyalty.* Cambridge, MA: Harvard University Press.

Hirschman, Albert (1977) *The Passions and the Interests.* Princeton: Princeton University Press.

Hirschman, Albert (1982) *Shifting Involvements. Private Interest and Public Action.* Princeton: Princeton University Press.

Hirschman, Albert (1993) 'Exit, Voice and the Fate of the GDR', *World Politics,* 45, 173–202.

Hoffmann, Aline (2006) *The Construction of Solidarity in a German Central Works Council: Implications for European Works Councils.* Warwick: PhD Thesis, Warwick University.

Home Office (2009) *Accession Monitoring Report, May 2004—March 2009.* London: Home Office.

Höpner, Martin and Schäfer, Armin (2007) *A New Phase of European Integration. Organized Capitalisms in Post-Ricardian Europe.* Cologne: MPIfG Discussion Paper 2007/4.

Hyman, Richard (1999) 'Imagined Solidarities: Can Trade Unions Resist Globalization?' In *Globalization and Labour Relations,* edited by Peter Leisink, 94–115. Cheltenham: Elgar.

Hyman, Richard (2001) *Understanding European Trade Unionism.* London: Sage.

Hyman, Richard (2004) 'Is Industrial Relations Theory always Ethnocentric?' In *Theoretical Perspectives on Work and the Employment Relationship,* edited by Bruce Kaufman, 265–292. Ithaca: Cornell University Press.

Hyman, Richard (2005) 'Shifting Dynamics in International Trade Unionism: Agitation, Organisation, Diplomacy, Bureaucracy', *Labor History*, 46, 2, 137–154.

International labour Organisation (ILO) (2010) *Laborsta Database* (http://laborsta.ilo.org/).

Irish Independent (2009) 'Any Sad New Song Should Be, Perhaps, in Polish', 23rd September.

Jacoby, Wade (1999) 'Priest and the Penitent: The European Union as a Force in the Domestic Politics of Eastern Europe', *East European Constitutional Review*, 8, 1–2.

Janicko, Pavel and Sirucek, Pavel (2009) 'Three Pillars of Flexicurity: The Case of the Czech Republic', *Transfer*, 15, 3–4, 596–603.

Jarkowiec, Maciej (2007) 'Bóg kocha w Londynie', *Gazeta Wyborcza*, 19th May.

Jürgens, Ulrich and Krzywdzinski, Martin (2009) 'Work Models in the Central Eastern European Car Industry: Towards the High Road?' *Industrial Relations Journal*, 40, 6, 471–490.

Jürgens, Ulrich and Krzywdzinski, Martin (2010) *Die Neue Ost-West-Arbeitsteilung. Arbeitsmodelle und industrielle Beziehungen in der Europäischen Automobilindustrie*. Frankfurt: M: Campus.

Kadziauskas, Giedrius (2007) 'Lithuanian Migration: Causes, Impacts and Policy Guidelines'. In *Labor Mobility in the European Union: New Members, New Challenges*, edited by Jen Smith-Bozek, 80–100. Washington: Center for European Policy Analysis.

Kahancová, Marta (2010) *One Company, Diverse Workplaces. The Social Construction of Employment Practices in Western and Eastern Europe*. London: Palgrave.

Kahanec, Martin, Zaiceva, Anzelika, and Zimmermann, Klaus (2009) '*Lessons from Migration after EU Enlargement*'. In *EU Labor Markets After Post-Enlargement Migration*, edited by Martin Kahanec and Klaus Zimmermann, 3–46. Berlin: Springer.

Kallaste, Epp, Jaakson, Krista, and Eamets, Raul (2008) 'Two Representatives But No Representation', *Employee Relations*, 30, 1, 86–97.

Kaminska, Monika and Kahancová, Marta (2010) *Emigration and Labour Shortages. An Opportunity for Trade Unions in the New Member States?* Amsterdam: AIAS Working Paper 10–87.

Katz, Harry and Darbishire, Owen (2000) *Converging Divergences: Worldwide Changes in Employment Systems*. Cornell: Cornell University Press.

Kaufman, Bruce (2007) 'The Core Principle and Fundamental Theorem of Industrial Relations', *International Journal of Comparative Labour Law and Industrial Relations*, 23, 1, 5–33.

Kelly, John (1998) *Rethinking Industrial Relations: Mobilization, Collectivism and Long Waves*. London: Routledge.

Kennedy, Robert (2003) 'Smithfield Foods: The Truth behind its Pigs and Factories', *The Ecologist*, nr 10.

Keune, Maarten (2009) 'EU Enlargement and Social Standards: Exporting the European Social Model?' In *The European Union and the Social Dimension of Globalization. How the EU Influences the World*, edited by Jan Orbie and Lisa Tortell, 45–61. London: Routledge.

Keune, Maarten and Jespen, Maria (2007) 'Not Balanced and Hardly New: The European Commission's Quest for Flexicurity', *ETUI Working Paper* 01/2007.

Kilpatrick, Claire (2009) 'The ECJ and Labour Law: A 2008 Retrospective', *Industrial Law Journal*, 38, 2, 180–208.

Kim, Kee-Beom (2006) *Direct Employment in Multinational Enterprises: Trends and Implications*. Geneva: MULTI Working Paper, No. 101, International Labour Organization.

King, Lawrence (2007) 'Central European Capitalism in Comparative Perspective'. In *Beyond Varieties of Capitalism: Conflict, Contradiction, and Complementarities in the European Economy*, edited by Bob Hancké, Martin Rhodes, and Mark Thatcher, 307–327. Oxford: Oxford University Press.

Klenner, Christina and Leiber, Simone (eds) (2009) *Wohlfahrtsstaaten und Geschlechterungleichheit in Mittel- und Osteuropa*. Wiesbaden: VS Verlag.

Kofman, Eleonore, Phizacklea, Annie, Raghuram, Parvati, and Sales, Rosemary (2000) *Gender and International Migration in Europe: Employment, Welfare and Politics*. London: Routledge.

Kohl, Heribert and Platzer, Hans-Wolfgang (2004) *Arbeitsbeziehungen in Mittelosteuropa*. Baden-Baden: Nomos.

Kohl, Heribert and Platzer, Hans-Wolfgang (2007) 'The Role of the State in Central and Eastern European Industrial Relations: The Case of Minimum Wages', *Industrial Relations Journal*, 38, 6, 614–635.

Koleva, Petia (2009) 'La Responsabilité Sociale des Entreprises: Une Occasion de Repenser les Modes de Régulation en Europe Centrale dans le Contexte du Development Durable', *Revue d'Études Comparatives Est-Ouest*, 40, 2, 5–31.

Kowalik, Tadeusz (2009) *Polska transformacja*. Warsaw: Muza.

Kozek, Wiesława (1999) 'Społeczne organizacje biznesu i jego związki w Polsce'. In *Społeczne organizacje biznesu w Polsce a stosunki pracy*, edited by Wieslawa Kozek, 13–102. Warsaw: Wydawnictwo B-P.

Krieger, Hubert and Fernandez, Enrique (2006) *Too Much or Too Little Long-Distance Mobility in Europe? EU Policies to Promote and Restrict Mobility*. Dublin: European Foundation for the Improvement of Living and Working Conditions.

Krings, Torben (2009) 'A Race to the Bottom? Trade Unions, EU Enlargement and the Free Movement of Labour', *European Journal of Industrial Relations*, 15, 1, 49–69.

Krings, Torben, Bobek, Alicja, Moriarty, Elaine, Salamonska, Justyna, and Wickham, James (2009) 'Migration and Recession: Polish Migrants in Post-Celtic Tiger Ireland', *Sociological Research Online*, 14, 2.

Krzywdzinski, Martin (2009) 'Organisatorischer Wandel von Gewerkschaften in Postkommunistischen Ländern. Der Fall der Solidarność', *Industrielle Beziehungen*, 16, 1, 25–45.

Kubicek, Paul (2004) *Organized Labor in Postcommunist States: From Solidarity to Infirmity*. Pittsburgh: Pittsburgh University Press.

Kubik, Andrzej (2004) 'Hyundai wybrał Słowację', *Gazeta Wyborcza*, 3rd March.

Kurekova, Lucia (2010) *States, Welfare States and Migration in Central and Eastern Europe*. Budapest: Paper for the Annual Doctoral Conference of the Central European University.

Kusznir, Julia and Pleines, Heiko (eds) (2008) *Trade Unions from Post-Socialist Member States in EU Governance*. Stuttgart: Ibidem Verlag.

Krugman, Paul (2011) 'Can Europe Be Saved?', *The New York Times*, 12th February.

Kvinge, Torunn and Rezanow Ulrichsen, Aleksandra (2008) 'Do Norwegian Companies' Direct Investments in Poland Imply Exports of Labour Relations?' *Economic and Industrial Democracy*, 29, 1, 125–155.

Ladó, Maria (2001) 'Hungary: FDI and Its Impact on Industrial Relations'. In *CEE Countries in EU Companies' Strategies of Industrial Restructuring and Relocation*, edited by Grigor Gradev, 73–135. Brussels: ETUI.

Lane, Christel (1998) 'European Companies between Globalization and Localization: A Comparison of Internationalization Strategies of British and German MNCs', *Economy and Society*, 27, 4, 517–540.

Langewiesche, Renate and Tóth, András (2003) 'Introduction: Making Unification Work'. In *The Unity of Europe, Political, Economic and Social Dimensions of EU Enlargement*, edited by Renate Langewiesche and András Tóth, 7–68. Brussels: European Trade Union Institute.

Lawrence, Felicity (2010) 'Meat Packers United: Labour renaissance in the UK food industry', *The Guardian*, 24th April.

Lawrence, Peter (1991) 'The Personnel Function: An Anglo-German Comparison'. In *International Comparisons in Human Resource Management*, edited by Chris Brewster and Shaun Tyson, 131–44. London: Pitman.

Leiber, Sabine (2007) 'Implementation of EU Social Policy in Poland: Is There a Different "Eastern World of Compliance"?' *Journal of European Social Policy* 17, 4, 349–360.

Léonard, Evelyne (2005) 'Governance and Concerted Regulation of Employment in Europe', *European Journal of Industrial Relations* 11, 3, 307–326.

Levada, Yuri (2000) 'Soviet Man Ten Years Later: 1989–1999', *Russian Social Science Review* 41, 1, 4–28.

Levinson, Charles (1972) *International Trade Unionism*. London: Allen and Unwin.

Lillie, Nathan and Greer, Ian (2007) 'Industrial Relations, Migration, and Neoliberal Politics: The Case of the European Construction Sector', *Politics and Society*, 35, 4, 551–581.

MacKenzie, Robert and Forde, Chris (2009) 'The Rhetoric of the "Good Worker" versus the Realities of Employers' Use and the Experiences of Migrant Workers', *Work, Employment and Society* 23, 142–159.

Maduro, Miguel Poiares (1999) 'Striking the Elusive Balance between Economic Freedom and Social Rights in the EU'. In *The EU and Human Rights*, edited by Philip Alston, Mara Bustelo, and James Heenan, 449–472. Oxford: Oxford University Press.

Mailand , Mikkel (2008) 'The Uneven Impact of the European Employment Strategy on Member States' Employment Policies: A Comparative Analysis'. *Journal of European Social Policy* 18, 4: 353–365.

Mailand, Mikkel and Due, Jesper (2004) 'Social Dialogue in Central and Eastern Europe: Present State and Future Development', *European Journal of Industrial Relations* 10, 2, 179–197.

Malinowska, Ewa (2001) 'Kobiety i feministki', *Kultura i Społeczeństwo*, 45, 21–38.

Makó, Csaba and Novoszáth, Peter (1995) 'Employment Relations in Multinational Companies: The Hungarian Case'. In *Industrial Transformation in Europe*, edited by Eckhard Dittrich, Gert Schmidt, and Ricahrd Whitley, 255–276. London: Sage.

Mansfeldová, Zdenka (2007) *Trade Union and Employers' Associations on the Way to Multi-level Social Dialogue—Comparison between Czech Republic, Slovakia and Slovenia*. EUSA Conference, Montreal.

Marginson, Paul, and Meardi, Guglielmo (2006) 'EU Enlargement and the FDI Channel of Industrial Relations Transfer', *Industrial Relations Journal*, 37, 2, 92–110.

Marginson, Paul and Meardi, Guglielmo (2009) *Multinational Companies and Collective Bargaining*. Dublin: European Foundation for the Improvement of Working and Living Conditions.

Marginson, Paul and Sisson, Keith (2004) *European Integration and Industrial Relations*. Basingstoke: Palgrave.

Martin, Philip (2009) 'Recession and Migration: A New Era for Labor Migration?' *International Migration Review*, 43, 3, 671–691.

Martínez Lucio, Miguel, and Walker, Steve (2005) 'The Networked Union? The Internet as a Challenge to Trade Union Identity and Roles', *Critical Perspectives in International Business*, 1, 2–3, 137–154.

Mau, Steffen and Burkhardt, Christoph (2009) 'Migration and Welfare State Solidarity in Western Europe', *Journal of European Social Policy*, 19, 3, 213–229.

McKay, Sonia and Markova, Eugenia (2010) 'The Operation and Management of Agency Workers in Conditions of Vulnerability', *Industrial Relations Journal*, 41, 5, 446–460.

McMenamin, Iain (2002) 'Polish Business Associations: Flattened Civil Society or Super Lobbies?' *Business and Politics*, 4, 3, 301–318.

Meardi, Guglielmo (2000) *Trade Union Activists, East and West. Comparisons in Multinational Companies.* Aldershot: Gower.

Meardi, Guglielmo (2002) 'The Trojan Horse for the Americanization of Europe? Polish Industrial Relations towards the EU', *European Journal of Industrial Relations* 8, 1, 77–99.

Meardi, Guglielmo (2004) 'Short Circuits in Multinational Plants. The Extension of European Works Councils to Poland', *European Journal of Industrial Relations*, 10, 2 161–178.

Meardi, Guglielmo (2005) 'The Legacy of Solidarity. Class, Democracy, Culture and Subjectivity in the Polish Social Movement', *Social Movements Studies*, 4, 3, 261–280.

Meardi, Guglielmo (2006a) 'Social Pacts on the Road to EMU: A Comparison of the Italian and Polish Experiences', *Economic and Industrial Democracy* 27, 2, 197–222.

Meardi, Guglielmo (2006b) 'I sindacati nell'Europa postcomunista: attori scomparsi?' In *Guida ai Paesi dell'Europa Centrale Orientale e Balcanica*, edited by Luisa Chiodi and Francesco Privitera, 15–24. Bologna: Il Mulino.

Meardi, Guglielmo (2007) 'Voice after More Exit? Unstable Industrial Relations in Central Eastern Europe', *Industrial Relations Journal* 38, 6, 503–523.

Meardi, Guglielmo and Tóth, András (2006) 'Who Is Hybridising What? Insights on MNCs' Employment Practices in Central Europe'. In *Multinationals and the Construction of Transnational Practices: Convergence and Diversity in the Global Economy*, edited by Anthony Ferner, Xavier Quintamilla, and Carles Sánchez-Rundes, 155–183. London: Palgrave.

Męcina, Jacek (2009a) 'Prawo pracy w przebudowie—kierunki i cechy ewolucji zmian w prawie pracy'. In *Polacy pracujący a kryzys fordyzmu*, edited by Juliusz Gardawski, 258–306. Warsaw: Scholar.

Męcina, Jacek (2009b) 'Najważniejsze cechy i wyzwania polskiego rynku pracy'. In *Polacy pracujący a kryzys fordyzmu*, edited by Juliusz Gardawski, 307–342. Warsaw: Scholar.

Melucci, Alberto (1996) *Challenging Codes: Collective Action in the Information Age.* Cambridge: Cambridge University Press.

Menz, Georg (2008) *The Political Economy of Managed Migration. Nonstate Actors, Europeanization, and the Politics of Designing Migration Policies.* Oxford: Oxford University Press.

Milkman, Ruth (ed) (2006) *L.A. Story: Immigrant Workers and the Future of the U.S. Labor Movement.* New York: Russell Sage Foundation.

Minkenberg, Michael (2011) 'A l'Est, l'Obsession des Frontières', *Le Monde Diplomatique*, 682.

Molnar, Margit, Pain, Nigel, and Taglioni, Daria (2008) *Globalisation and Employment in the OECD.* Paris: OECD Economic Studies.

Morley, John and Sanoussi, Fadila (2009) *Comparative Analysis of Working Time in the European Union.* Dublin: European Foundation for the Improvement of Working and Living Conditions.

Mrożowicki, Adam, Pulignano, Valeria, and Van Hootegem, Geert (2009) 'Reinvention of Activism: a Chance for Union Renewal in New Market Economies?— The Case of Poland'. In *The Future of Union Organising. Building for Tomorrow*, edited by Gregor Gall, 79–96. London: Palgrave.

Myant, Martin (2010) 'Trade Union Influence in the Czech Republic since 1989', *Czech Sociological Review*, 44, 6, 899–911.

Myant, Martin and Drahokoupil, Jan (2010) *Transition Economies: Political Economy in Russia, Eastern Europe, and Central Asia*. Hoboken: Wiley.

Neumann, Laszló (2007) 'European Labour Standards' Impacts on Accession Countries: The Hungarian Case'. In *Industrial Relations in the New Europe: Enlargement, Integration and Reform*, edited by Peter Leisink, Bram Steijn, and Ulke Veersma, 63–80. Cheltenham: Edward Elgar.

Newell, Andrew and Socha, Mieczyslaw (2007) 'The Polish Wage Inequality Explosion', *Economics of Transition*, 15, 4, 733–758.

Nölke, Andreas and Vliegenthart, Arjan (2009) 'Enlarging the Varieties of Capitalism: The Emergence of Dependent Market Economies in East Central Europe', *World Politics*, 61, 4, 670–702.

OECD (2008) *Employment Outlook 2008*. Paris: OECD.

OECD (2009) *Social and Welfare Statistics* (http://stats.oecd.org/Index.aspx? DataSetCode=INEQUALITY)

OECD (2010a) Employment Database (www.oecd.org/employment/database).

OECD (2010b) Statistics on Measuring Globalisation Database (http://oecd-library.org/ finance-and-investment/data/oecd-statistics-on-measuring-globalisation_global-data-en).

Offe, Claus and Wiesenthal, Helmut (1985) 'Two Logics of Collective Action'. In *Disorganized Capitalism*, edited by Claus Offe, 170–220. Cambridge, MA: Polity.

Office for National Statistics (2009) *Labour Force Survey*. Newport: Office for National Statistics.

Onaran, Özlem and Stockhammer, Engelbert (2008) 'The Effect of FDI and Foreign Trade on Wages in the Central and Eastern European Countries in the Post-Transition Era: A Sectoral Analysis for the Manufacturing Industry', *Structural Change and Economic Dynamics*, 19, 66–80.

Organization for Economic Co-operation and Development (OECD) (2009) *OECD Science, Technology and Industry Scoreboard*. Paris: OECD.

Ost, David (2000) 'Illusory Corporatism: Tripartism in the Service of Neoliberalism', *Politics and Society*, 28, 4, 503–530.

Ost, David (2002) 'The Weakness of Strong Social Movements: Models of Unionism in the East European Context', *European Journal of Industrial Relations*, 8, 1, 33–51.

Ost, David (2005) *The Defeat of Solidarity. Anger and Politics in Postcommunist Europe*. Ithaca: Cornell University Press.

Ost, David (2009) 'The Consequences of Postcommunism: Trade Unions in Eastern Europe's Future', *East European Politics and Societies*, 23, 1, 13–33.

Ostrowski, Piotr (2009) *Powstawanie związków zawodowych w sektorze prywatnym w Polsce*. Warsaw: Friedrich Ebert Stiftung.

Pankowski, Rafal (2010) *The Populist Radical Right in Poland*. London: Routledge.

Państwowa Inspekcja Pracy (PIP) (2005) *Przestrzeganie Przepisów Prawa Pracy w Supermarketach, Hipermarketach I Sklepach Dyskontowych w Latach 1999–2005*. Warsaw: Państwowa Inspekcja Pracy.

Państwowa Inspekcja Pracy (PIP) (2008) *Sprawozdanie Głównego Inspektora Pracy z działalności Państwowej Inspekcji Pracy w 2007 roku*. Warsaw: Państwowa Inspekcja Pracy.

Państwowa Inspekcja Pracy (PIP) (2009) *Sprawozdanie Głównego Inspektora Pracy z działalności Państwowej Inspekcji Pracy w 2008 roku*. Warsaw: Państwowa Inspekcja Pracy.

Parent-Thirion, Agnès, Fernández Macías, Enrique, Hurley, John, and Vermeylen, Greet (2007) *Fourth European Working Conditions Survey*. Dublin: European Foundation for the Improvement of Living and Working Conditions.

Parlevliet, Jante and Xenogiani, Theodora (2008) *Report on Informal Employment in Romania*. Paris: OECD Development Centre, Working Paper 271.

Passerini, Luisa, Lyon, Dawn, Capussotti, Enrica, and Laliotou, Ioanna (eds.) (2007) *Women Migrants from East to West: Gender, Mobility, and Belonging in Contemporary Europe*. New York: Berghahn Books.

Pedersini, Roberto (2004) *Industrial Relations in the Automotive Sector*. (http://www.eurofound.europa.eu/eiro/2003/12/study/tn0312101s.htm)

Pellegrin, Julie (2001) *The Political Economy of Competitiveness in an Enlarged Europe*. Basingstoke: Macmillan.

Peña-Casas, Ramón and Pochet, Philippe (2009) *Convergence and Divergence of Working Conditions in Europe: 1990–2005*. Dublin: European Foundation for the Improvement of Living and Working Conditions.

Phillips, Leigh (2010) 'What's Left in Eastern Europe', *Red Pepper*, 24th January.

Pilat, Dirk, Cimper, Agnès, Olsen, Karsten, and Webb, Colin (2006) *The Changing Nature of Manufacturing in OECD Economies*. Paris: STI Working Paper 9, OECD.

Piore, Michael (1979) *Birds of Passage: Migrant Labour and Industrial Societies*. Cambridge: Cambridge University Press.

Polanyi, Karl (1944) *The Great Transformation*. Boston, MA: Beacon Press.

Pollert, Anna (1999) 'Trade Unionism in Transition in Central and Eastern Europe', *European Journal of Industrial Relations*, 5, 2, 209–234.

Pollert, Anna (2003) 'Women, Work and Equal Opportunities in Post-Communist Transition', *Work, Employment and Society*, 12, 2, 331–357.

Portet, Sylvaine and Sztandar-Sztanderska, Karolina (2008) 'Pologne. Indeminisation du Chômage: le Spectre de l'Illégitimité', *Chronique Internqtionale de l'IRES*, 115, 147–160.

Pries, Ludger (2004) 'New Production Systems and Workers' Participation: A Contradiction? Some Lessons from German Automobile Companies'. In *Work and Employment Relations in the Automotive Industry*, edited by Elise Charron and Paul Stewart, 76–102. London: Palgrave.

Pringle, Tim and Clarke, Simon (2010) *The Challenge of Transition: Trade Unions in Russia, China and Vietnam*. Bainsgstoke: Palgrave.

Pulignano, Valeria (2007) 'Co-Ordinating across Borders: The Role of European Industry Federations within European Works Councils'. In *Towards a European Labour Identity. The Case of the European Works Council*, edited by Michael Whittall, Herman Knudsen, and Fred Huijgen, 74–93. London: Routledge.

Pulignano, Valeria (2009) 'International Cooperation, Transnational Restructuring and Virtual Networking in Europe', *European Journal of Industrial Relations*, 15, 2, 187–205.

Purcell, John (2010) *Individual Disputes at the Workplace: Alternative Disputes Resolution*. (http://www.eurofound.europa.eu/eiro/studies/tn0910039s/tn0910039s.htm).

Radosevic, Slavo, Varblane, Urmas, and Mickiewicz, Tomasz (2003) 'Foreign Direct Investment and Its Effect on Employment in Central Europe', *Transnational Corporations*, 12, 1, 53–90.

Ramsey, Harvie (1999) 'In Search of International Union Theory', in *Globalization: Patterns of Labour Resistance*, edited by Jeremy Waddington, 192–219. London: Mansell.

Rekacewicz, Philippe and Rucevska, Ieva (2009) 'La Crise Vue de Léttonie', *Le Monde Diplomatique*, 666.

Rogers, Joel and Streeck, Wolfgang (eds) (1995) *Works Councils: Consultation, Representation, and Cooperation in Industrial Relations*. New York: University of Chicago Press.

Romano, Serena (2009) *Poverty and Welfare Reforms in Eastern Europe*. Poznań: Paper for the ISA Workshop on Migration and Inequalities.

Rosenzweig, Philip and Nohria, Notia (1994) 'Influences on Human Resource Management Practices in Multinational Corporations', *Journal of International Business Studies*, 25, 2, 229–251.

Rueschemeyer, Dietrich, Stephens, Evelyne, and Stephens, John (1992) *Capitalist Development and Democracy*. Cambridge: Polity.

Rugraff, Eric (2006) 'Firmes Multinationals et Relations Industrielles en Europe Centrale: une Approche Institutionnaliste', *Relations Industrielles*, 61, 3, 437–464.

Sayad, Abdelmalek (1999) *La Double Absence: Des Illusions de l'Émigré aux Souffrances de l'Immigré*. Paris: Seuil.

Scharpf, Fritz (2009) *Legitimacy in the Multilevel European Polity*. Cologne: MPIfG Working Paper 09/1.

Schierup, Carl-Ulrik, Hansen, Peo, and Castles, Stephens (2006) *Migration, Citizenship, and the European Welfare State. A European Dilemma*. Oxford: Oxford University Press.

Schneider, Friedrich and Buehn, Andreas (2007) 'Shadow Economies and Corruption All Over the World: Revised Estimates for 120 Countries', *Economics: The Open-Access, Open-Assessment E-Journal*, 1.

Schulten, Torsten (2008) 'Towards a European Minimum Wage Policy? Fair Wages and Social Europe', *European Journal of Industrial Relations*, 14, 4, 421–439.

Shlyk, Aleksander (2009) 'Social Movement Unionism in Poland: Towards Revitalization of Organized Labor?', *Theory in Action*, 2, 1, 158–190.

Silver, Beverley (2003) *Forces of Labor: Workers' Movements and Globalization since 1870*. Cambridge: Cambridge University Press.

Sinn, Hans-Werner and Ochel, Wolfgang (2003) 'Social Union, Convergence and Migration', *Journal of Common Market Studies*, 41, 5, 869–896.

Sissenich, Beate (2005) 'The Transfer of EU Social Policy to Poland and Hungary'. In *The Europeanization of Central and Eastern Europe*, edited by Frank Schimmelfennig and Ulrich Sedelmeier, 156–177. Ithaca: Cornell University Press.

Sissenich, Beate (2007) *Building States without Society: European Union Enlargement and Social Policy Transfer to Poland and Hungary*. Lanham: Lexington.

Smith, Chris and Meiksins, Peter (1995) 'System, Society and Dominance Effects in Cross-National Organisational Analysis', *Work, Employment and Society*, 9, 2, 241–267.

Sommers, Jeff (2009) 'The Anglo-American Model of Economic Organization and Governance: Entropy and the Fragmentation of Social Solidarity in Twenty-First Century Latvia', *Debatte: Journal of Contemporary Central and Eastern Europe*, 17, 2: 127–142.

Sommers, Jeff and Woolfson, Charles (2008) 'Trajectories of Entropy and "the Labour Question": The Political Economy of Post-communist Migration in the New Europe', *Debatte: Journal of Contemporary Central and Eastern Europe*, 16, 1, 53–69.

Spatz, Julius and Nunnenkamp, Peter (2004) 'Globalization of the Automobile Industry: Traditional Locations under Pressure?' in *European Industrial Restructuring in a Global Economy: Fragmentation and Relocation of Value Chains*, edited by Michael Faust, Ulrich Voskamp, and Volker Wittke, 105–129. Göttingen: SOFI.

Sperling, Hand Joachim (2004) 'Going East: A Volkswagen Version of Globalization'. In *European Industrial Restructuring in a Global Economy: Fragmentation and Relocation of Value Chains*, edited by Michael Faust, Urlrich Voskamp, and Volker Wittke, 181–200. Göttingen: SOFI.

Spiegel (2003) 'Autoindustrie: die Job-Maschine'. 8th September.

Spiegel (2004) 'Bye-Bye "Made in Germany"'. 25th October.

Spieser, Catherine (2009) *Institutionalising Market Society in Times of Systemic Change: The Construction and Reform of Social and Labour Market Policies in Poland in a Comparative Perspective (1989–2004)*. Florence: PhD Thesis, European University Institute.

Standing, Guy (2009) *Work after Globalization. Building Occupational Citizenship*. Cheltenham: Edward Elgar.

Stanojević, Miroslav (2003) 'Workers' Power in Transition Economies: The Cases of Serbia and Slovenia', *European Journal of Industrial Relations*, 9, 3, 283–301.

Stanojević, Miroslav (2005) 'The Slovenian Pattern'. In *Working and Employment Conditions in the New EU Member States*, edited by Daniel Vaughan-Whitehead, 339–381. Geneva: ILO.

Stanojević, Miroslav (2010) 'Social Pacts in Slovenia'. In *Social Pacts in the European Union*, edited by Philippe Pochet, Maarten Keune, and David Natali, 317–344. Brussels: European Trade Union Institute.

Stanojević, Miroslav (2011) 'Post-EMU Slovenia: The Decline of Social Dialogue?', *Transfer*, 17, 3, 415–420.

Stark, David and Bruszt, Laszló (1998) *Postsocialist Pathways: Transforming Politics and Property in East Central Europe*. Cambridge: Cambridge University Press.

Stewart, Rosemary, Kieser, Alfred, and Barsoux, Jean-Louis (1994) *Managing in Britain and Germany*. Basingstoke: Macmillan.

Streeck, Wolfgang (1987) 'The Uncertainties of Management in the Management of Uncertainty', *Work, Employment and Society*, 1, 2, 317–349.

Streeck, Wolfgang (1997) 'German Capitalism: Does It Exist? Can It Survive?' In *Political Economy of Modern Capitalism: Mapping Convergence and Diversity*, edited by Colin Crouch and Wolfgang Streeck, 33–54. London: Sage.

Streeck, Wolfgang (1998) 'The Internationalization of Industrial Relations in Europe: Prospects and Problems', *Politics and Society*, 26, 4, 429–459.

Streeck, Wolfgang (1999) *Competitive Solidarity: Rethinking the "European Social Model"*. Cologne: MPIfG Working Paper 99/8.

Streeck, Wolfgang (2009) *Re-Forming Capitalism. Institutional Change in the German Political Economy*. Oxford: Oxford University Press.

Sumption, Madelaine and Somerville, Will (2010) *The UK's New Europeans. Progress and Challenges Five Years After Accession*. Manchester: Equality and Human Rights Commission.

Surdykowska, Barbara (2008) 'Prześwietlanie rad pracowniczych', *Dialog. Pismo Dialogu Społecznego*, 2, 14–21.

Svetlik, Ivan and Ilič, Branko (eds) (2005) *HRM's Contribution to Hard Work: A Comparative Analysis of Human Resource Management*. Bern: P. Lang.

Szewczyk, Robert and Unterschütz, Joanna (2009) 'Labour Emigration: Government and Social Partner Policies in Poland'. In *EU Labour Migration since Enlargement*, edited by Béla Galgóczi, Janine Leschke, and Andrew Watt, 211–227. Aldershot: Ashgate.

Sztanderska, Urszula (2005) *Efektywna polityka zatrudnienia*. Presentation at the Conference on the National Lisbon Strategy, Warsaw, 19 December.

Taguieff, Pierre-André (2004) *L'Illusion Populiste: de l'Archaïque au Médiatique*. Paris: Berg International.

Tarrow, Sydney (1994a) *Social Movements in Europe: Movement Society or Europeanisation of Conflict?* Florence: EUI Working Paper RSC 94/8.

Tarrow, Sydney (1994b) *Power in Movement. Social Movements, Collective Action and Mass Politics*. Cambridge: Cambridge University Press.

Tarrow, Sydney (2005) *The New Transnational Activism*. Cambridge: Cambridge University Press.

Taylor, Sally, Beechler, Shon, and Napier, Nancy (1996) 'Toward an Integrative Model of Strategic International Human Resource Management', *The Academy of Management Review*, 21, 4, 959–985.

Thompson, Edward (1963) *The Making of the English Working Class*. London: Gollancz.

Tholen, Jochen (2007) *Labour Relations in Central Europe. The Impact of Multinationals' Money*. Aldershot: Ashgate.

Tholen, Jochen and Hemmer, Eike (2004) *Die Auswirkungen von Direktinvestitionen deutscher Unternehmen in Mittel-/Osteuropa auf Arbeitsplätze in Deutschland*. Bremen: IAW.

Tischner, Józef (1992) *Etyka solidarności oraz homo sovieticus*. Krakow: Znak.

Tonin, Mirco (2007) 'The Wage Dimension of Flexibility and Security in Selected Central and South-Eastern European Countries'. In *Flexicurity: A Relevant Approach in Central and Eastern Europe*, edited by Sandrine Cazes and Alena Nesperova, 213–233. Geneva: ILO.

Tóth, András and Grajczjar, István (2007) 'Different Roads to the Siren Songs of the Extreme Right in Hungary'. In *Changing Working Life and the Appeal of the Extreme Right*, edited by Jörg Flecker, 201–215. Aldershot: Ashgate.

Tóth, András and Neumann, Laszló (2004a) *Works Councils Examined*. (http://www.eurofound.europa.eu/eiro/2004/01/feature/hu0401106f.htm).

Tóth, András and Neumann, Laszló (2004b) *National-Level Tripartism and EMU in the New EU Member States and Candidate Countries*. Dublin: European Foundation for the Improvement of Living and Working Conditions.

Tóth, András and Neumann, Laszló (2006a) *Three-Year Central Agreement Reached on Minimum Wage Rises and Pay Policy Guidelines*. (http://www.eurofound.europa.eu/eiro/2005/12/feature/hu0512104f.htm).

Tóth, András and Neumann, Laszló (2006b) *Renewed Tensions at Suzuki Car Assembly Plant*. (http://www.eurofound.europa.eu/eiro/2006/03/articles/hu0603019i.htm)

Touraine, Alain (1966). *La Conscience Ouvrière*. Paris: Seuil.

Touraine, Alain (1978). *Le Voix et le Regard*. Paris: Seuil.

Touraine, Alain (1997) *Pourrons-Nous Vivre Ensemble? Egaux et Différents*. Paris: Fayard.

Touraine, Alain (2006) *Le Monde des Femmes*. Paris: Fayard.

Towalski, Rafał (2010) 'Poland: Individual disputes at the workplace—alternative dispute resolution' (http://www.eurofound.europa.eu/eiro/studies/tn0910039s/pl0910039q.htm)

Trades Union Congress (TUC) Commission on Vulnerable Employment (2008) *Hard Work, Hidden Lives. Commission Report*. London: TUC.

Trappmann, Vera (2012) *Fallen Heroes in Global Capitalism. Workers and the Restructuring of the Polish Steel Industry*. London: Palgrave.

Traxler, Franz (2010) 'Corporatism(s) and Pacts: Changing Functions and Structures under Rising Economic Liberalism and Declining Liberal Democracy'. In *Social Pacts in the European Union*, edited by Philippe Pochet, Maarten Keune, and David Natali, 45–82. Brussels: European Trade Union Institute.

Traxler, Franz, Brandl, Bernd, Glassner, Vera, and Ludvig, Alice (2008) 'Can Cross-Border Bargaining Coordination Work? Analytical Reflections and Evidence from the Metal Industry in Germany and Austria', *European Journal of Industrial Relations*, 14, 2, 217–237.

Traynor, Ian (2010) 'Hungary Party to Follow's European extremism's Move Away from Fringes', *The Guardian*, 8th April.

Trif, Aurora (2008) 'Opportunities and Challenges of EU Accession: Industrial Relations in Romania', *European Journal of Industrial Relations*, 14, 2, 461–478.

Turner, Lowell (2009) 'Institutions and Activism: Crisis and Opportunity for a German Labor Movement in Decline', *Industrial and Labor Relations Review*, 62, 3, 294–312.

Turner, Lowell and Cornfield, Daniel (eds) (2007) *Labor in the New Urban Battlegrounds: Local Solidarity in a Global Economy*. Ithaca: ILR Press.

Tüselmann, Heinz-Jozef, Heise, Arne, McDonald, Frank, Allen, Matthew, and Voronkova, Svitlana (2008) *Employee Relations in Foreign-Owned Subsidiaries. German Multinational Companies in the UK*. London: Palgrave.

Unite (2009) *Acas inquiry into the recent unofficial action: "The law wasn't broken the law was wrong"* (http://www.unitetheunion.org/news__events/latest_news/acas_inquiry_into_the_recent_u.aspx).

United Nations Conference on Trade and Development (UNCTAD) (2005) *World Investment Report 2005*. New York: United Nations.

United Nations Conference on Trade and Development (UNCTAD) (2010) *World Investment Report 2010*. New York: United Nations.

Untied Nations' Conference on Trade and Development (UNCTAD)—Division on Investment, Technology, and Enterprise (DITE) (2004) *Global Investments Prospects Assessment 2004*. New York: UNCTAD–DITE.

Vandenbrande, Tom (ed) (2006) *Mobility in Europe. Analysis of the 2005 Eurobarometer Survey on Geographical and Labour Market Mobility*. Dublin: European Foundation for the Improvement of Living and Working Conditions.

Van Gyes, Guy, De Witte, Hans, and Pasture, Patrick (eds) (2000) *Can Class Still Unite? The Differentiated Workforce, Class Solidarity and Trade Unions*. Aldershot: Ashgate.

Van Gyes, Guy, Vandenbrande, Tom, Lehndorff, Steffen, Shilling, Gabi, Schief, Sebastian, and Kohl, Heribert (2007) *Industrial Relations in EU Member States, 2000–2004*. Dublin: European Foundation for the Improvement of Living and Working Conditions.

Vanhuysse, Pieter (2006) *Divide and Pacify. Strategic Social Policies and Political Protests in Post-Communist Democracies*. Budapest: CEU Press.

Vasilescu, Lucian and Contescu, Valentina (2003) 'Romania: The Role of the Trade Unions in Labour Relations'. In *Labour Relations in South East Europe: A Legal Overview in 2003*, edited by Wiebke Düvel, Isabelle. Schömann, Stefan Clauwaert, and Grigor Gradev, 149–162. Brussels: ETUI.

Vaughan-Whitehead, Daniel (2003) *EU Enlargement versus Social Europe? The Uncertain Future of the European Social Model*. Cheltenham: Edward Elgar.

Verband der Automobilindustrie (VDA) (2004) *Die Deutsche Automobilindustrie in der Erweiterten EU—Motor der Integration*. Frankfurt a.M.: Verband der Automobilindustrie.

Verschueren, Herwig (2008) 'Cross-Border Workers in the European Internal Market: Trojan Horses for Member States' Labour and Social Security Law?', *International Journal of Comparative Labour Law and Industrial Relations*, 24, 2, 167–199.

Verschuur, Christine (2008) 'Neighbourhood Movements, Gender and Social Justice: The Cultural Reinvention of Politics by Women', *International Social Science Journal*, 59, 193–194: 409–420.

Visser, Jelle (2011) *ICTWSS: Database on Institutional Characteristics of Trade Unions, Wage Setting, State Intervention and Social Pacts in 34 countries between 1960 and 2007*. Amsterdam: Amsterdam Institute of Advanced Labour Studies.

Vliegenthart, Arjan and Overbeek, Henk (2009) 'Corporate Tax Reform in Neoliberal Europe: Central and Eastern Europe as a Template for Deepening the Neoliberal European Integration Project?' In *Contradictions and Limits of Neoliberal European Governance*, edited by Bastiaan Van Apeldoorn, Jan Drahokoupil, and Laura Horn, 143–162. Basingstoke: Palgrave.

Wallace, Clare and Pichler, Florian (2008) 'Working Conditions and Quality of Work: A Comparison of Eastern and Western Europe'. In Handbook of Quality of Life in the Enlarged European Union, edited by Jens Alber, Tony Fahley, and Chiara Saraceno, 162–174. London: Routledge.

Warneck, Wiebke (2007) *Strike Rules in the EU27 and Beyond. A Comparative Overview*. Brussels: ETUI Report 103.

Waterman, Peter (2001) 'Trade Union Internationalism in the Age of Seattle'. In *Place, Space and the New Labour Internationalism*, edited by Peter Waterman and Jane Wills, 8–32. Oxford: Blackwell.

Webster, Edward, Lambert, Rob, and Bezuidenhout, Andries (2008) *Grounding Globalization: Labour in the Age of Insecurity*. Oxford: Blackwell.

Weinstein, Marc (2000) 'Solidarity's Abandonment of Worker Councils: Redefining Employee Stakeholder Rights in Post-Socialist Poland', *British Journal of Industrial Relations*, 38, 1, 49–73.

Wever, Kirsten (1995) 'Human Resource Management and Organizational Strategies in German- and US-Owned Companies', *International Journal of Human Resource Management*, 6, 3, 606–625.

Weyland, Kurt (1999) 'Neoliberal Populism in Latin America and Eastern Europe', *Comparative Politics*, 31, 4, 379–401.

Whitley, Richard (1999) *Divergent Capitalisms: The Social Structuring and Change of Business Systems*. Oxford: Oxford University Press.

Whittall, Michael, Knudsen, Herman, and Huijgen, Fred (eds) (2007) *Towards a European Labour Identity. The Case of the European Works Council*. London: Routledge.

Williams, Colin (2009) 'Illegitimate Wage Practices in Central and Eastern Europe: A Study of the Prevalence and Impacts of "Envelope Wages"', *Debatte: Journal of Contemporary Central and Eastern Europe*, 17, 1, 65–83.

Wodecka, Dorota, Kulczycka, Agata, Szlachetka, Małgorzata, Kępka, Agnieszka, Warchala, Magdalena (2008) 'Co czują EUrosieroty?' *Gazeta Wyborcza*, 12th May.

Woolfson, Charles (2006) 'Working Environment and "Soft Law" in the Post-Communist New Member States', *Journal of Common Market Studies*, 44, 1, 195–215.

Woolfson, Charles (2007a) 'Pushing the Envelope: The "Informalization" of Labour in Postcommunist New EU Member States', *Work, Employment and Society*, 21, 3, 551–564.

Woolfson, Charles (2007b) 'Labour Standards and Labour Migration in the New Europe: Post-Communist Legacies and Perspectives', *European Journal of Industrial Relations*, 13, 2, 199–218.

Woolfson, Charles (2010) '"Hard Times" in Lithuania: Crisis and "Discourses of Discontent" in Post-communist Society', *Ethnography*, 11, 4, 487–514.

Woolfson, Charles and Calite, Dace (2008) 'Working Environment in the New EU Member State of Lithuania: Examining a "Worst Case" Example', *Policy and Practice in Health and Safety*, 1, 3–29.

Woolfson, Charles, Calite, Dace, and Kallaste, Epp (2008) 'Employee "Voice" and Working Environment in Post-Communist New Member States: An Empirical Analysis of Estonia, Latvia and Lithuania', *Industrial Relations Journal*, 39, 4, 314–334.

Woolfson, Charles, Kallaste, Epp, and Bernzins, Janis (2011) 'Illusory Corporatism "Mark 2" in the Baltic States', *Warsaw Forum of Economic Sociology*, 2, 1.

Woolfson, Charles and Likic-Brboric, Branka (2008) 'Migrants and the Unequal Burdening of "Toxic" Risk: Towards a New Global Governance Regime', *Debatte: Journal of Contemporary Central and Eastern Europe*, 16, 3, 291–308.

Wright, Erik Olin (2000) 'Working-Class Power, Capitalist-Class Interests, and Class Compromise', *American Journal of Sociology*, 105, 4, 957–1002.

ZSSS (2003) *Bili smo na ulicah 1991–2003*. Ljubljana: Prima.

Index